Scott
Conant's
new Italian
Cooking

More than 125 recipes
for everyday eating,
relaxed weekend cooking,
and elegant entertaining

Scott
Conant's
new Italian
Cooking

Scott Conant
with Joanne McAllister Smart

Broadway Books
New York

BROADWAY

PRINTED IN HONG KONG

BROADWAY BOOKS and its logo, a letter B bisected on the diagonal, are trademarks of Random House, Inc.

Visit our Web site at www.broadwaybooks.com

First edition published 2005

Book design by Stark Design
Photography by Shimon and Tammar

Library of Congress Cataloging-in-Publication Data
Conant, Scott.
    Scott Conant's new Italian cooking : more than 125 recipes for everyday eating, relaxed weekend cooking, and elegant entertaining / Scott Conant, with Joanne McAllister Smart.— 1st ed.
        p.   cm.
    Includes index.
    1. Cookery, Italian. I. Smart, Joanne McAllister. II. Title.
TX723.C6173 2005
641.5945—dc22
                                                        2004060060

ISBN 0-7679-1682-4

10 9 8 7 6 5 4 3 2 1

To my mom and dad.
Not a day goes by that I don't honor
and celebrate the life and lineage that
I grew up with. I am still learning and
marveling at the depth of your
knowledge, understanding, and
wisdom. *All* of this is because of you.

Thank you!

Contents

Introduction

WHEN YOU ASK A BOY WHAT HE WANTS TO BE when he grows up, "firefighter," "doctor," "astronaut," and even "cowboy" are typical responses—and ones I never uttered. I can't recall wanting to be anything other than a cook. I think it's because I always loved to eat. (I have photos of me as a chubby little kid to prove it.) When I was eleven, I started taking cooking classes at our local community center. At the trade high school I attended, most of the guys were there to work on cars; I was one of the few who wanted to work in the kitchen.

When I was nineteen and a student at the Culinary Institute of America, the idols of all of us young chef hopefuls were David Burke, Charlie Palmer, and Larry Forgione. These guys were advancing the cuisine that came to be known as New American. The emphasis was on using the best ingredients possible and treating them simply to create sophisticated, satisfying fare. We all wanted to be like them. Yet I can still remember that while I thought their food was groundbreaking and delicious, I wanted my cooking to include more of the warmth, the joy, the comfort of Italian cooking. What I knew of traditional Italian cooking, however, lacked the vibrancy I was so fond of in New American–style cooking. During and after school, I worked on creating my own style, combining the best aspects of New American cooking with the best of Italian cuisine.

While at the CIA, I interned at the famous San Domenico in New York City under chef Paul Bartolotta. There I began to learn the craft of *alta cucina*, the refined, upscale Italian cuisine that contrasts with the more homey *cucina rustica*. I then spent a year cooking in Germany, stealing away to Italy whenever I could. The year abroad did wonders for my pastry skills, but when I got home, I went straight back to San Domenico, this time for two years as sous chef under Theo Schoenegger. (During this stint, our kitchen earned three stars from the *New York Times*.)

In 1995, I moved to Pino Luongo's Il Toscanaccio as chef de cuisine. Working with chef Cesare Casella, a master of rustic Tuscan fare, taught me to simplify and even further refine my cooking style. I also learned a lot about running a restaurant from Pino, and I started visualizing what my own restaurant would be like someday. A stint at Chianti, on the Upper East Side, where I recreated the restaurant from the kitchen to the front of the house (and to good reviews), taught me even more about running a restaurant.

I knew that when I opened my own place, my cooking style would not be easily labeled, that it would lie somewhere between *cucina rustica* and *alta cucina*. It would be sophisticated but not fussy, straightforward yet exciting, traditional but pushing convention.

In the fall of 2002, I, along with partners Chris Cannon, Jane Epstein, and Vincente Wolf, opened L'Impero, which is Italian for "empire." The restaurant struck a chord. People came in. They came back. They told their friends. Their friends came. Then they told their friends. During our first year, the *New York Times* gave us three stars and we were honored with a James Beard award for best new restaurant in the country. In 2004, *Food & Wine* named me as one of the ten best new chefs in the country. That same year, Ruth Reichl, editor of *Gourmet*, included L'Impero in her list of favorite places to eat in New York.

L'Impero, however, is not your father's Italian restaurant. "If you consider all the characteristics typically associated with Italian restaurants, it's hard at first to see where L'Impero fits in," Eric Asimov wrote in his *Times* review. "No Italian accents greet you at the door, or anywhere else. No long list of daily specials recited at the table, and almost no Italian language on the menu." Yet, Asimov concludes, "at its heart, L'Impero is decidedly Italian." And while this was something most critics immediately understood, some of our patrons were still a little puzzled. While they loved the food, they wanted to know, just what kind of Italian food was I cooking?

After thinking long and hard about how I could concisely describe my cooking style, I came up with the words "New Italian" as a good way to describe it. For one thing, I want to immediately erase the image that comes to mind for most Americans when they hear the words "Italian food": huge portions of cheese-filled pasta topped with tomato sauce and tons of garlic on everything. Like New American cooking, the dishes I cook rely on handling high-quality ingredients simply in order to let the true flavors of the ingredients shine.

I also want to steer away from the notion that for Italian cooking to be "authentic," it has to focus on a region of Italy. Sure, the cooking in Italy changes as you move north and south, east and west. Obviously, seafood plays a huge role in the cooking of the coast, while in inland Emilia-Romagna, one of the most famous food regions in the world, there's wheat for pasta, cows for Parmigiano-Reggiano, and pigs for prosciutto. In those places where it's easier to grow olives than it is to herd cows, cooking with butter gives way to cooking with olive oil. But it seems to me that the top young chefs in Italy, while respectful of these regional traditions, are less mired in them than we often are here.

I love all of Italian cooking, which is why I don't pursue one region only. Almost all of my cooking begins with olive oil, but I make my polenta amazingly rich and smooth with the addition of cream. A fish dish I like to serve was inspired by a meal I enjoyed while gazing out over the Adriatic. Yet I pair it with little potatoes prepared in a way I first experienced while living near the Italian Alps. So another "new" aspect of my style of Italian cooking is that I don't let traditional cooking boundaries hem me in. I look to the past for inspiration, but I look to the ingredients, the plate, and my customers to decide what will work best for a certain dish. My raw fish appetizers are a good example of this. People love them, but they are also puzzled. The flavorings I pair with the fish are almost wholly Italian: rosemary, lemon, crushed red pepper, olive oil, parsley. But because of the popularity of sushi bars here, raw fish has become almost completely associated with Japanese cuisine. On a recent trip to Italy, however, I enjoyed many raw fish dishes, some traditional but most created by modern Italian chefs putting their own stamp on a dish.

Why label my cooking at all? Why even categorize my cooking as Italian, albeit "New Italian"? The most important reason for me is hardly tangible. Sure, I look to traditional Italian ingredients and techniques as a starting point. I also look to my Italian heritage for inspiration: My mother's maiden name is Varrone, so I really do have some Italian blood in me; I grew up enjoying classic Neapolitan dishes cooked by my grandmother, whose *taralle,* a not-too-sweet knot-shaped biscuit, I serve as part of L'Impero's cheese course. Extensive travels in Italy as well as cooking with Italian masters have also had an enormous impact on my cooking. And although you might be hard pressed to find the exact same dishes I prepare anywhere in Italy, I have had many people—food critics included—tell me that my food is the kind of food they *wish* they could have been eating when they actually were in Italy. But by far the most important thing is that my cooking has an Italian soul. That might sound a little hokey, but my hope is that when you sit down to enjoy the food you create from these recipes, you will immediately understand what I mean.

HOW TO USE THIS BOOK

WHENEVER I COOK, I strive for a balance of flavor, tasting all the time for the sweet, sour, bitter, and salty elements of the dish and tweaking a recipe to make sure they're in harmony. But what I'm after is really more than that. Consider a bowl of creamy polenta topped with beautifully browned wild mushrooms glistening from a drizzle of truffle oil. The aroma wafts upward, presenting you not only with the tangible, earthy, musky fragrance of the dish but also stimulating within you thoughts of comfort, well-being, and intrigue. When you take a bite, you experience the flavor in your mouth, of course, but its essence also seems to immediately fill your entire head. You shut your eyes for a moment, your shoulders relax downward, you slowly exhale through your nose to further extend the flavor of that first bite. Wow, you think. Then, This is *really* good.

This combination of a beguiling aroma followed by flavors that come together to match—if not to exceed—the promise of that initial aroma is what I am after with every recipe in this book, from the humblest pasta to a risotto topped with seared foie gras. The Cumin-Spiced Roast Chicken on page 208, for example, will make you want to linger over your plate and just breathe in the good-ness of the dish, and this before you even have taken a bite. The chicken has an irresistible aroma: While a little on the exotic side, it also includes warm notions of family and home, even if your fam-ily never ate roast chicken and your thoughts of home are not particularly warm.

WHEN THINKING ABOUT WRITING A COOKBOOK, a chef has to take a hard look at what he does, at things that feel like second nature, at techniques developed over many years of trial and error, of irrational-seeming flavor combinations created in a flash of inspiration. And then he has to figure out how to present this information in a way that would be inspiring, helpful, and successful to the home cook. As a thirty-three-year-old single guy who has spent almost every night of his adult life cooking in a restaurant kitchen, I can't say that I have much firsthand experience with cooking at home. (Currently, my refrigerator holds eggs, white truffles, and *bottarga*, not your usual staples, I'm sure.) I know people, including me, look to cookbooks for inspiration. I also believe that some of the people buying this book will have eaten my food and want to learn how to cook some of our signature dishes.

So before I set out to write, I asked friends, family, and customers to tell me what they look for in a cookbook. The most commonly cited answer I got was "dinner." Something different, something delicious, but also something fairly quick and easy to prepare. I also heard from people who love the cooking as much as they love the eating and happily spend all of a weekend afternoon in the kitchen, making soups and stews and, yes, even fresh pasta.

Both of these approaches fit in very well with Italian cuisine in general, and my style in particular. Because I strive for simplicity and balance in my cooking, my plates are not fussy and overblown. I don't like too many ingredients all vying for attention. For that reason, many of my quick-cooking fish, chicken, and meat dishes would be perfect for a Tuesday night. Yet many of my most favorite recipes, including my creamy polenta, my braises, and my gnocchetti, fall into the category of longer, more leisurely cooking. What can be frustrating to cookbook readers, however, is not being able to quickly tell which kind of recipe is which. You know the feeling: You open a favorite cookbook and an inviting recipe catches your eye. It looks pretty simple, so you think you might try it—right now—for dinner. Then you read that it has to marinate overnight. Or what looked like a short ingredients list actually refers to two other recipes in the book with ten ingredients each. I'm not saying that marinating, long slow cooking, or multi-component recipes are bad things. (In fact, you'll find some of these recipes in this book.) But these are just not the kinds of recipes you want when you've worked all day and you'd like to eat at a reasonable hour.

Here is what we have done to make choosing the right recipe to fit your schedule and your mood easier. The recipes that you can make in about forty-five minutes or less, and which require no special ingredients, have been designated "weeknight" recipes. You can flip through the book and find them by ✳. These recipes include all of the salads, the dried pastas, a couple of soups, many of the risottos (contrary to what many people think, risotto doesn't take long to prepare), almost all of the vegetable side dishes, and many quick-cooking meat, chicken, and fish dishes. Yet it's my firm belief that dinner, even on a Tuesday night, ought to be delicious, and many of these quick-to-cook recipes have appeared, exactly as represented here, on our menus.

You have to promise me that you won't *only* make the quick-cooking recipes (as wonderful as they are). When you want to make something truly sumptuous, choose among the remaining recipes, the braises, the roasts, the stuffed pastas. These are the recipes to turn to for relaxed weekend cooking. Many of my favorite Italian dishes are not difficult at all to make, but they do take time. Time in the oven is what transforms a peasant cut like short ribs into a culinary treasure; time in the pot turns coarse cornmeal into pudding-like polenta. You may be thinking: Time? I wish. But since much of the time is hands off, you'll be able to do other things while the lamb braises, the soup gently bubbles, or the chicken marinates overnight. For me, these kinds of dishes are the heart of this book. Maybe it's the anticipation that comes from slowly building a dish: braising the meat one day, shredding it the next, and stuffing it into that fresh pasta before finally bringing it all together for serving—but these recipes satisfy in a way that's different from the quick-cooking ones.

These longer-cooking dishes are also *easier* to serve when entertaining. Preparing a dish *à la minute*, while often quick, can get a little hairy. When my customers ask me to recommend dishes for them to cook for a dinner party, I ask them: "Are these people you want to hang out with or not?" If they're not, go ahead and look for something that will keep you away from your guests in the kitchen. But if you want to have fun and socialize at your own gathering, look to these longer-cooking recipes. Most of the work is done well before the guests arrive, with just a little bit of last-minute cooking before the food is brought to the table.

You can even make fresh pasta—something that is truly an enjoyable experience when you are unstressed by the other demands of the meal—weeks ahead of serving it. That's because when I make fresh pasta, I always freeze it before cooking it. I know this sounds a little odd. This is supposed to be *fresh* pasta, right? While there's no denying the freezing of the pasta is very convenient for the professional restaurant kitchen (as well as the home cook), I would never do it if I didn't believe that the freezing improves the product. But it does (see page 88 for more on this). Freezing your fresh pasta also works well for having a dinner party since pretty much all that's left to do is boil some water. It also means that you can have an amazingly delicious dinner of fresh pasta anytime you want. (This also holds true for soups and braises—not only can they be made ahead of serving but also taste better for it. So even though the dish may take some time to make initially, it can then become a quick weeknight meal when reheated.)

Finally, a few of the recipes designated for weekend cooking don't take long to cook but do include what most people would consider special-occasion food. For example, searing sliced foie gras is quick and easy, but it's expensive. Other times the ingredient is not so much costly as it is hard to find, such as goat or *guanciale*. Even if you never actually make these dishes, I hope you find the information about these ingredients, if not exactly useful to you at this moment in your life, at least interesting.

The book ends, appropriately, with a chapter on desserts and cheeses. Here the recipes run the gamut from very straightforward, easy-to-prepare treats, such as a (practically) flourless chocolate truffle cake to those desserts that might take a little more time, finesse, or are comprised of a few delicious components, such as my Sesame Cannoli with Orange Mascarpone Mousse (page 285). Another option for ending a meal is the cheese course. I like to pair select cheeses with condiments that excite the palate while complementing the cheese. On page 256, you'll find information on how to serve cheeses this way, followed by recipes for some of the condiments.

A FEW WORDS ON INGREDIENTS AND PANTRY RECIPES

HERE IS A LITTLE INFORMATION on some of the staples in my restaurant kitchen, from the most common—shallots and crushed red pepper—to the more exotic—*guanciale* and *bottarga*. Let me be clear about this: You will find many more recipes containing the former two ingredients than the latter two. My cooking is not "out there." I'm not looking to startle anyone at dinner. In fact, all of the "exotic" ingredients I use are commonplace in Italy. For the most part, the ingredients listed here are used throughout the chapters of this book. You'll also find recipes here for my customized pantry staples, such as flavored oils and broths. I've left the discussion of ingredients like risotto to the chapter bearing its name. Look in Sources (page 288) for buying guides for harder to find ingredients.

Anchovies: Most of the time when I am using anchovies, I am using them as a seasoning rather than the focus of the dish. They are usually chopped and cooked until they melt away completely into the dish, leaving behind only their full flavor. I think the best-flavored anchovies are imported from Italy and packed in salt. These need a rinse in a few changes of water before using them and often their tiny skeletons need to be lifted away from the meat. Oil-packed anchovies can also be quite tasty and need less preparation; a quick rinse in water and they are good to go.

Bottarga: *Bottarga di muggine* is the salted, pressed, and air-dried roe of the grey mullet fish (there is also a tuna roe version, but I prefer the mullet). It hails from southern Italy as well as Sicily and Sardinia and even parts of the Middle East and Africa. *Bottarga* has a very strong flavor, which breeds very strong feelings toward it. Some people can't stand it at all while others love nothing more than eating paper-thin slices garnished with a bit of olive oil. I like it in moderation; just a bit finely grated over a pasta (page 97) or raw scallops (page 26) adds an indescribable aromatic accent to the dish. When using *bottarga*, peel off the very thin membrane before slicing or grating.

Bread crumbs: My Italian grandmother would roll over in her grave if she knew this, but for bread crumbs, I often prefer the Japanese-style bread crumbs called *panko* over homemade. *Panko* (also called *panko* flakes) create a crisp, light, and delicate coating in fried foods that seems to stay crisper longer. Fast becoming a common sight at most supermarkets, *panko* is more often shelved with other international ingredients than it is with other bread crumbs. You will also find it at Asian markets and through mail order. If you don't have any *panko*, dry out a few pieces of bread in a low oven and then grind them in a food processor until they are between medium and finely ground.

Capers: Capers are the flower bud of a Mediterranean bush. Why anyone ever thought of eating these things, which are exceedingly bitter right off the bush, is beyond me. But once preserved, whether in salt or in a vinegary brine, capers add a wonderful piquant flavor to all kinds of dishes. As with anchovies, I generally prefer salt-packed, which need to be rinsed in a few changes of water before using them. The other kind simply needs a quick rinse. Which size to use? That depends on how much of a briny bite you are looking for. In general, Italians use a slightly larger size bud than the French.

Chicken broth: Relax. If you can boil water, you can make a chicken broth better than anything offered at the supermarket (see recipe, page 14). I especially like to use homemade broth in the instances where its superior flavor will be especially noticeable, as in risotto and light soups. Otherwise, you can get away with using a low-salt, good-quality packaged brand.

Chicken reduction: When I first started cooking professionally, I used a veal reduction in just about everything except dessert. A veal reduction gives foods an intensely rich and deep flavor. But to tell you the truth, it can become a crutch. Sure, things taste delicious with it, but its strong flavor can obscure the other flavors of the dish; in other words, it *becomes* the dish. As I developed my own style of cooking, I began to replace veal reduction with a less intense chicken reduction to create lighter, brighter tasting dishes. With this chicken reduction—the recipe is on page 15—I still get an added depth of flavor but without muting the other flavors in the dish. An unintended benefit of this switch is that making a chicken reduction is less arduous for the home cook than making a veal reduction. In other words, you might actually take a look at the recipe for chicken reduction (and even consider trying it), whereas if the first line of the ingredients list called for veal bones, you might have turned the page.

If you don't make the chicken reduction but want to make one of the dishes calling for it (such as the roasted chicken on page 208 or the beef short ribs on page 168 or the vinegar reduction that follows it), experiment with some of the commercial chicken reductions out there (see Sources). But keep in mind that because I reduce mine until it's just a little thicker than chicken stock, you will likely need to reconstitute any packaged version you buy. One that I have tried with success is Glace de Poulet Gold, which is made by More Than Gourmet. A classic reduced chicken stock, it can be reconstituted by 6 to 1 to get a flavorful chicken reduction that, while not exactly what I make, is exceedingly convenient.

Crushed red pepper: I use it. A lot. I didn't realize this was such an entrenched habit of mine until we were testing the recipes for this book and our recipe tester, Meg Suzuki, joked that she was heading out to buy a ten-pound bag of it. I'm not always looking to add heat to the dish, however. It's more about enlivening the overall flavor, exciting the palate. Because different brands of crushed red pepper (*peperoncino* in Italian and also called red pepper flakes) offer different levels of heat and because people respond to the heat differently, I usually suggest a range for using crushed red pepper if it's more than a pinch.

Grating cheeses: Grating cheeses are just that: hard cheeses that are often grated as a garnish for pasta, polenta, risotto, soups, and salads. As a category, they are referred to as grana, which points to their slight granular texture. Parmigiano-Reggiano is the most famous and revered of the grating cheeses, the one everyone wants to use. It's also very expensive. At L'Impero, we go through a $700 wheel of it about every ten days. (You do the math.) Most of the really good stuff is served in small chunks as part of our cheese course so that the flavor nuances of the cheese as well as its melt-in-your-mouth texture can be fully appreciated. While many dishes benefit hugely from this premium cheese being grated over it, you can often turn to a less expensive but good-quality "generic" grana, such as grana Padano. Grana Padano, like Parmigiano-Reggiano, is a cow's milk cheese made in Emilia-Romagna, but it's usually aged for about six months, as opposed to the fourteen-month minimum for Parmigiano. Grana's creation is also not as regulated as that of Parmigiano-Reggiano, which must follow very strict standards regarding where the milk is from, when it is made, and how it is aged. Grana Padano will look a lot like Parmigiano-Reggiano but will be priced considerably less and will taste like a paler version of Parm. (Be sure that if you are paying Parmigiano-Reggiano prices, you are getting the real thing; by law, the words Parmigiano-Reggiano must be stamped everywhere over the cheese's rind.)

Pecorino Romano, while a wonderful grating cheese in its own right, should not be used interchangeably with Parmigiano-Reggiano or grana Padano. Real pecorino Romano, made from sheep's milk in the province of Rome, has a sharp flavor that's so intense that eating it out of hand can make your mouth pucker in the same way an overly tannic wine can. But pecorino Romano's sharpness works beautifully in many dishes, such as my salad with toasted hazelnuts (page 61) or a pasta featuring corn, asparagus, and jalapeño (page 96). A grana or even a Parmigiano in those dishes would taste fine but not nearly as exciting.

Guanciale: I hope that *guanciale,* instead of being this trendy ingredient that will help pinpoint the publishing of this book as early in the millennium, will become, as pancetta and prosciutto have become, a pretty common—and easily purchased—ingredient for the enthusiastic cook. *Guanciale,* brined, seasoned, and dried pig jowls, is a staple of the cooking of central Italy and is used basically in the same way as pancetta, although it's actually more delicate in flavor and less fatty than pancetta. Try it in place of bacon or pancetta in your favorite pasta alla carbonara and you will understand the beauty of this product. As I write this, *guanciale* is not easy to find in the United States. I get mine from Salumeria Biellese in New York City, which also sells the best salamis and sausages outside of Italy. It's located at 378 Eighth Avenue at 29th Street. If you live in the city, you can head on over and wallow in the wonderful smells there. Otherwise, you can mail order by calling 212–736–7376. On the West Coast, Niman Ranch in California also makes a *guanciale* that they can barely keep in stock, it's so popular. You can visit their website at *www.nimanranch.com* or call them at 510–808–0340.

Infused oils: I know it's very chefy to have a bunch of squeeze bottles in the kitchen filled with different oils. But we use them for good reason. A little flavored oil squirted from a bottle (or drizzled off of a spoon) adds another layer of flavor to a dish. (The squirt bottle itself just adds convenience and accuracy to the process.) Two oils that I just love include one made with fresh ginger and one made from steeping crushed red pepper. (You will find the recipes on page 19.) They are used in specific recipes in the book, but you can use them in your own cooking as well. The red pepper oil gives a little kick to pasta while the ginger oil would taste great over simply grilled fish. Don't cook with them or you will lose their flavor; instead add them to a dish just before serving.

Microgreens: Microgreens are teeny, tiny greens picked just when their first leaves arrive and sold with their silks or stems still attached, which makes them look a little like sprouts, but they are not. Cresses, mustard greens, chard, beet greens, and many more greens are cultivated this way. Their flavor is delicate and their tiny stems add a wonderful texture, but with their steep price microgreens are best reserved for garnishes, as in the raw fish *assagini* on page 27. In the past, microgreens went directly from farmer to chef, but they are now turning up at upscale food markets and farmers' markets. Some seed companies also provide seeds and directions for growing your own microgreens (see Sources), which sounds fun, especially for gardeners tight on space. Baby greens—greens picked a little later in their life—are a more common sight at most supermarkets and can be substituted for microgreens in these recipes.

Olive oil: I use a lot of olive oil in my cooking. Most of the time, I use regular olive oil for sautéing and frying and save the extra virgin olive oils for finishing. I always use Italian olive oil, although Spain and Greece make some good ones, too. Olive oils can vary tremendously in flavor from very fruity to quite peppery. How to choose? To tell the truth, a lot of knowing about food and wine has to do with knowing a little about geography. Although I am generalizing a bit, you can usually rely on the fact that most northern olive oils tend to be more full-bodied, spicier, with a very rich feel. Further south, you find lighter, milder, grassy olive oils. You might want to choose an olive oil from, say, Capania, Abruzzo, or Basilicata when you don't want an overtly olive flavor to permeate the dish, such as when you add a drizzle to a light risotto or pasta or fish. The oils from Tuscany and Umbria, however, with their more assertive flavors, can stand up to richer stews, seared meats, and grilled fare.

Polenta: I use an imported Italian cornmeal for my polenta, called polenta *bramata*, *bramata* referring to a coarse grind of the cornmeal. I think the Italian corn and age-old method employed for grinding and drying the corn offer a fresher, more full-bodied flavor than any other cornmeal. That said, my polenta cooking method was tested using cornmeal made by a major supermarket brand and the results were still deemed delicious. (You can find polenta *bramata* at many gourmet grocery stores and even in some supermarkets. Most of the Italian vendors listed in the Sources also carry it.) Whichever cornmeal you use, keep in mind that it is perishable. Keep it in a cool place, even the refrigerator, and smell it before using it to be sure it's fresh.

Salt: You will find many kinds of salts in my kitchen with the exception of the fine-grained table salt we all grew up on. For most of my cooking, whether adding salt to the pasta water or seasoning lamb shanks before braising, I use kosher salt, which is coarser than table salt and does not contain the additives table salt does that keep it from clumping. I save the best (and most costly) kind of sea salt—*fleur de sel*—for sprinkling over foods just before serving, more like a condiment. *Fleur de sel*, from Brittany, is harvested by hand from shallow salt marshes as the seawater evaporates. The white, more delicate *fleur de sel* is the top layer of saline found at the marshes, while *sel gris* is the more abundant lower layer. I like to play with both types as well as the sea salt from Hawaii that's colored via a process using the natural red clay from the area. Aside from its good flavor, the red sea salt adds a little color, which is fun. Sample different brands and styles of sea salt to determine which you like best; that's what I have done over the years. For more on when and how to add salt, see page 172.

Shallots: When I call for shallots, I'm picturing something about the size of my thumb. A shallot this size, finely chopped, gives you about a tablespoon. A lot of supermarkets carry jumbo shallots. If you're using those, use just one clove when I call for a whole shallot. But don't sweat over this too much; in recipes where a little more or a little less shallot would make a significant difference in flavor, I call for an exact measurement.

Truffles and truffle products: My first experience with fresh white truffles was unforgettable. I was eighteen years old and working at a restaurant that was having a party to celebrate truffle season. We were hosting more than one hundred fifty people, offering six courses, and running an auction to raise money for City Meals on Wheels, a New York City charity. The chef purchased $30,000 worth of the most fabulous and fragrant truffles I have ever seen since. The aroma from these three huge piles of truffles, which were stacked in the downstairs kitchen, permeated the whole restaurant. You could even smell the truffles out on the sidewalk nearby. Really amazing.

I still love truffle season and all the excitement surrounding their coming to market. For most people, however, owning even just a single whole, fresh truffle of their own is an unlikely scenario. (If you are lucky enough to have one, try grating a little over scrambled eggs or plain risotto and take a moment to breathe in that exquisite aroma.) Although nothing can match fresh truffles, you can still get a wonderful truffle essence from some of the better-quality truffle products. In our kitchen, we use the oil from preserved, jarred white truffles. Home cooks can do the same or substitute white truffle oil. A tiny drizzle of this potently flavored and aromatic oil adds a final flourish to finished dishes; you can get a sense of its power when you make the truffle vinaigrette on page 70 or the mushroom fricassee on page 37. Don't blanch at the high price of truffle oil; you use so little that it will last a while. In fact, a smaller bottle may be the better investment, since the ephemeral flavor of the oil can dissipate with age and exposure to air. (It also gets wiped out with heat, which is why you never cook with truffle oil and even take foods off of the heat before adding a touch of the oil.)

When I want some flecks of truffles throughout a dish, I reach for sliced truffles packed in oil or for truffle butter. Truffle butter especially is a convenient way to add some truffle flavor to pastas, risotto, and purees. (I don't eat mashed potatoes much, but I might be more inclined to if they had a little truffle butter mixed in.)

Vinegar: There are all kinds of vinegars, and once again, I suggest you keep tasting different ones until you find the few you like best. In many of my preparations, especially in vinaigrettes, I use both a little balsamic vinegar and red wine vinegar. The balsamic adds a toasty, sweet undertone, while the red wine vinegar punches up the acidity. A favorite red wine vinegar that we use by the case is Trucioleto (see Sources), which is obtained from the grape's first press and aged in oak wood. It's also quite a bang for the buck. As for balsamic vinegars, you can spend tons on them. But save the really expensive, thick, long-aged elixir for special occasions—a little drizzled over a chunk of Parmigiano-Reggiano is pure heaven—and use more moderately priced, less-aged balsamic for your everyday cooking. Do check, however, that what you are using does not contain coloring, added sugar, or preservatives. Even with inexpensive balsamic vinegar, you'll likely get the best flavor from the ones in Modena, just north of Bologna.

PANTRY RECIPES

WE ALWAYS HAVE THE FOLLOWING RECIPES made and on hand in the kitchen. Each of these recipes makes more than any single recipe will call for, but all of these staples keep either refrigerated or frozen.

LOBSTER-TOMATO BROTH

You can gather cooked lobster shells as you use whole lobster, freeze the shells, and then make this stock when you have a pound of them; or simply make the lobster with chickpeas and *guanciale* on page 48 and save the lobster shells to make this easy broth the next day. (Your fishmonger may also have spent lobster shells that he's willing to part with.)

MAKES **7** CUPS

1 to **2** tablespoons olive oil

1 onion, sliced

Pinch of crushed red pepper

One **14.5**-ounce can of tomatoes, drained, seeded, and chopped (1^1/2 cups)

1 pound cooked lobster shells (from **2** lobsters), coarsely chopped

2 cups dry white wine

12 basil leaves, coarsely chopped

IN A LARGE SOUP POT, heat the oil over medium heat. Add the onion and cook, stirring occasionally, until the onion is soft, 12 minutes. Add the crushed red pepper, tomatoes, and lobster shells. Increase the heat to medium-high, and cook, stirring occasionally for another few minutes. Add the wine, bring it to a boil, and let it cook until reduced by about half. Add 8 cups of water to the pot, bring it to a boil, reduce to a simmer, and cook for 40 minutes. Add the basil and cook for another minute before straining the broth through a mesh strainer. Use the broth immediately, refrigerate it for up to three days, or freeze it. Season with salt and pepper as you use it.

CHICKEN BROTH

Every day we make huge pots of chicken broth. My guys come in, throw a few chickens in a pot, add some carrots, celery, onion, and thyme, fill the pot with water, put it on the stove, and two hours later, it's done. Go ahead and add a bay leaf, some parsley, or a whole clove; about the only thing I am adamant about with my chicken broth is that it contains a little thyme. Instead of saving chicken necks and backs for stock, go ahead and spend a few bucks on a couple of whole chickens. Cut off the breasts to use for another dish. But leave the rest of the meat on the bone; for me, taking the chicken out of the pot and picking at the thigh meat is the best part of making broth. You could also throw the cooked meat into a soup. Use the broth within a few days or freeze it.

MAKES **10** CUPS

Two **3**- to **4**-pound whole chickens, giblets removed, rinsed inside and out, and breasts removed and saved for another dish

1 carrot, washed and cut into **6** to **8** pieces

1 celery stalk, rinsed and cut into **6** to **8** pieces

1 small onion, peeled and quartered

3 to **4** sprigs fresh thyme

PUT THE CHICKENS, carrot, celery, onion, and thyme in a very large (about 10-quart) stockpot. Add cold water to cover, about 4 quarts. Bring to a bubbling simmer over high heat, and then lower the heat to maintain a gentle simmer over the course of the couple hours it takes to extract the flavor from the chickens. Every so often, skim the scum that floats to the top of the pot. After a couple of hours, dip a ladle deep into the pot so you can taste the actual broth and not the fat floating on top. Add a little salt to the ladle and taste the broth. If it's pleasingly chickeny flavored, the broth is done. If not, allow the birds to cook another half hour or so.

Remove the chicken and strain the broth several times through a chinois or other fine strainer. Cool the broth in the refrigerator. Once cooled, the fat will float to the top; remove about 90 percent of this fat. (A little fat is good for flavor.) Use the broth within a few days or freeze it.

Scott Conant's New Italian Cooking

CHICKEN REDUCTION

I use this chicken reduction, essentially a brown chicken stock reduced until full-bodied and intensely flavorful, for braising and to make sauces. Freeze it in varying amounts so you can easily pull out just the amount called for in a recipe. In this case, chicken bones make more sense to use because the bones get roasted first for added flavor. Some supermarkets sell packages of chicken bones, and you can save the chicken carcass after boning it as described on page 210.

MAKES 1 QUART

6 pounds chicken bones

3 to 4 tablespoons olive oil

1 medium onion, coarsely chopped

1 clove garlic, coarsely chopped

1 carrot, coarsely chopped

2 stalks celery, coarsely chopped

4 whole canned tomatoes (4 ounces), coarsely chopped

4 sprigs rosemary, bruised with the dull side of a chef's knife

2 cups dry white wine

HEAT THE OVEN TO 425°F. Rinse the chicken bones and pat dry. Spread them out in a single layer with a little room between the bones on one large or two smaller sheet pans. Roast until golden brown, flipping and turning the bones every 15 minutes or so, about 1 hour.

In a large stockpot, heat the olive oil over medium heat. Add the onion, garlic, carrot, and celery and cook, stirring occasionally, until the vegetables are well browned, 20 minutes. Add the tomatoes, rosemary, wine, and bones to the stockpot. Add enough water to cover everything by 2 inches (6 quarts). Cook over medium heat (you want a gentle simmer, *not* a boil) until the chicken is falling off of the bone and the stock has a full flavor, 1 1/2 hours.

Remove the chicken and strain the broth several times through a chinois or other fine strainer. If you want to make and use the reduction right away, spoon off any visible fat floating on top of the stock. Otherwise, chill the stock until the fat solidifies on top and then scrape off and discard most of it. Pour the

Introduction

defatted stock into a saucepan, bring to a boil over high heat, and then reduce the heat slightly so the stock is not boiling so furiously. As the stock reduces, it will glaze the sides of the saucepan; use a spoon or ladle to pour some of the stock over this glaze to incorporate it. (This will further increase the intensity of the flavor.) Continue simmering until the stock has darkened and has reduced to about 1 quart. The time this will take will vary, but it will likely take at least 20 to 30 minutes. Use right away, refrigerate for up to three days, or freeze.

VINEGAR REDUCTION

This simple sauce has a really full flavor with a slight hint of the herbs. You can make it ahead of time and use it to finish a simple piece of beef, lamb, or chicken. I especially like it with the Spice-Crusted Lamb on page 190.

MAKES **2/3** CUP

1 teaspoon olive oil

1 shallot, thinly sliced

1 sprig thyme

Small pinch of crushed red pepper

3 tablespoons red wine vinegar or balsamic vinegar

1/4 cup homemade Chicken Broth (page 14) or purchased low-salt chicken broth

1 cup homemade Chicken Reduction (page 15) or purchased chicken reduction diluted with water until a little thicker than chicken stock

HEAT THE OLIVE OIL in a small saucepan over medium heat. Add the shallot, thyme, and crushed red pepper and cook, stirring occasionally, until the shallot is golden brown. Add the vinegar, increase the heat to medium high, and cook until reduced by half. Add the chicken broth and the chicken reduction and cook until reduced and somewhat thickened, 15 minutes.

MARINATED RED ONIONS

I love to keep marinated onions on hand. They will last at least a week in the fridge, and add a tangy (and not overly oniony) note to salads and sandwiches. They are also a crucial element in one of my raw fish starters (page 27). If, like me, you get hooked on these onions, know that the recipe is easily doubled.

MAKES **3/4** CUP

1 medium red onion, sliced thinly

1/2 cup red wine vinegar

1$\frac{1}{2}$ teaspoons kosher salt

1/2 cup water

MIX ALL THE INGREDIENTS TOGETHER and let sit, covered and refrigerated, for a minimum of 24 hours.

OLIO DI ZENZERO (GINGER OIL)

> Man, this is good stuff. Try some drizzled over sautéed asparagus or grilled fish.

MAKES **3/4** CUP

3/4 cup olive oil

1/2 ounce (2-inch piece) fresh ginger, peeled and chopped into about **4** pieces

1/2 teaspoon kosher salt

HEAT THE OVEN TO 250°F. Put the olive oil in a small saucepan and add the ginger and salt. Cover and put in the oven for 3 hours. Remove from the oven and let cool. When cool, puree in blender. Pass the oil through a fine strainer and refrigerate for up to a month.

PEPERONCINO OIL
(RED PEPPER OIL)

> When you want to add some subtle heat to a dish, reach for this. It's no more difficult to make than a pot of tea.

1 cup olive oil

$2\frac{1}{2}$ teaspoons crushed red pepper

COMBINE THE OLIVE OIL and red pepper in a small saucepan. Heat over medium heat until it just starts to bubble lightly. Immediately remove it from the heat and allow the red pepper to steep in the olive oil until cool. Strain the oil and refrigerate it for up to a month.

WHICH WINE?

LIKE MOST GOOD ITALIANS, I view wine as an integral component of a great meal. It's celebratory, fun, and by breaking down inhibitions, it generally promotes genial moods. Aside from all that good stuff, wine whets the palate and balances taste sensations, making a much better accompaniment to delicious food than, say, a Coke.

Throughout the book, wine pairings are suggested for most recipes. The wines are exclusively Italian. The obvious reason for this is that this is a book about Italian cooking, and it's not a bad idea to enjoy the wine from a certain region with the food from that region. But really my overriding goal is to get more people to learn more about and drink more Italian wine.

Italian wines can be challenging to promote for two reasons. Until relatively recent times, the wine exported from Italy was not of high quality, and also most people are not familiar with the grapes grown there. For example, if you offer someone a glass of Merlot, he or she can know (at least generally) what to expect, whether the wine is from France, California, or Australia. That's not true with many of the most famous grapes of Italy. Try this the next time you are feeling a little frisky: Tell your guests you're pouring a Nebbiolo and watch the blank stares you get in return. While Nebbiolo is one of the world's most-renowned wine grapes, it's really only grown in Italy. But even those who regularly drink Italian wines might not know Nebbiolo, as the wines made with the grape are not referred to as such; instead they go by their regional names, such as Barolo and Barbaresco.

This brings us to another somewhat confusing aspect of Italian wines: Sometimes they are named for the grape, sometimes the place, and (maybe most confusingly) sometimes the name and the place. Since the grapes may not be immediately familiar to most readers in the way that Chardonnay and Zinfandel are, I will point out whether the wine is being called by its regional name by putting in parenthesis DOC and DOCG where applicable. These labels—Italian appellations, really—stand for Denominazione di Origine Controllata (DOC) and Denominazione di Origine Controllata e Garantita (DOCG). In a nutshell, DOC and DOCG are government specifications that include primarily the geographic production of the wine but also such variables as alcohol content, grape varieties used, and aging. DOCG is more demanding than the DOC category, although neither branding guarantees the wine's quality level. (Indeed, those highly regarded Super Tuscans don't technically fall into either category.) I don't mean to go on about this as there are many food books about wine out there (my best friend Sergio Esposito, owner of Italian Wine Merchants in New York City, is working on one as I write this); I simply want to use the DOC and DOCG designations as shorthand for "this is not (in most cases) the name of the grape." You'll see what I mean as you read through the wine notes.

I have kept the wine notes very simple and do not offer up specific vintages (which will become harder and harder to get as time goes by) or even specific winemakers. Seek out a smart person at the wine store and have him or her help you choose wines based on the parameters given here. You will have more fun (and feel less futile) searching for good wines that way than being hell-bent on a particular grape, year, style, and maker.

Finally, while I know my food better than anyone, I asked Chris Cannon, a partner in L'Impero and creator of our wine list, and the aforementioned Sergio to assist in making these recommendations.

Small Tastes

Raw Bluefin Tuna with Baby Tomato Salad and Mint
* Scallop Carpaccio with Scallions and Lemon
Fluke with Citrus Salad and Peperoncino Oil
Yellowtail with Olio di Zenzero and Marinated Onions
Citrus-Cured Salmon
Citrus-Cured Salmon with Baby Greens
and Horseradish Cream
* Fried Zucchini with Anchovy Mayonnaise
Creamy Polenta with a Fricassee of Mushrooms
Baked Polenta "Croutons" with
Sautéed Chicken Livers and Capers
Baked Polenta Margarita
Seared Scallops with Farro and Seafood Ragu
Stewed Fresh Squid in Spicy Guazzetto
Polenta-Crusted Soft-Shell Crabs
Roasted Lobster with Chickpeas and Guanciale
Parsley and Vegetable Salad
Olive Oil–Poached Rabbit with Baby Greens
and Shaved Parmigiano-Reggiano

MANY RECIPES IN THIS BOOK—soups, salads, risottos, and pastas—can all work very well as first courses. The recipes in this chapter are really more about the little bites offered at the very start of a dinner or gathering, often before anyone even sits down at the table. In Italy, these are called *assagini*.

Think of these recipes as opportunities for you to try out new ingredients and flavor combinations that you might shy away from were the dish to be the bulk of the meal. With these small bites you are neither gustatorily nor financially overcommitted. For instance, raw yellowtail with ginger oil and marinated onions (page 29) is a starter my customers clamor for. But you know your crowd better than I do and maybe they are not so sure about raw fish; by serving it as a small bite you relieve yourself and them from any pressure. If it's not to their liking, they know there is more food to come, while you have not broken the bank on what the same amount of fish as a main course would have cost. Admittedly, some of these dishes are on the fancier side. So my suggestion is this: If you are planning on making one of the more elaborate dishes here, keep the pasta course (if you're having one) and the main course simple. A braise, for instance, would be an ideal main course, since you can make it ahead of time and then reheat it on the night you want to serve it. Finally, a few of the recipes contained here, such as the rabbit salad (page 53) and the scallop and farro ragu (page 42), can also make a delicious light lunch.

RAW BLUEFIN TUNA WITH BABY TOMATO SALAD AND MINT

Baby greens or the even smaller microgreens are simply greens that have been picked while still very tiny. They are tender, tasty, and sized right for these small appetizer plates. You'll find them at some supermarkets and specialty stores. Other options include pea shoots, mizuna, and watercress. You could also trim larger leafy greens to size. This starter comes together in minutes if you already have some Peperoncino Oil made; you can also try substituting a good purchased chile oil in place of my homemade infused oil.

MAKES **6** SERVINGS

4 ounces sashimi-quality tuna, preferably bluefin

10 baby tomatoes (pear or cherry, for example), cut into eighths

1 teaspoon extra virgin olive oil

1/2 teaspoon red wine vinegar

1 to **2** leaves fresh mint, finely chopped

1/4 teaspoon snipped fresh chives

A couple pinches of sea salt

A handful of baby or microgreens

1 teaspoon homemade Peperoncino Oil (page 19)

WITH A VERY SHARP KNIFE, slice the tuna into six equal slices. In a small bowl, gently toss the tomatoes with the oil, vinegar, mint, chives, and a pinch of sea salt. Divide the tomato salad among six plates. Top each with a slice of tuna. Sprinkle just a smidge of sea salt on each slice of tuna. Top with the baby greens and a drizzle of the Peperoncino Oil. Serve immediately.

WHICH WINE?

This is wonderful with a bubbly glass of rosé; try a spumante from Franciacorta (DOCG) in Lombardy, a region made famous by the outstanding quality of its sparkling wines.

SCALLOP CARPACCIO WITH SCALLIONS AND LEMON

When you eat this dish you may ask yourself: "Why would I ever eat a cooked scallop again?" This recipe is the simplest thing in the world—the *bottarga* is optional—but within simplicity lies restraint. Make sure the scallops you buy are "dry," have not been treated with chemicals, and are exceedingly fresh.

MAKES **6** SERVINGS

4 large sea scallops, preferably diver scallops

1 teaspoon fresh lemon juice

2 tablespoons olive oil

1 to **2** scallions, sliced very, very thin on the bias

1 cup micro or baby greens

Sea salt

Bottarga (see page 6), shaved very thin (optional)

SLICE THE SCALLOPS CROSSWISE into very thin rounds, each $1/8$ inch thick. Lay the slices in a single layer on a large plate and drizzle with the lemon juice and olive oil. Sprinkle about a teaspoon of the scallions over the scallops, wrap them in plastic wrap, and refrigerate until very cold, at least an hour and up to 4 hours ahead of serving.

When ready to serve, divide the baby greens among six plates and top with the slices of scallops. Sprinkle just a tiny bit of sea salt over each. Finish with the tiniest bit of shaved *bottarga*. (A bit of *bottarga*, with its strong fish flavor, can make this dish sing, but too much is unpleasant. You can also leave it off completely.) Drizzle the plate with any remaining olive oil and lemon juice from the scallops and serve immediately.

WHICH WINE?

These sweet scallops would enjoy being paired with a full-bodied **Pigato** from Liguria, a white wine with enough flavor to stand up to the *bottarga*.

Raw Fish, Italian Style

DURING A VISIT TO ITALY IN 2003, I was surprised to see how popular raw fish is there. But I really shouldn't have been, as *crudo*, as it's called in Italy, is gaining popularity there. I took such a liking to the way raw fish was handled by young Italian chefs that I started to serve similar dishes in the restaurant. I had no idea that it would be a potential quandary. Customers wanted to know why I was serving sashimi. Well, call it what you want, but in my mind each of these raw fish appetizers has an Italian soul, relying for the most part on classic Italian herbs, robustly flavored oils, and sea salt to complement the subtle flavor of the raw fish.

Maybe this is obvious, but because you are serving the fish raw, it has to be pristine—as fresh and as high a quality as there is. That, in fact, is the only challenging aspect to these recipes. Seek out a trusted fishmonger, and be sure to buy what would be considered sushi or sashimi-quality fish. (Be aware that there are some people, including children, pregnant women, the elderly, and people with impaired immune systems, who should not eat any raw fish.)

Once the warnings have been heeded and you have in your possession some beautiful fish, these are actually fun dishes to make. I give amounts for these recipes, but once you make them, you will no longer need to measure. Just bear in mind that the fish is the main attraction and that the other items are there to accent it—so use them sparingly.

The raw fish starters each make six "two-bite" servings; if you want more, serve fewer people or multiply the recipe. It would be easy (if expensive) to make a lot of these small bites for a party, especially if you get all of the ingredients lined up assembly-line style. Consider them when you're doing some serious entertaining.

FLUKE WITH CITRUS SALAD
AND PEPERONCINO OIL

> Tiny, triangular pieces of orange, lemon, and lime shimmer on the plate like little jewels. Very sexy looking food! If you can't find fluke, also called summer flounder, try yellowfin tuna.

MAKES **6** SERVINGS

4 ounces sashimi-quality fluke

1 lemon

1 lime

1 small orange

1/4 teaspoon fresh lemon juice

1 teaspoon extra virgin olive oil

1 teaspoon Peperoncino Oil (page 19)

A couple pinches of sea salt

Freshly ground black pepper

WITH A VERY SHARP KNIFE, slice the fluke into twelve very thin slices. Segment the lemon, lime, and orange in the following way: Cut both ends off of the fruit. Using a sharp, flexible knife and a sawing motion, cut the skin and white membrane away from top to bottom following the contours. Free two segments from each fruit by cutting along the seams that separate one segment from the other. Squeeze some of the remaining lemon to get some fresh juice. Cut the segments into small pieces and toss them with the lemon juice and extra virgin olive oil.

Put one slice each of the fluke on 6 small plates. Top with half of the citrus segments. Dot each piece with a little Peperoncino Oil and season very lightly with the sea salt and pepper. Top with another layer of fish, citrus, Peperoncino Oil, sea salt, and black pepper. Serve immediately.

WHICH WINE?
Try a **Verdicchio di Matelica** (DOC), which is dry, soft, and harmonious, with a brilliant pale yellow color that makes it a wonderful pour with delicately flavored raw fish starters.

Scott Conant's New Italian Cooking

YELLOWTAIL WITH OLIO DI ZENZERO AND MARINATED ONIONS

This is my favorite raw fish. Even though they are used sparingly, the marinated red onions add an amazing depth and roundness; their texture is also a welcome surprise. While ginger isn't exactly thought of as an Italian ingredient (even though I do write it in Italian here and on my menu), its personality becomes somewhat subdued when infused in olive oil. It is not the main flavor, but rather it adds an intriguing background to the dish. Yes, this dish calls for not one but two infused oils as well as marinated onions. But you will have made these ahead of time so that when it comes to assembly, you're done in just a few minutes. People just go crazy over the flavors of this dish. In fact, you may want to double the recipe because everyone is going to want more!

MAKES **6** SERVINGS

4 ounces sashimi-quality yellowtail

1 teaspoon Peperoncino Oil (page 19)

1 teaspoon Olio di Zenzero (page 19)

Pinch of sea salt

Freshly ground black pepper

1 tablespoon finely chopped Marinated Red Onions (page 18)

WITH A VERY SHARP KNIFE, slice the fish into six pieces and place each on a small plate. Top each with a "dot" of the Peperoncino Oil and about three "dots" of the Olio di Zenzero. Sprinkle with just a touch of sea salt and black pepper. Sprinkle some of the chopped red onions over the fish and serve immediately.

WHICH WINE?
With this, my favorite raw fish dish, I like a glass of **Soave Classico** (DOC) **Superiore**; its elegant aroma, full of peaches and piecrust, works magic with the bright gingery flavor of this dish.

CITRUS-CURED SALMON

A side of cured salmon is a beautiful sight on a table full of hors d'oeuvres. You can serve it as is with little toasts and some honey mustard or crème fraîche and let people slice it themselves. If you're feeling more formal, dice the silken salmon and gently mix it with fresh snipped chives and a little olive oil, or use it as part of a colorful little salad topped with horseradish cream (recipe follows). This is really simple to make, but it requires the best-quality salmon you can get and needs to cure for three days before it's ready to be served.

MAKES 15 TO 20 SERVINGS

1 whole side of fresh salmon, filleted and skin on

1 1/4 cups kosher salt

1 cup dark brown sugar

1 tablespoon yellow mustard seeds

1 teaspoon coarsely ground black pepper

1 bunch fresh dill

1 bunch fresh parsley

1 medium onion, thinly sliced

1 lemon, thinly sliced

1 lime, thinly sliced

1 orange, thinly sliced

1/4 cup olive oil (not extra virgin)

1/4 cup white wine

REMOVE ANY PINBONES FROM THE SALMON. Trim the stomach flaps if necessary for a neater presentation. On a sided platter or sheet pan large enough to hold the fish, gently rub the salt onto both sides of the salmon. Lay the salmon skin side down and cover with plastic wrap. Place another sheet pan, platter, or a cutting board on top of the length of the fish and weight it lightly. Refrigerate the salmon for 12 to 24 hours.

Remove the weights, unwrap the salmon, and gently wipe off the excess salt and moisture. (Do not rinse it!) Lay the salmon skin side down on the platter. Sprinkle the sugar, mustard seeds, and black pepper over the length of the fish. Next cover the fish with the dill, parsley, onion, lemon, lime, and orange, distributing and layering the ingredients as evenly as you can along the length of the fish. Drizzle the olive oil and white wine over everything. Cover the salmon with plastic wrap, weight it again, and refrigerate for 24 hours.

Unwrap the salmon and spoon any accumulated juices onto it.

Carefully turn the salmon over (don't worry about rearranging the marinade ingredients, just let them fall onto the platter and rest the fish on top of everything). Once again cover the fish with plastic wrap, weight it, and refrigerate for 24 to 36 hours. Unwrap the fish, gently scrape any remaining marinade mixture off the salmon, and pat it dry. The salmon will keep in the refrigerator for a week.

TO SLICE THE SALMON

Use a long, thin, very sharp knife and begin at the tapered, tail end. Cut thin slices across the grain at an angle almost parallel to the work surface.

TO DICE THE SALMON

Remove larger "blocks" of flesh and dice.

WHICH WINE?

A dry (secco) **Moscato**, especially one from Alto Adige, would taste terrific with the cured salmon.

CITRUS-CURED SALMON WITH BABY GREENS AND HORSERADISH CREAM

This bright and lively salad is an excellent way to feature the Citrus-Cured Salmon.

MAKES **8** SERVINGS

1/2 cup crème fraîche

1 tablespoon red wine vinegar

2 tablespoons grated fresh horseradish

Citrus-Cured Salmon (page 30)

4 cups tiny baby greens or pea shoots

1 tablespoon snipped fresh chives

STIR TOGETHER the crème fraîche, red wine vinegar, and horseradish. Mound a couple slices of salmon on each of eight plates. (Alternatively, dice the salmon and put 2 tablespoons of diced salmon on each plate.) Drizzle some of the horseradish cream over the salmon. Top each plate with a small handful of greens and drizzle just a little of the horseradish cream over the greens. Sprinkle each plate with some chives and serve.

FRIED ZUCCHINI WITH
ANCHOVY MAYONNAISE

These are a fun way to kick off a meal. The fried zucchini taste best eaten right away, so have everyone nearby with their plates at the ready while you do the frying. Otherwise, keep the fried zucchini warm in a low oven until ready to serve. The recipe for this loose mayonnaise makes more than you need, but any left over will keep for a couple of days in the refrigerator.

For the mayonnaise

1 large egg yolk
(see Note)

1 1/2 teaspoons fresh lemon juice, more to taste

1 1/2 teaspoons red wine vinegar, more to taste

1/2 teaspoon finely chopped fresh parsley

Kosher salt and freshly ground black pepper to taste

1/2 cup vegetable oil, such as canola, corn, or grapeseed oil

1 anchovy fillet, rinsed (if oil-packed) or soaked in a couple changes of water (if salt-packed), and finely chopped (1 tablespoon)

1 1/2 teaspoons capers, rinsed (if oil-packed) or soaked in a couple changes of water (if salt-packed), and finely chopped

Worcestershire sauce to taste

FOR THE MAYONNAISE: In a medium bowl, whisk together the egg yolk and 1 teaspoon each of the lemon juice and red wine vinegar. Add the parsley, season with a little salt and pepper, and whisk again to combine. Begin adding the oil very slowly, almost drop by drop, whisking the whole time. Once about a third of the oil has been added, and the mixture has thickened considerably, you can add the oil more steadily, but only add more oil as each addition becomes thoroughly blended. Stir in the anchovy and capers as well as a few drops of the Worcestershire sauce. Taste and add more lemon juice or vinegar and Worcestershire sauce to taste. Serve the mayonnaise soon after making it or refrigerate it for up to 2 days. *(continued)*

For the zucchini

1 cup all-purpose flour

1 teaspoon kosher salt, more to taste

Freshly ground black pepper

2 whole eggs, beaten with
2 tablespoons water

2 cups dry, unseasoned bread crumbs, preferably *panko* (see Sources)

2 medium zucchini (**7** ounces each), washed and sliced **1/4** inch thick on a slight diagonal

Olive oil for frying

To coat the zucchini: Put the flour on a plate or in a wide bowl and season it with the salt and a little pepper. Position the beaten eggs near the flour. Have the bread crumbs also nearby on a plate or in a wide bowl. Dip each slice of zucchini in the flour, then the eggs, then the flour again, and then the eggs. Finally, dip the slices into the bread crumbs, patting them on if necessary to make them adhere. If you have the time, refrigerate the breaded zucchini on a plate or wire rack for 15 to 20 minutes before frying; this helps the coating firm up, making it adhere better as it cooks.

TO PAN-FRY THE ZUCCHINI

Have ready a paper towel–lined plate. In a large, heavy-based skillet heat 1/4 cup vegetable oil over medium-high heat. Add the zucchini in one layer (you may need to do this in batches), and cook until well browned on one side. Flip the pieces over and cook on the other side until well browned and tender. Transfer the zucchini to the lined plate to drain and immediately season with salt.

TO DEEP-FRY THE ZUCCHINI

Have ready a paper towel–lined plate. Pour enough oil into a heavy-based, high-sided saucepan so that the oil is at least 2 inches deep. (Be sure the pot is less than halfway full to prevent the oil from bubbling over during frying.) Heat the oil until it reads 350°F on a frying thermometer (also called a candy thermometer). Fry the zucchini in batches, if necessary, until tender and deep golden brown, 3 minutes. Adjust the heat as needed to keep the temperature close to 350°F. Lift the zucchini out of the oil using a slotted spoon or a Chinese skimmer and drain it on the lined plate. Immediately season with salt. Serve the fried zucchini while still hot with some of the mayonnaise on the side.

> NOTE While the risk for contracting salmonella from raw or undercooked eggs is extremely small, you may want to look for eggs pasteurized in the shell, a new product becoming available at supermarkets (see Sources, page 288).

WHICH WINE?

A **Montepulciano d'Abruzzo** would make a good, reasonably priced companion for this humble yet delicious fried fare.

CREAMY POLENTA WITH A
FRICASSEE OF MUSHROOMS

This polenta dish has become a signature starter at L'Impero. Waiters bring the mushrooms to the table in tiny copper saucepans. The lid to the pan is ceremoniously lifted and the mushrooms and their heavenly cooking juices are spooned over a waiting bowl of our Creamy Polenta (page 234). You probably won't go to such lengths at home, but I do suggest serving the mushrooms piping hot just after the addition of the truffle oil, so that, like our patrons, you appreciate the aroma of this dish at its peak. My favorite mushrooms to use in the fricassee include blue foots, black trumpets, and hen-of-the-woods, but even if you use only cultivated mushrooms, say a mix of creminis and shiitakes, your results will be delicious.

MAKES **4** SERVINGS

1/4 cup olive oil

2 medium shallots, thinly sliced

8 ounces mixed domestic and wild mushrooms, sliced or cut into naturally occurring pieces, **2** cups

1/2 cup homemade Chicken Reduction (page 15) or purchased chicken reduction, diluted with water until a little thicker than chicken stock

Creamy Polenta (page 234)

1 tablespoon snipped fresh chives

1/2 teaspoon white truffle oil

IN A LARGE SAUTÉ PAN, heat the oil over medium heat. Add the shallots and cook, stirring, until they just begin to color on their edges. Add the mushrooms and cook until the liquid is released. Add the chicken reduction, bring to a boil, reduce to a bubbling simmer, and cook until the liquid is reduced by half. (You can prepare the mushrooms ahead up to this point; reheat them over medium-high heat just before serving.)

Have the polenta portioned out into warm bowls. Just before serving, reheat the mushrooms if necessary. Toss the mushrooms with the chives and drizzle a little of the truffle oil over the mushrooms. Be careful not to cook the truffle oil more than a few seconds, because the flavor and aroma dissipate quickly.

(continued)

Spoon some mushrooms and some of the cooking juices over each serving of polenta.

WHICH WINE?

This is a dish that takes time to cook and needs nurturing. It deserves a wine that is special. Splurge on an older **Barbaresco** (DOCG).

BAKED POLENTA "CROUTONS" WITH **SAUTÉED CHICKEN** LIVERS AND CAPERS

MAKES **8** APPETIZER SERVINGS
OR **4** MAIN-DISH SERVINGS

3 cups water

1 cup milk

2 teaspoons kosher salt

1 cup cornmeal, preferably coarse (see page 10)

3 to **4** tablespoons olive oil

1/4 cup grated Parmigiano-Reggiano

1 medium onion, chopped

4 sprigs fresh thyme

1 pound chicken livers, well trimmed and halved

Kosher salt and freshly ground black pepper

1 tablespoon rinsed capers, chopped

2 tablespoons sherry vinegar

1/2 cup homemade Chicken Reduction (page 15) or purchased chicken reduction diluted with water until a little thicker than chicken stock

IN A MEDIUM SAUCEPAN, bring the water and milk to a boil. Whisk in the salt and the cornmeal and cook, still whisking, for a couple of minutes. Reduce the heat to low and cook, stirring occasionally, until the polenta has thickened and tastes tender, 45 minutes.

Lightly grease a 9-inch-square baking pan with a little olive oil. Spoon all of the polenta into the prepared pan. Refrigerate the polenta until quite cold and firm, about 4 hours.

Twenty minutes before serving, heat the oven to 350°F and lightly oil a sided sheet pan. Cut the polenta into four squares and the squares into triangles and place the triangles on the baking sheet. Drizzle with a little olive oil and sprinkle with cheese. Bake until the polenta is heated through and the cheese has melted, 20 to 25 minutes. (If you would like to brown the cheesy tops, go ahead and place the baking sheet under the broiler briefly.)

Meanwhile, heat 2 tablespoons olive oil in a large sauté pan over high heat. Add the onion and thyme sprigs, and cook, stirring, until the onion begins to brown, about 5 minutes. Season the chicken livers well with salt and pepper, add them to the pan, and cook them for about one minute on each side. Add the capers and vinegar and cook until the vinegar is reduced almost completely. Add the chicken reduction and cook until reduced by half.

Divide the baked polenta triangles among four or eight warm plates and top with the chicken livers and the sauce from the pan. Serve immediately.

WHICH WINE?

A **Nebbiolo d'Alba** (DOC) has rich fruit and is quite luscious, which makes it a good match for roasted or braised meats and game or gamey flavors, as in the case of the chicken livers. A good-quality Nebbiolo d'Alba makes a wise choice while you're waiting for that more expensive Barolo to age.

When I make polenta to be baked or fried, I use a combination of milk and water to make the polenta firm up and hold together better. (The exception to this is the pan-fried Polenta and Speck Canederli on page 236, which uses a creamy polenta but also includes bread crumbs to help hold the polenta together during frying.) Cut small, these polenta squares work well as an appetizer. Cut a little larger, they can be lunch. If chicken livers are not your thing, you can substitute boneless, skinless chicken thighs, cut into small pieces and cooked just a bit longer. It's a different dish, but also delicious.

BAKED POLENTA MARGARITA

This pizzalike polenta is fun, casual food; play around with it, adding different toppings.

MAKES **8** APPETIZER SERVINGS
OR **4** MAIN-DISH SERVINGS

3 cups water

1 cup milk

2 teaspoons kosher salt

1 cup cornmeal, preferably coarse
(see page 10)

1/4 cup plus **2** tablespoons grated
Parmigiano-Reggiano or grana Padano

3 to 4 tablespoons olive oil

4 cloves garlic

Pinch of crushed red pepper

1 pint cherry tomatoes, halved

2 tablespoons Fresh Tomato Sauce
(page 104) or other good-quality,
lightly seasoned tomato sauce

4 ounces fresh mozzarella,
grated or cut into small cubes

8 to **10** whole basil leaves,
torn into pieces

IN A MEDIUM SAUCEPAN, bring the water and milk to a boil. Whisk in the salt and the cornmeal and cook, still whisking, for 2 minutes. Reduce the heat to low and cook, stirring ccasionally, until the polenta has thickened, 45 minutes. Stir in the $1/4$ cup grated cheese and cook until the cheese has melted.

Lightly grease a 9-inch-square baking pan with olive oil. Spoon all of the polenta into the prepared pan. Refrigerate the polenta until quite cold and firm, about 4 hours.

To serve, heat the oven to 350°F and lightly oil a sided sheet pan. Cut the polenta into 4 squares and place on the sheet. Drizzle with a little olive oil and bake until heated through. Heat 2 tablespoons olive oil in a large sauté pan over medium heat. Add the garlic and crushed red pepper and cook, stirring 2 minutes. Add the tomatoes and cook 10 minutes. Add the tomato sauce and bring to a boil. Season to taste and keep warm.

Divide the mozzarella among the polenta. Top with the tomato mixture and a little cheese. Bake in the oven until the mozzarella is fully melted, 20 minutes. Sprinkle with the basil and serve.

WHICH WINE?
I like a **Cerasuolo di Vittoria** (DOC) with this.

SEARED SCALLOPS WITH
FARRO AND SEAFOOD RAGU

MAKES **4** SERVINGS

3 spot prawns or **4** extra-large shrimp, peeled, deveined, and chopped

1/4 teaspoon chopped fresh rosemary

Small pinch of crushed red pepper

1/2 garlic clove, finely chopped

2 tablespoons plus **1** teaspoon olive oil

Kosher salt

1/2 cup farro

8 small clams, such as Manila clams, tiny littlenecks, or even cockles, cleaned

8 mussels, cleaned and beards trimmed

8 large sea scallops (be sure to get dry, untreated scallops)

Freshly ground black pepper

1 tablespoon finely chopped scallions

1/4 cup chopped cooked lobster meat (optional)

IN A SMALL BOWL, toss the shrimp with the rosemary, crushed red pepper, garlic, and 1 teaspoon olive oil.

Bring a medium saucepan full of salted water to a boil. (Farro will expand to about three times the volume you started with, so be sure your pot is big enough to accommodate the finished amount.) Add the farro, reduce the heat to a gentle boil, and cook until just tender, adding more water if needed. The time can vary depending on the grain, and whether it has had a soak, from 25 to 45 minutes. Drain and reserve.

In another saucepan, combine the clams, mussels, and $1/4$ cup water. Cover the pan and cook the mollusks until they open. Drain in a colander set over a bowl to catch the cooking liquid. Remove the meat from the shells; reserve the meat and discard the shells. Carefully strain the liquid through a fine strainer, leaving any sediment behind, and reserve the cooking liquid. (All of the preceding can be done earlier in the day and kept refrigerated.)

Remove the muscle on the side of the sea scallops and discard. Season the scallops with salt and pepper. Combine the cooked farro, the liquid from cooking the mussels and clams, and the scallions in a large sauté pan and heat over medium heat. In a separate sauté pan, heat the remaining 2 tablespoons olive oil over high heat. Add the scallops and brown thoroughly on one side, 2 to 3 minutes. Turn the scallops over, remove the pan from the heat, and let the residual heat from the pan finish cooking them for 5 minutes to a medium rare. In the meantime, add the shrimp, the reserved mussels and clams—and the lobster if you're going all out—to the pan with the farro and heat thoroughly to cook the shrimp.

To serve: Divide the farro mixture among four plates and top with two scallops each.

WHICH WINE?

This is actually a very full-flavored dish and can therefore be paired with an intense wine, although I would keep it white. A **Verdicchio dei Castelli di Jesi (DOC) Riserva** has been described by some as Italy's premier wine to serve with fish, and I would agree.

This is a really elegant starter for a serious dinner party. It has a fabulous, intense, oceany flavor and, despite having no butter or cream, it is also quite rich. This richness, which comes mainly from the scallops, is why I like to serve it with chewy, earthy farro. Also known as spelt, farro looks like barley and is available at Italian groceries and gourmet markets (see Sources). I cook it like pasta in a lot of boiling salted water until al dente. If you want to go all out with this dish, add about a quarter cup of chopped, cooked lobster to the ragu.

STEWED FRESH SQUID
IN SPICY GUAZZETTO

The first time I heard the word *guazzetto* I turned to my good friend Roberto DeAngelis, who is from Capri, and asked him to tell me what the word means. The word he came up with was *splashy*. That makes perfect sense to me as a guazzetto is kind of like a soup with a lot of ingredients but with only enough broth to cover the bottom of the bowl by about 1/4 inch. You could look at this as just enough liquid for the ingredients to splash around in. Or just enough splash to ruin a good shirt. The actual dish comes together quite fast; the way to avoid overcooking the squid is to have all of the ingredients ready and at arm's reach as the total cooking time for the squid from the moment it hits the pan should be about three minutes.

MAKES **4** SERVINGS

2 cloves garlic, finely chopped

1/4 cup olive oil

2 cups Lobster-Tomato Broth (page 13), homemade Chicken Broth (page 14), or purchased low-salt chicken broth

1 pound fresh squid, cleaned

1/2 cup finely diced (1/4 inch) potatoes

Kosher salt to taste

1/2 cup finely diced (1/4 inch) zucchini

1 teaspoon crushed red pepper

1 teaspoon chopped fresh parsley

1/2 cup quartered baby or cherry tomatoes

1 teaspoon chopped fresh scallion

4 slices Italian bread, grilled or broiled

Soak the garlic in the olive oil for at least $^1/2$ hour and up to a day.

Heat the broth over medium-low heat.

Rinse the squid under cold water and pat dry with paper towel. Cut the bodies of the squid crosswise into $^1/4$-inch-wide rings. Cut the tentacles in half lengthwise and, if long, crosswise into 2-inch pieces.

Cook the potatoes in a small pot of salted boiling water until just tender, 3 to 5 minutes. Drain and pat dry.

Heat a very large—ideally 14-inch—sauté pan over high heat. Strain the garlic oil into the pan and let it get hot. Add zucchini and the potato followed by the calamari and crushed red pepper; remove the pan from the heat. As soon as the calamari start to curl, add the broth, parsley, tomatoes, and scallion. Divide the calamari, vegetables, and broth among four warm bowls and serve with the bread.

WHICH WINE?

I seem to be favoring Alto Adige wines for my starters, but here again a wine from that DOC, particularly a **Pinot Bianco**, which has an almost aperitif quality, would work really nicely with this spicy stew.

POLENTA-CRUSTED
SOFT-SHELL CRABS

Polenta shows up in a lot of dishes in my kitchen. Here I use cornmeal in the dredging flour to add a nice crunch to the crab coating. If your ideal way of eating soft-shell crab is a sandwich, you can use this recipe with your favorite garnishes. I, however, prefer to serve the fried crab with a crisp, parsley-dominated vegetable salad (page 52). You can serve the crabs one per person for a first course, or you can cut the crabs in half (after they are cooked) and serve them on small bread plates, or even in wide-rimmed coffee saucers, as a smaller taste if a large meal is to follow. Providing cocktail forks makes the presentation more elegant and the crabs more accessible.

MAKES **4** SERVINGS

4 soft-shell crabs, cleaned (see Note)

1 cup milk

1 cup flour

2 tablespoons cornmeal

Kosher salt and freshly ground black pepper

2 cups soy oil or peanut oil for pan frying

Sea salt to taste

PLACE THE CLEANED CRABS in the milk and let sit for 10 to 15 minutes. Combine the flour and cornmeal on a plate and season with about $1/2$ teaspoon salt and a few grinds of pepper. Position the soaking crabs and the flour mixture near the stove. Also have a few layers of paper towels nearby for draining the oil from the crabs.

Pour the oil into a deep, heavy skillet and heat over medium-high heat. When a bit of the crab-coating mixture sizzles immediately when added to the oil, you are ready to fry.

Lift a crab from the milk and dredge it in the flour mixture, coating both sides well. Shake off the extra flour and place the crab in the hot oil "shell" side down. Let the crabs get golden brown on one side and then flip. Be careful while the crabs are frying; they have a tendency to pop and spray their now hot juices. If they're spraying a lot, use a paring knife to poke the crabs once or twice in the belly. After turning the crabs, let them cook for another 3 to 4 minutes. Remove them from the oil, drain briefly on paper towels, and serve immediately sprinkled with a little sea salt.

NOTE TO CLEAN SOFT-SHELL CRABS For the freshest "softies," the crabs must be alive when you buy them. If you are going to make them the second you get home, you can have the fishmonger clean them for you; if not, you should clean them yourself, which is easy. To clean a crab, cut off the head approximately 1/4 inch below the eyes. (Unlike, say, lobster, soft-shell crabs are quite sluggish, so don't worry about one trying to escape while you clean it.) Press on the crab a little to squeeze out an unpleasantly flavored green bubble. Remove the gill filaments on each side of the crab by peeling back the pointed soft shell and scraping these inedible gills out with a paring knife. On the belly side, bend back the apron (or tail flap) and pull it off using a slight twisting motion.

WHICH WINE?

A fresh, fruity **Vermentino** from the Maremma coast is a perfect white wine to have with this particular crab as well as to sip in the warmer weather when soft-shell crab season kicks off.

ROASTED LOBSTER WITH
CHICKPEAS AND GUANCIALE

Although the lobster is the star of this dish, the *guanciale* works like the best character actor: absolutely natural in the role, vital for an excellent result, but not stealing the show. You won't find *guanciale*, which is cured pig jowl, in most (or any) supermarkets. So check out page 9, where I describe why I love it so much and tell you where you can get it. Then go ahead and order some. Because if I say that you can substitute pancetta for it in this recipe you probably will—and you may never seek out this wonderful product. So here's the deal: You can't make this dish without the *guanciale*. Really. I mean it. The *guanciale* adds a voluptuousness that just can't be matched by any other ingredient. So go pick up the phone and get your supply; you'll be thanking me every time you use it.

MAKES **4** SERVINGS

2 whole pound lobsters, each 1$\frac{1}{2}$ pounds, boiled in salted water for **5** minutes to parcook them, drained

8 slices (1/4 inch thick) *guanciale*, julienned

1 shallot, sliced

Pinch of crushed red pepper

2 sprigs rosemary

1 cup canned or cooked chickpeas

6 Concentrated Tomatoes (page 244), julienned

3 teaspoons fresh lemon juice

2 tablespoons extra virgin olive oil, plus more for finishing

Kosher salt and freshly ground black pepper

1 teaspoon snipped fresh chives

Baby greens for garnish (optional)

REMOVE THE MEAT from the large lobster claws and the tail. Cut the tails lengthwise and remove and discard the intestinal tract. Put the pieces on a small sheet pan and reserve. (You can do this up to a day ahead; wrap the lobster meat in plastic wrap and refrigerate.) Rinse the shells and save them for making the lobster broth on page 13, if you like.

Heat the oven to 300°F. In a medium ovenproof sauté pan over medium heat, cook the *guanciale* to lightly brown it (don't crisp it), 8 to 10 minutes. Add the shallot, crushed red pepper, and rosemary to the pan and cook until the shallot loses its crunch. Toss in the chickpeas and tomatoes and cook in the oven until the chickpeas are very tender, 20 to 25 minutes. (Check on them after about 15 minutes; if the pan is very dry, add a few tablespoons of water to the pan.)

When the chickpeas have about 10 minutes left to go, sprinkle the lobster pieces with 2 teaspoons lemon juice, olive oil, and a little salt and pepper. Heat the lobster in the oven until just cooked through, 6 to 7 minutes. Remove the lobster to a cutting board but reserve any juices in the pan. Slice the meat into bite-size pieces and keep warm.

To the liquid in the sheet pan, add the chives, a drizzle of olive oil, and a teaspoon of lemon juice and stir. To serve, divide the chickpea mixture among four warm dishes. Place the lobster meat on top of the chickpeas. Spoon the liquid over the lobster and chickpeas and serve garnished with some greens, if you like.

WHICH WINE?

Chardonnay is a classic paring for lobster. A big **Chardonnay Riserva** from Abruzzo would also stand up to the salty *guanciale* and earthy chickpeas.

PARSLEY AND VEGETABLE SALAD

This light, bright, yet delicate salad would go well with all kinds of fried fare, from calamari to zucchini blossoms, as well as the Polenta-Crusted Soft-Shell Crabs on page 46.

MAKES **4** SERVINGS

1$\frac{1}{2}$ cups well-washed and dried flat-leaf parsley leaves

3 tablespoons extra virgin olive oil

1$\frac{1}{2}$ teaspoons red wine vinegar

3/4 cup very fine julienne of zucchini (**1** small zucchini)

15 cherry or grape tomatoes, quartered

1/2 cup very finely julienned carrot (**1** small carrot)

15 halved baby radishes (if available) or **3** larger ones, shaved with a vegetable peeler

Kosher salt to taste

TOSS ALL OF THE ingredients together just before serving.

OLIVE OIL–POACHED RABBIT WITH **BABY GREENS** AND **SHAVED** PARMIGIANO-REGGIANO

You won't believe just how tender and wonderful rabbit can become when cooked so long and so gently. And I mean long. I generally let the rabbit cook in a very low oven for six hours. The key word in that sentence is *let* as you need do nothing to the rabbit during those six hours. The cooked rabbit will then keep, refrigerated in the strained olive oil, for a few weeks, so you may even want to double the recipe to make more. In the fall, I like to add shaved porcini to the salad and switch the sunflower seeds to walnuts. I generally serve this dish as a first course, but it would also work as a light supper or a fine lunch.

MAKES **4** SERVINGS

For poaching the rabbit

4 rabbit legs (see Note)

Kosher salt and freshly ground black pepper

4 sprigs fresh thyme

2 rosemary sprigs

3 shallots, sliced

2 cups olive oil, more if needed

Pinch of crushed red pepper flakes

TO POACH THE RABBIT: Heat the oven to 250°F. Season the rabbit legs with a little salt and pepper and lay them in one layer in a baking pan. Cover with all of the poaching ingredients and cover the pan with aluminum foil. Carefully put the pan in the oven and cook until the meat is easy to pull off of the bone with a fork, $5^1/2$ to 6 hours.

Remove the rabbit from the oil, reserving both the rabbit and oil, and let both cool to room temperature. Ladle or pour the oil through a strainer into a clean container that can hold all of the rabbit legs, preferably one with a lid. As you strain the fat, you'll notice the juices from the rabbit have settled to the bottom. You don't want these juices to go into the container, just the fat, so stop pouring while there's still a little oil left in the pan. *(continued)*

For the salad

2 tablespoons red wine vinegar

1 tablespoon balsamic vinegar

Salt and freshly ground black pepper

4 cups baby greens

2 tablespoons sunflower seeds, lightly toasted in a dry skillet

1/4 cup blanched and peeled fresh fava beans (optional; see page 245)

1 ounce Parmigiano-Reggiano

Remove the meat from the rabbit legs and put the pieces of meat in the strained oil. Cover the container and store the rabbit in the refrigerator. The rabbit can be kept up to three weeks if very cold and covered completely with the oil. (Add some additional olive oil if the rabbit pieces are not completely submerged.)

Put the rabbit and its oil in a baking dish or saucepan. Warm the rabbit meat in a 200°F oven or over very low heat on the stove. (Don't let it get too hot, or the rabbit will toughen and your six hours of gentle cooking will have been in vain.)

Reserve about 6 tablespoons of the warm oil. Remove the rabbit meat from the remaining oil and let it drain briefly on some paper towels. Combine the 6 tablespoons oil with the red wine vinegar and balsamic vinegar. Season with salt and pepper to taste.

To serve: Divide the rabbit meat among four plates and drizzle it with a little of the vinaigrette. Divide the greens among the four plates, piling the leaves on top of the rabbit. Drizzle with a little more vinaigrette. Sprinkle the sunflower seeds and fava beans, if using, over the greens. Use a peeler to shave some Parmigiano-Reggiano over the salad and serve.

NOTE I use just the meatier hind legs of the rabbit for this dish. The tiny front legs are barely worth the bother and the loin can turn out too dry for my taste. If you can buy only whole rabbit, buy a couple (rabbit is not expensive). Use the hind legs for this recipe and sear or grill the loin and front legs another night. Go ahead and freeze the rabbit if you would rather spread out your rabbit enjoyment.

WHICH WINE?

An intense, fragrant red, such as a **Roero** (DOC), made primarily from Nebbiolo grapes, is just the match for the subtly gamey rabbit and the autumnal salad.

Plating Food to Look Its Best

WHILE HOW GOOD THE FOOD TASTES will always be more important than how pretty it looks, visual appeal definitely adds to the appreciation of a good meal. This first impression offers a clue (especially at a restaurant) that care and thought was put into the making of the food. I know that some restaurants take this too far, and it can look like more effort and energy was put into assembling that edible tower of food than was put into actually cooking it, but I really do believe food should look good. And it doesn't take much more time at all to plate food simply but attractively.

Here is perhaps the single best piece of practical advice I can give as far as making food look good on the plate: Don't place your cooked protein—whether it's beef, chicken, or fish—directly on the plate. Now, I am not a proponent of "tall" food, but there is a very good reason why you don't want to simply lay the main component down flat on the plate. While that meat (or fish or chicken) was heating up, its interior juices began moving and flowing. When it's then put flat on a plate, a bit of a suction is created and those juices get pulled right out of the meat. The result is an unattractive puddle that proceeds to run haphazardly all over the plate. How to avoid this? Instead of keeping the various elements of the plate separate, the way we all demanded our food to be presented when we were kids, integrate the elements by resting the cooked protein either on top of or against the polenta, fregola, potatoes, or what have you. In my recipes that include a side dish with the main attraction, such plating directions are given. You can also take a look at the pictures in the book and get the idea.

At the restaurant we often place metal rings in the center of a large plate (you can use a large round cookie cutter at home) and fill the ring with, say, some risotto or lentils. We lay the vegetables or fish or whatever on top and then pull the ring up and off. You're not looking to have a perfect circle of food, but this little trick does make the plate look both clean and appealing with the focus—thanks to that white space on the edge of the plate—perfectly centered on the food.

Squeeze bottles? Yeah, we use them. We don't have the inclination or time during service to use them to create works of colorful modern art that you sometimes see on fussier presented food, but I do like how you can add a very controlled amount of a flavoring, for example, the ginger oil that we pair with our raw fish appetizers, to the dish. And if it looks good, all the better.

Finally, a bit of green is almost never a bad thing. But it doesn't always have to be parsley. I often use scallions, snipped very tiny, to add not only a bright color but also a dose of flavor.

Oh, one last thing: Stick with white plates. Think about it: How many really good restaurants have you been to that served their food on colored plates? I thought so.

Salads and Soups

* Mixed Greens with Balsamic Vinaigrette, Pecorino, and Toasted Hazelnuts
* Warm Pear and Taleggio Salad
* Heirloom Tomato Salad
* Raw Mushroom Salad with Oregano Vinaigrette and Toasted Ricotta Salata

Warm Fagiolini and Goat Cheese Salad with Truffle Vinaigrette and Baby Greens

* Garlicky Mussel and Green Bean Soup

Chilled Roasted Red Pepper Soup with Eggplant Caponata

Spring Pea Soup with Herbed Goat Cheese Croutons

Puree of Caramelized Onion with Rosemary

White Bean and Escarole Soup with Rosemary and Sage

Curried Butternut Squash Soup with Crispy Shallots and Goat Cheese

LAYERS OF FLAVOR are a hallmark of all good cooking, but I find them especially important when creating a superb salad or a delicious soup. Whether served as a first course to start a meal or at the end as a refreshing conclusion, a good salad presents flavors that are integrated in such a way that the flavors get more interesting with every bite. Once you understand the basics, a superb salad takes no more time to make than a mediocre one.

"Begin with the best ingredients." I know every chef says that about almost every dish, but for salads, where most of the ingredients remain in their raw state, we really, really mean it. Once you have your fabulous ingredients, think about how to best maximize flavors and textures: Should I toast the nuts? Should I marinate the onion? Should I warm the cheese? Of course any greens or herbs should be well washed, but it's just as important to dry them well. When it comes time to dress the salad, I don't always toss the greens and the vinaigrette. For better control, I'll assemble the elements on the salad plate and drizzle a little dressing over each layer.

The same kind of care goes into building a great soup. As with the salad, the ingredients must come together in a way that feels natural yet stimulating. Aromatics, such as garlic, shallots, or red pepper, create a deeply flavored foundation. There is the main ingredient, whether mussels, butternut squash, or peas, and herbs or spices for added intrigue. As for the liquid, a well-balanced homemade broth is the gold standard, but good-quality purchased broth works very well, especially since most of the soups are a puree of flavorful ingredients. To a pureed soup I add something chunky—reserved beans, sautéed vegetables, or fried shallots—for flavor, color, and, most important, texture. At the restaurant, we often do this with a little pomp and circumstance. A water brings to the table a bowl that's empty save for a tiny pile of, say, beans or caponata, and then pours the soup into the bowl over the pile. This is not only good theater but it also lets the person eating the soup catch a glimpse of what fun and flavor are in store. Most of the recipes here simply direct you to add the non-pureed ingredients to the pot or bowl and then serve, but you never know: You might one day want to give your dinner guests a little show.

A final thought about these soups: If you don't have an immersion blender (also called a hand blender or a stick blender), you might want to buy one. With an immersion blender, you can puree the soup right in the pot it cooked in instead of ladling it batch by batch into a food processor or conventional blender. An immersion blender also makes adding and emulsifying olive oil (something I do often with soups) a much easier proposition.

MIXED GREENS WITH BALSAMIC VINAIGRETTE, PECORINO, AND TOASTED HAZELNUTS

> Toasted hazelnuts and Pecorino cheese make a great, slightly unexpected combination in this salad. The vinaigrette calls for a lot of black pepper, which punches up the flavor of the entire salad.

MAKES **4** SERVINGS

For the vinaigrette

1 teaspoon Dijon mustard

2 tablespoons balsamic vinegar

1 tablespoon red wine vinegar

1/2 cup olive oil

1 teaspoon freshly ground black pepper

Kosher salt to taste

For the salad

1 small head Belgian endive, root trimmed, quartered lengthwise, and cut into matchstick pieces

1 small head radicchio, cored, quartered, and cut into matchstick pieces

2 handfuls mixed leafy greens

2 tablespoons finely chopped, toasted hazelnuts

2 tablespoons freshly (preferably finely) grated pecorino Romano

COMBINE ALL OF THE VINAIGRETTE INGREDIENTS and shake or whisk until emulsified. You can make this up to three days ahead. Cover and refrigerate until ready to use.

(continued)

In a large bowl, toss together the endive, radicchio, greens, hazelnuts, and cheese. Toss gently with enough vinaigrette to lightly coat the leaves. Heap the salad onto plates and serve.

WHICH WINE?

A **Trebbiano d'Abruzzo** (DOC). I mentioned before that Italian wines can be confusing. Here's a perfect example of why. Trebbiano is a grape, but it's not the one used in this wine. The grape used is actually Bombino Bianco, which is not related to Trebbiano at all. Go figure. The toastiness of the Trebbiano d'Abruzzo matches the toasted nuts nicely and soothes the sharpness of the Pecorino.

WARM PEAR AND
TALEGGIO SALAD

In place of the hit-you-over-the-head flavor of blue cheese typically served with this style salad, barely soft slices of Taleggio, a rich cow's milk cheese from Lombardy, offer more nuance and intrigue. The idea here is to achieve full, rounded flavors with little fuss. I like to keep the slices of pear and Taleggio on the larger side. At this size, they're easy to find under all that lettuce. I also like that, because you need to cut into them yourself, you create different flavor combinations—a bit more cheese, a bit more pear—with every mouthful. This is a knife and fork salad.

MAKES **4** SERVINGS

3 ripe pears, peeled, quartered, and cored

1 tablespoon honey

2 medium or **4** small heads red oak leaf lettuce

2 tablespoons balsamic vinegar

1 tablespoon red wine vinegar

1 teaspoon Dijon mustard

1/2 cup extra virgin olive oil

Salt and freshly ground black pepper to taste

6 ounces Taleggio cheese, cut into **8** slices

1 1/2 tablespoons crispy shallots (see page 84; optional)

HEAT THE OVEN to 250°F. Toss the pears with the honey and put the pears on a baking sheet. Warm them in the oven for 15 minutes.

Meanwhile, if you have small heads of lettuce, trim the root ends but keep the heads intact. If you have larger heads, separate the leaves. Wash and dry the lettuce well.

In a small bowl or in a squeeze bottle, combine the balsamic vinegar, red wine vinegar, mustard, and olive oil. Whisk or shake well to emulsify. Season to taste with salt and pepper.

To serve, divide the warm pear quarters among four large plates. Position two slices of Taleggio among the pear slices. If using loose leaves of lettuce, pile the leaves on the pears and Taleggio in the center of the plate, hiding most of the fruit and cheese. If using whole heads, cut them in half lengthwise and lay the halves on the pears and cheese. Using the squeeze bottle or a tablespoon, drizzle the dressing on the salad. Top with some crispy shallots, if you like.

WHICH WINE?

Try an **Arneis** from Piedmont; this white wine has great acidity and a fruity, rich finish that won't clash with the Taleggio.

HEIRLOOM TOMATO SALAD

This salad (perhaps obviously) is best at the height of tomato season. However, if you have a hankering for tomatoes in the dead of winter, this salad can still be pretty damn good, although you will want to marinate winter tomatoes for longer than summer tomatoes, as they need a bigger flavor boost. Whatever the weather outside, the tomatoes are best when seasoned in advance. Ripe, juicy tomatoes will benefit from as little as a half hour, but for all tomatoes, 8 to 24 hours ahead works best. (After more than a day, however, the tomatoes start to break down and become mushy.) You can use whatever size and shape (and color) tomato you like for this salad. I cut cherry tomatoes in half, plum tomatoes in quarters or sixths. When I have those really large tomatoes, I cut them in half and then slice the halves.

MAKES **4** TO **6** SERVINGS

2 pounds tomatoes

3 tablespoons extra virgin olive oil

3 to **4** tablespoons red wine vinegar

5 fresh basil leaves, finely chopped

1 teaspoon kosher or coarse salt

Freshly ground black pepper to taste

4 cups mixed leafy greens

1/2 cup shaved Parmigiano-Reggiano

4 to **6** slices ciabatta bread, drizzled with more olive oil, and grilled (or broiled) at the last moment

CUT THE TOMATOES INTO HALVES, quarters, or slices, depending on their size. Put them on a rimmed plate or something similar. Drizzle the olive oil and vinegar over them, and then sprinkle on the basil, salt, and pepper. In an ideal world, the tomatoes would bathe in the marinade for at least 3 hours. If you don't have that much time, don't worry about it. Allow the tomatoes to marinate for as long as possible while you get the rest of the meal ready. If there is liquid collecting on the plate—the salt will prompt the tomatoes to release their liquid—baste the tomatoes with it.

Divide the greens among four or six plates. Place the tomatoes on top of the greens. Spoon or pour the marinade that remains behind on the plate over the greens and the tomatoes. Sprinkle with the Parmigiano, top with some fresh cracked pepper, and serve with the grilled ciabatta bread.

(continued)

Salads and Soups

WHICH WINE?

A **Frascati** (DOC) from Latium on the western coast of central Italy is a good, summery choice, especially if you choose a spumante-style (sparkling) wine.

The Best Meals Offer More Than One Course

THINK OF THE BEST MEALS IN YOUR LIFE. Me? I have had lots of them. From dinner at my grandmother's house in Connecticut culminating with her biscuitlike *taralle* to tasting menus at Daniel in New York City to a truffle-studded dinner on the back roads of Piedmont cooked by two sisters in their eighties. They run the gamut. But when I recall my favorite meals, what they have in common is that the flavors of the food as well as the conversation at the table increased in depth and intensity as the courses came and went, until by the time dessert arrived, everyone at the table was satiated, contented, and relaxed.

Now, most of us don't eat this way all of the time. And that's fine. But when you are entertaining, or having a special dinner at home, you might want to think about the sequence of the food you are presenting. Having something placed in front of you at the wrong time can throw off the balance of the experience. Earlier courses should generally be bright and light. If made with a rich ingredient, such as scallops or foie gras, less is actually more for these courses.

At L'Impero, it's strongly recommended that when ordering for dinner, one begins with an appetizer, either a special small bite or some soup, salad, or a small portion of polenta. That's followed by a risotto or pasta course and then a main course. Ideally, the meal continues with a cheese course and dessert.

Every chef wants his customers to eat on his terms. And nothing makes me happier than when someone orders my full tasting menu; that way I know they are fully experiencing my vision of what a good meal should be. But I've had some people come in and eat all starches: a polenta dish, some risotto, and, finally, some spaghetti. It's not necessarily how I think one should eat, but those customers left satisfied.

With this book in your hands, you can go all out and serve a multicourse meal, something that's really nice to do once in a while, especially if you enjoy having friends linger at the table. That said, sometimes a risotto and a salad is the perfect meal for dinner, no "entrée" needed. Other times, all you want (or maybe have time for) is a really good bowl of pasta. But do take into consideration that the recipes in this book are portioned so that they will not be served completely on their own.

RAW MUSHROOM SALAD WITH

OREGANO VINAIGRETTE AND

TOASTED RICOTTA SALATA

Ricotta salata is a smooth, firm, sheep's milk cheese with a mild, sweet milk flavor. Made from curd that's pressed, dried, and then aged for at least three months, it's originally from Sicily. Toasting the ricotta salata in the oven dries it out a bit more and deepens its mild nutty flavor. I always have marinated red onions on hand, so it's easy for me to toss some in. They add a nice tang and crunch to the salad, but the salad is fine without them as well.

MAKES **4** SERVINGS

3 ounces ricotta salata

2 tablespoons balsamic vinegar

2 tablespoons red wine vinegar

1 tablespoon chopped fresh parsley

1$\frac{1}{2}$ teaspoons chopped fresh oregano

1/2 cup olive oil

1/4 cup Fresh Tomato Sauce (page 104) or other good-quality, lightly seasoned tomato sauce, pureed to thin it

Salt and freshly ground black pepper to taste

3 small hearts of romaine, cut into quarters

1$\frac{1}{4}$ cups sliced mushrooms (I like to use 3/4 cup shiitake mushrooms and 1/2 cup fresh porcinis, but use what you like and what you can find)

Marinated Red Onions, optional (page 18)

HEAT THE OVEN to 350°F. Bake the cheese in a small pan or on a baking sheet until it's lightly browned on the outside, 10 to 15 minutes. In a small bowl or squeeze bottle, combine the balsamic vinegar, red wine vinegar, parsley, oregano, olive oil, and tomato sauce. Whisk or shake to emulsify and season with salt and pepper. At the restaurant, I layer the hearts of romaine, mushrooms, and onions, squeezing a little vinaigrette on each layer. This might be a little fussy for home, but give it a try if you're in the mood for a pretty presentation. Otherwise, divide the romaine hearts, mushrooms, and onions, if using, among four plates and squeeze or drizzle some of the vinaigrette over each plate.

Using the side of a box grater or a vegetable peeler, shave off slices of the ricotta salata and top the salads with the slices. Drizzle or squeeze on a bit more dressing, season with a bit more salt and pepper, and serve.

WHICH WINE?

Try a white wine from **Offida Pecorino** (DOC) in the Marches region of central Italy. Its pale yellow color and crisp acidity go well with the slightly salty ricotta and the meaty mushrooms.

WARM FAGIOLINI AND GOAT CHEESE SALAD WITH TRUFFLE VINAIGRETTE AND BABY GREENS

Fagiolini means string bean in Italian. I generally make this salad with French green beans (also called haricot verts) and yellow wax beans. But you could just as easily use the flatter Romano beans (similar to green beans) or even dragon tongue beans, which have cool purple striping. Whichever kind of bean I use, I halve or quarter them lengthwise. They look less clunky on the plate that way and have a better mouthfeel. As for the potatoes and lentils in this dish, one or both could be omitted and life would still go on with its lovely swift pace. But if you have the time (and all of the salad's components can be prepared ahead), the lentils and potatoes add contrast and interest. I like Peruvian blue potatoes simply because they are so beautiful.

MAKES **4** SERVINGS

4 ounces soft, fresh goat cheese

1 teaspoon chopped fresh parsley

1 teaspoon chopped fresh thyme

1 teaspoon snipped fresh chives

Salt and freshly ground black pepper to taste

1/2 cup plus **1** tablespoon extra virgin olive oil

1/4 cup French lentils (also called European lentils and lentils du Puy)

1/2 cup finely diced potatoes, preferably Peruvian blue potatoes

15 to **20** green beans

15 to **20** yellow wax beans

2 tablespoons red wine vinegar

1 tablespoon balsamic vinegar

1 teaspoon white truffle oil

3 cups baby greens

IN A SMALL BOWL, mix together the goat cheese, parsley, thyme, and chives. Season with a little salt and pepper. Divide

the herbed cheese into four balls, put them on a small baking pan, drizzle them with 1 tablespoon olive oil, and reserve.

In a small saucepan, cover the lentils by 2 inches with well-salted water. Bring to a boil, reduce to a simmer, and cook the lentils until they are tender, 18 to 20 minutes. Meanwhile, cook the potatoes in the same way in another small saucepan; they should be tender in 5 minutes. Drain and reserve the lentils and the potatoes separately.

Have ready a large bowl of ice water. Boil the green beans and wax beans in ample salted water until they are just tender, 4 to 5 minutes. Plunge them into the ice water. Drain the beans, pat them dry, and slice them lengthwise into halves or quarters, depending on their thickness.

Combine the red wine vinegar, balsamic vinegar, and $1/2$ cup extra virgin olive oil in a small bowl or squeeze bottle. Whisk or shake until emulsified.

Five minutes before serving, heat the oven to 300°F. Heat a large sauté pan over medium-low heat. Add the beans, potatoes, and lentils and just a touch of the vinaigrette and warm everything gently. At the same time, bake the goat cheese for 5 minutes, just to warm it through.

Just before serving, add the truffle oil to the pan of warm beans, potatoes, and lentils, toss gently, and season to taste with salt and pepper. Divide the bean mixture among four plates. Place the warm goat cheese on top. Toss the baby greens with just enough of the vinaigrette to coat the leaves lightly. Lay the greens on top of the goat cheese and serve immediately.

WHICH WINE?

There is a lot going on in this salad, so it needs wine that will cut through it, all while still allowing the focus to be on the dish. A nice **Sauvignon Blanc** from Friuli, with its tart, citrus notes and its acidic fruit qualities, would taste fresh yet subtle.

GARLICKY MUSSEL AND GREEN BEAN SOUP

You know when you get a bowl of steamed mussels, the best part comes at the end when you get to dunk your bread into the brothy liquid waiting at the bottom of the bowl? That's what this soup is all about. You'll note that I don't add wine to the mussels. You'll see why when you taste this; without the wine, the soup tastes mainly and quite vibrantly of the sea. I've added the green beans primarily for color; feel free to substitute tiny broccoli florets or—less colorfully—cooked white beans or chickpeas.

MAKES **4** SERVINGS

1/4 cup olive oil, plus a little more for the bread

4 cloves garlic, sliced very thin, plus another peeled clove for rubbing on the bread

2 sprigs thyme

Crushed red pepper

2 pounds mussels, rinsed

1/2 teaspoon kosher salt

2 cups water

4 slices good-quality Italian bread

24 green beans, sliced into pieces on the diagonal

1/2 cup diced potatoes (optional)

1 tablespoon chopped fresh parsley

HEAT THE OIL in a large, wide pan. Add the garlic, thyme, and red pepper. Add the mussels, salt, and water. Cover and cook until the mussels open. As soon as they open, remove them with a slotted spoon, reserving the liquid. Strain the mussel cooking liquid into a clean saucepan. When cool enough to handle, take the mussels out of their shells and reserve the meat. (You can chuck the shells.) *(continued)*

Rub the bread with a little olive oil and toast both sides under the broiler or on the grill. Rub the toasted bread with the cut clove of garlic.

Add the green beans and potatoes, if using, to the mussel cooking liquid. Bring to a boil. Reduce to a simmer and cook until tender, 4 to 5 minutes. Add the parsley, remove the pan from the heat, and add the mussels. Serve the soup with the toasted bread.

WHICH WINE?
The **Vermentino** wines made in Liguria are particularly crisp. I can eat this soup and drink this wine all day.

CHILLED ROASTED RED PEPPER

SOUP WITH **EGGPLANT CAPONATA**

If you are in the mood for this soup but don't have the ingredients or the time to make the caponata to go with it, don't worry. This soup is delicious—vibrant and full of flavor—on its own. Come to think of it, the caponata would also do well on its own, spread on some bruschetta, say, or as a little side dish. Another option: Serve this soup (with or without the caponata) with the herbed goat cheese on page 70. Roasting peppers over an open flame gives them the best flavor, but you can also broil them. Halve them lengthwise, stem and seed them, put them on a baking sheet, skin side up, and broil until well blackened.

MAKES **4** SERVINGS

For the soup

4 red bell peppers

1/2 cup extra virgin olive oil, plus more for brushing on the peppers

1/4 cup thinly sliced shallots

Pinch of crushed red pepper

2 tablespoons sherry vinegar, plus more to taste

2 cups homemade Chicken Broth (page 14) or purchased low-salt chicken broth or vegetable broth

Kosher salt and freshly ground black pepper to taste

TO MAKE THE SOUP: Heat your grill (gas or coal) to medium-high. Brush the red peppers with a little of the olive oil. Place on a hot grill and char the peppers on their exterior, turning them as needed, until well blackened on all sides. Immediately put the peppers in a container that can close completely, such as a bag that can be sealed or tied or a bowl with a tight-fitting lid. When the peppers are cool enough to handle easily, stem and seed them and peel off their blackened skin. Please do not run water over the peppers to remove the blackened skin or the roasty flavor of the peppers will go down the drain with the charred bits. Instead, use your fingernails or the tip of a paring knife to carefully remove any stubborn specks. *(continued)*

For the caponata

1 medium eggplant, cut into small dice

1 teaspoon kosher salt, plus more to taste

2 tablespoons olive oil

1 small onion, sliced thin

1 plum tomato, stemmed, seeded, and diced

1 tablespoon capers

1/2 teaspoon chopped fresh oregano

1/4 cup Fresh Tomato Sauce (page 104) or other good-quality tomato sauce

In a large saucepan, heat a tablespoon of the olive oil over medium-high heat and sauté the shallots and crushed red pepper. When the shallots are golden, add the peeled roasted red peppers, sherry vinegar, and broth. Season with a little salt and pepper. Bring the soup to a boil and then turn off the heat. Allow the soup to cool a bit and then puree it while adding $1/2$ cup olive oil to create a smooth, emulsified consistency. I like to do this right in the pot with a hand-held mixer, adding the oil as I mix. But you can also puree the soup in batches in a blender, dividing the olive oil among the batches. Refrigerate the soup to serve it slightly chilled. (You can refrigerate the soup for up to three days or freeze it.)

To make the caponata: Put the diced eggplant in a colander and toss with kosher salt. Put the colander in a clean sink, weight the eggplant, and allow the salt to draw out the excess moisture for at least 10 minutes. Do not rinse the eggplant. Pat it dry with paper towels.

Heat the olive oil in a large, straight-sided sauté pan over medium heat. Add the onion and a pinch of salt and sauté until it takes on some color. Add the diced tomato, capers, oregano, tomato sauce, and the eggplant and stir to combine well. Reduce the heat to low, cover the pan, and cook until the eggplant is soft and the mixture stewlike, 25 minutes.

To serve the soup: If the soup is super cold, let it warm up a bit before serving or the flavors will be muted. Before serving, taste the soup and add an additional teaspoon or so of sherry vinegar and more salt and pepper, if needed, to balance the flavor. Divide the soup among four shallow soup bowls. Place a rounded spoonful of the caponata in the center of the bowl and serve.

WHICH WINE?

Try a Sauvignon Blanc from northeast Italy, specifically a **Colli Orientali del Friuli** (DOC).

SPRING PEA SOUP WITH HERBED
GOAT CHEESE CROUTONS

To give this soup a creamy quality, I puree it with ample olive oil. This is really easy to do with an immersion blender, so if you have always wanted one of those gadgets, here's your excuse to go out and buy one. Otherwise, you can simply puree the soup in batches in a standard blender. The soup can go right from blender to bowl, but if you are a fan of cold soups, you might want to try it chilled. Just don't serve it so cold that the flavors become muted. The herbed goat cheese croutons make a satisfying accompaniment—for even more flavor, use an olive-studded baguette. A few poached shrimp, especially ones that have been marinated in a little rosemary, garlic, and parsley, as directed on page 134, would also make a lovely addition.

MAKES **6** SERVINGS OF SOUP
AND **6** CROUTONS

For the soup

$3^1/2$ pounds fresh peas in their pods, shelled to yield $3^1/2$ cups

3 tablespoons plus $^1/2$ cup extra virgin olive oil, divided

3 shallots, thinly sliced

Pinch of crushed red pepper

3 cups homemade Chicken Broth (page 14) or low-salt purchased broth, more if needed

1 cup (a small handful) well-washed and dried spinach leaves

1/2 cup finely diced zucchini

1/2 cup finely chopped leeks

1 tablespoon chopped fresh tarragon

1/2 teaspoon chopped fresh chives

1/2 teaspoon chopped fresh parsley

Kosher salt to taste

For the croutons

3 tablespoons fresh goat cheese

3/4 teaspoon chopped fresh parsley

3/4 teaspoon chopped fresh thyme

3/4 teaspoon snipped fresh chives

Kosher salt and freshly ground black pepper to taste

6 slices baguette

2 teaspoons extra virgin olive oil

FOR THE SOUP: Reserve $1/2$ cup peas. Have ready a large bowl filled with ice and a little water. Heat about 3 tablespoons olive oil in a large saucepan over medium heat. Add the shallots and crushed red pepper and sauté until the shallots are golden. Add the 3 cups of shelled peas and chicken broth. Cook until the peas are soft and just tender, 10 minutes. Don't overcook the peas or the soup will lose its vibrant green color and will feel less fresh. Take the soup off the heat, pour it into a bowl, and place the bowl in the ice bath to quickly cool the soup down. Add the spinach.

If you have an immersion blender, add the remaining $1/2$ cup olive oil now and puree the soup. If not, puree the soup in a blender in batches, adding some of the $1/2$ cup olive oil to each batch to create an emulsion.

Return the soup to a clean saucepan. Add the zucchini, leeks, and reserved peas. Cook over medium heat until the vegetables just begin to lose their "rawness" but are still crisp, 5 minutes. Add the tarragon, chives, and parsley and season to taste with salt. Serve the soup warm or chill it in the refrigerator and serve it cool. Float a goat cheese crouton (see page 80) on top or serve alongside the soup.   *(continued)*

For the croutons: Mash together the goat cheese and herbs and season with salt and pepper. Drizzle the bread with the olive oil. Lightly toast the bread under the broiler and spread the goat cheese on the toasted bread.

WHICH WINE?

A crisp, cold **Sauvignon Blanc** from Alto Adige would go so well with this soup, as both the wine and the soup have lovely herbal undertones.

PUREE OF CARAMELIZED ONION
WITH ROSEMARY

> I like to garnish this with caramelized carrots, stewed rabbit, and roasted chanterelles, which not only tastes wonderful but also makes people feel better about shelling out ten bucks for a bowl of soup. But, truthfully, this soup, although quite humble, is so full of flavor that it doesn't even need a garnish.

MAKES **4** TO **6** SERVINGS

1/4 cup olive oil, plus a tablespoon or so of extra virgin olive oil to finish the soup

2 medium Spanish onions, chopped into large pieces

2 medium red onions, chopped into large pieces

1 to **2** cloves garlic

1/8 teaspoon crushed red pepper, more to taste

1 tablespoon chopped fresh rosemary

6 cups homemade Chicken Broth (page 14) or purchased low-salt chicken broth or vegetable broth

1/4 cup finely diced carrots, sautéed in a bit of olive oil until golden brown (optional)

IN A LARGE SOUP POT, heat the olive oil over medium-high heat. Add the onions, garlic, crushed red pepper, and rosemary. Reduce the heat to medium-low, and cook, stirring occasionally, until the onions become soft and beautifully brown, 35 to 40 minutes. Lower the heat, if need be, to cook the onions gently. Add the broth and increase the heat to bring it to a boil. Reduce the heat so that the soup is bubbling gently and simmer for 15 minutes. Puree the soup with an immersion blender (a hand-held mixer) right in the pot or puree it in batches in a blender. Just before serving, cook the diced carrots, if using, in a little olive oil over medium-high heat until nicely browned. Serve the soup hot with a drizzle of extra virgin olive oil. If using the carrots, sprinkle them right on top of the soup.

WHICH WINE?
An **Albana di Romagna** (DOCG) with its smooth texture and toasty flavor would match in personality the smooth, deep sweetness of this soup.

WHITE BEAN AND ESCAROLE
SOUP WITH ROSEMARY AND SAGE

The sage and the ample crushed red pepper make the flavor of this classic Italian soup a little edgier and more interesting than usual. The pepper gives it heat, while the sage adds a slightly smoky, slightly astringent element to the creamy white beans. I know you can supposedly cook beans using the quick-boil method, but I think a long soak dramatically improves their texture. If you plan to make the soup a day or two before serving, leave out the escarole and add it when you reheat the soup.

MAKES ABOUT 8 CUPS; SERVES 6 TO 8

1/2 cup extra virgin olive oil

1 onion, cut into large pieces

3 whole cloves garlic

1/2 teaspoon crushed red pepper

2 sprigs fresh rosemary

2 sprigs fresh sage

6 ounces pancetta, left in big pieces

2 cups dried white beans, such as cannellini or cranberry beans, rinsed, soaked in water for 24 hours, and drained

3 quarts homemade Chicken Broth (page 14) or purchased low-salt chicken broth

Kosher salt and freshly ground black pepper

3 cups shredded escarole (from 1 head)

IN A LARGE SOUP POT, heat half of the olive oil over medium heat. Add the onion and cook until translucent, about 5 minutes. Add the garlic, crushed red pepper, rosemary, sage, and pancetta. Cook, stirring occasionally, for about 5 minutes to allow the flavors to intermingle and develop. Add the beans and chicken stock. Bring the liquid to a boil, reduce to a gentle simmer, and cook until the beans are tender, 1 1/2 to 2 hours.

With a slotted spoon, transfer the herbs, pancetta, and onion pieces as well as about half of the beans to a sided baking sheet. Pick out some of the pancetta and chop it for a garnish for the soup, if you like. Then discard all but the beans. (Putting it all on the sided sheet makes it easier to pick out the pieces to discard, but you could also pick them out right from the pot.) Puree the removed beans with a couple of tablespoons of olive oil and some salt and pepper and return the puree to the pot. Add the shredded escarole and cook until wilted. Taste and add additional salt and pepper if needed. Serve in warm bowls with any reserved pancetta and an additional drizzle of olive oil.

WHICH WINE?
Although the soup is jazzed up a bit, it still feels pretty traditional and would match nicely with a good Chianti (DOCG), such as a **Chianti Colli Senesi**.

CURRIED BUTTERNUT SQUASH SOUP WITH CRISPY SHALLOTS AND GOAT CHEESE

Maybe curry is not exactly Italian, but I had to include this soup because not only is it a favorite of mine but it's also simple to make, and it freezes beautifully. You can even fry the shallot a day or two ahead of serving the soup. Keep the shallot at room temperature in a bowl covered in plastic wrap or simply wrapped in a paper towel. But be warned: If you do cook the shallot in advance, it will be hard to keep from nibbling—the crisp texture and sweet flavor make the shallot irresistible. You may want to make extra to be sure you have some left for the soup.

MAKES **6** TO **8** SERVINGS

For the soup

1/2 cup extra virgin olive oil

2 medium onions, chopped

1$\frac{1}{2}$ teaspoons curry powder

2 medium (2$\frac{1}{4}$ pounds) butternut squash

2 quarts homemade Chicken Broth (page 14) or purchased low-salt chicken broth

Kosher salt

FOR THE SOUP: Peel and seed the squash, then dice it into 1-inch pieces (about 6 cups). Heat half of the olive oil in a large soup pot. Add the onions and cook for 5 minutes. Add the curry powder and cook, stirring, until the onions are tender, 10 minutes. Add the squash and chicken broth. Bring the soup to a boil, reduce it to a simmer, and cook until the squash is tender, 30 to 40 minutes. Remove the soup from the heat. If you have an immersion blender, add the remaining $\frac{1}{4}$ cup olive oil now and puree the soup in the pot. If not, puree the soup in a blender or food processor in batches, adding some of the olive oil to each batch to create an emulsion. Season to taste with salt.

For the crispy shallots: Heat the vegetable oil in a small sauté

For the crispy shallots

2 shallots, thinly sliced

2 to 3 tablespoons vegetable oil, such as canola, corn, or grapeseed oil

To finish

Fresh goat cheese, plain or herbed (page 70)

pan over medium heat. Add the shallots and cook, stirring occasionally, until well browned all over and crisp. This will take a while, 10 to 12 minutes, but be patient. If you rush, the shallots won't be as sweet or crispy. Drain the shallot slices on paper towels.

To serve: Reheat the soup if necessary and divide it among bowls. Top each with about a teaspoon of the goat cheese and a sprinkling of the shallots.

WHICH WINE?

This soup has a lot going on. A **Freisa d'Asti** (DOC) will help rein it all in. The Freisa grape produces a pale red wine that's very balanced, soft, and amiable.

Pasta and Gnocchi

* Fettuccine with Escarole and Wild Mushrooms
* Ziti with Fried Eggplant, Tomato, Oregano, and Ricotta Cheese
* Spaghetti Puttanesca (Scotty's Style)
* Rigatoni with Sausage, Spinach, and Goat Cheese
* Farfalle with Fresh Corn, Asparagus, and Jalapeño
  Orecchiette with Caramelized Cauliflower and Shallots, Herbed Bread Crumbs and Bottarga
* Linguine with Mussels and Kale
* Spaghetti with Spicy Garlic Shrimp, Baby Tomatoes, and Bread Crumbs
* Penne with Roasted Butternut Squash, Pancetta, and Sage
* Spaghetti with Fresh Tomato Sauce and Basil
* Spaghetti with Garlic, Olive Oil, and Anchovies
* Penne with Chickpeas, Rosemary, and Black Pepper
* Linguine with Tuna, Olives, and Tomatoes

* Rigatoni with Pancetta (or Prosciutto) and Pepper

Farfalle with Crispy Sweetbreads, Bitter Greens, and Chanterelles

Tagliatelle with Bolognese Sauce

Pasta Dough

* Melted Tomatoes

Ricotta Raviolini with Melted Tomatoes

Short Rib Agnolotti with Horseradish and Brown Butter

Pumpkin and Amaretto Cookie Cappellacci

Wild Mushroom Ravioli with Thyme, Truffle Oil, and Pancetta

Yukon Gold Potato Gnocchetti

Potato Gnocchetti with Shrimp, Peas, and Scallion

Spinach and Ricotta Gnocchi

Spinach and Ricotta Gnocchi with Fava Beans, Tomatoes, and Guanciale

EVERYBODY COOKS DRIED PASTA FOR DINNER. And why not? It cooks quickly and satisfies immensely. The challenge is not to make the same old dish time after time. For the dried pastas in this chapter, I've provided lots of options, whether bold and meaty like the sausage and onion pasta on page 95 or a light, summery pasta made with spicy shrimp and baby tomatoes (page 101). But if I had to eat one thing for the rest of my life, it would be my signature spaghetti with Fresh Tomato Sauce (page 104). As it is now, I eat it for lunch just about every single day. I'd like to pretend that this sauce, which *Gourmet* has called perfect, is difficult to make. Or that I am the only one who can make it both delicious and absolutely comforting. But it is actually a very easy sauce to make. The only hard part is peeling the tomatoes, which is not so hard as a little tedious. So there you go—my secret is out; you can make my tomato sauce anytime you want. (At the restaurant, we pair the sauce with fresh spaghetti, but it also works its magic with boxed pasta.)

Dried pasta is perfect for many recipes, and is so very convenient, but if you really love Italian cooking, I strongly recommend making your own stuffed pasta once in a while. I know some people are a little wary about trying their hand at making pasta at home. My hope is to convince you by including recipes so tempting, you just *have* to try them. Like most things, the more you make fresh pasta, the better and more proficient you will become. The recipe I give here for the actual pasta dough cooks up tender and delicious, yet is very easy to handle. But if you want to give the fillings a try without making your own dough, you can either buy pre-made pasta sheets at a good Italian market or substitute those wonton wrappers available at just about every supermarket.

Freeze your homemade pasta to serve when you want. I always freeze my fresh pasta before cooking it. I do this not only for convenience but also to create a product that's tender but strong. When submerged in hot water, the frozen fresh pasta does not absorb as much liquid as would just-made pasta. It holds its shape without expanding so much that it becomes flabby, and its flavor does not become diluted with excess water.

For the same reason, I always freeze my light-as-air gnocchi. Those who have floundered at trying to roll these tiny dumplings off of fork tines (or simply find it tedious) will be relieved to know that I make my tiny gnocchetti without those little ridges because I prefer their texture to be smooth. You simply roll the gnocchi dough into thin strips (just like you used to do with Play-Doh), and cut the strands into pieces.

The sauces for the homemade gnocchi and the fresh pasta are very simple and quick to make. The reason for the simplicity is to let the flavor of the gnocchi or the stuffed pasta shine. In most cases the sauce gets created in a sauté pan as the pasta cooks. A little of the pasta cooking water is added to the sauté pan with the pasta to finish cooking the pasta in the sauce. This technique, which is also used in the dried pasta recipes, encourages the flavor of the sauce to permeate the pasta while the released starch from the pasta adds body to the sauce.

Finally, a very basic element to making the actual pasta and gnocchi taste their best is often overlooked. The pasta cooking water must be amply salted. My mother advised salting the water "until it tastes like soup" and she was right. A couple of tablespoons of salt, preferably kosher salt, which dissolves quickly, usually does the trick.

FETTUCCINE WITH ESCAROLE

AND **WILD MUSHROOMS**

> The key to bringing out the flavors in this simple pasta is to amply salt both the pasta cooking water and the sauce.

MAKES **4** SERVINGS

1/3 cup olive oil

5 cloves garlic, sliced very thin

1/4 to 1/2 teaspoon crushed red pepper

8 ounces domestic or wild mushrooms (a mix is nice), wiped clean, stemmed, and sliced or broken into bite-size pieces

Kosher salt and freshly ground black pepper to taste

1 medium head of escarole, any wilted outer leaves discarded, well washed and dried, and chopped into **1**- or **2**-inch pieces

1 pound fettuccine

Chopped fresh parsley (optional)

1/4 cup freshly grated Parmigiano-Reggiano cheese

BRING A LARGE POT OF SALTED WATER TO A BOIL. In a large sauté pan, heat the olive oil over medium-high heat. Add the garlic and red pepper flakes. Cook the garlic, swirling it off the heat to prevent scorching, until it just takes on some color. Return the pan to the heat, add the mushrooms, season with ample salt and pepper, and cook, stirring, until the mushrooms release most of their liquid, 4 to 6 minutes. Add the chopped escarole and cook, stirring, until wilted. Keep warm.

Meanwhile, cook the pasta until just al dente. Reserve about 1 cup of the pasta water and drain the pasta. Toss the pasta and about $1/4$ cup of the reserved water with the escarole and the mushrooms over medium-high heat. Taste and add additional salt and pepper. If the sauce looks too dry, add a bit more of the cooking liquid. Divide the pasta among four warm bowls and sprinkle each with some parsley and cheese.

WHICH WINE?

A **Barbera d'Asti** (DOC) from Piedmont would be great with this. Less full-bodied than Barbera d'Alba, it's a nice wine for a midweek meal because it won't necessarily break the bank.

ZITI WITH FRIED EGGPLANT, TOMATO, OREGANO, AND RICOTTA CHEESE

Instead of mixing the ricotta cheese into the pasta, I top each bowl with a spoon-ful just before serving. Adding the ricotta cheese at the last minute makes its pres-ence more pronounced, and it adds a wonderful supple creaminess to the dish. Deep frying the eggplant is actually less messy than pan frying, but I include both methods in the recipe, so you can choose.

MAKES **4** SERVINGS

1 medium eggplant (1^1/4 pounds), peeled and cut into **3/4**-inch dice

Kosher salt

1/4 cup vegetable oil, such as canola, corn, or grapeseed oil if pan frying, more if deep frying

3/4 pound ziti or similar pasta

1/4 cup extra virgin olive oil

1 clove garlic, thinly sliced

6 plum tomatoes, cored and chopped

1/4 teaspoon crushed red pepper

1 teaspoon chopped fresh oregano

Freshly ground black pepper to taste

PUT THE DICED EGGPLANT IN A COLANDER and toss with 1 teaspoon of kosher salt. Put the colander in a clean sink, weight the eggplant, and allow the salt to draw out the excess moisture for at least 10 minutes. Do not rinse the eggplant. Pat it dry with paper towels.

TO PAN FRY THE EGGPLANT
Have ready a paper towel–lined plate. In a large, heavy-based skillet heat the vegetable oil over medium-high heat. Add the eggplant, and cook, stirring occasionally, until tender and deep golden brown, 5 minutes. Transfer the eggplant to the lined plate to drain.

TO DEEP FRY THE EGGPLANT
Have ready a paper towel–lined plate. Pour enough oil into a heavy-based, high-sided saucepan so that the oil is at least 2 inches deep. (Be sure the pot is less than halfway full to

2 tablespoons finely grated
Parmigiano-Reggiano

4 fresh basil leaves, cut into julienne

1/4 to 1/3 cup fresh ricotta cheese

prevent the oil from bubbling over during frying.) Heat the oil until it reads 350°F on a frying thermometer (also called a candy thermometer). Fry the eggplant in batches, if necessary, until tender and deep golden brown, 3 minutes. Adjust the heat as needed to keep the temperature close to 350°F. Lift the eggplant out of the oil using a slotted spoon or Chinese skimmer and drain it on the lined plate.

Bring a large pot of salted water to a boil and cook the ziti until al dente.

Meanwhile, heat the olive oil in a large sauté pan over medium-high heat. Add the garlic and cook until it just starts to go golden at its edges. Immediately add the tomatoes, crushed red pepper, and oregano. Season lightly with salt and fresh pepper. Cook the tomatoes until they release their juices and those juices reduce, about 5 minutes. Stir in the cooked pasta and eggplant and cook until the eggplant is heated through. Divide the pasta among four bowls. Sprinkle with the grated Parmigiano-Reggiano and basil. Top each with a spoonful of the ricotta and serve.

WHICH WINE?

A young **Aglianico** from Campania, with its garnet color and earthy, herby aroma, has the ability to remain deliciously distinct even while working in harmony with the full flavors of this dish.

SPAGHETTI PUTTANESCA
(SCOTTY'S STYLE)

I love the jumble of potent flavors typically found in puttanesca sauce: capers, black olives, anchovy, garlic, tomatoes. But often, there's just too much of it. I like to pull back a bit on the amounts, so that the flavors of the dish, instead of coming on in full force with diminishing returns, continue to build, until by the time you're done, you're wishing there was more. I like to use a mix of plum tomatoes and cherry tomatoes, but you can just as easily omit one and double the amount of the other.

MAKES **4** SERVINGS

1/2 cup extra virgin olive oil

2 anchovy fillets, rinsed (if oil-packed) or soaked in a couple changes of water (if salt-packed) and coarsely chopped

1 shallot, finely chopped

2 cloves garlic, finely chopped

2 pinches of crushed red pepper

1 tablespoon capers, rinsed (if oil-packed) or soaked in a couple changes of water (if salt-packed)

2 tablespoons pitted and quartered black olives, preferably Gaeta

1/2 pint cherry tomatoes, halved or quartered if large

2 plum tomatoes, peeled, and cut into **8** pieces

1 tablespoon chopped fresh parsley, plus more for garnish if you like

Pinch of chopped fresh oregano (optional)

1 pound dry spaghetti

IN A SMALL SKILLET, warm the olive oil over medium heat. Add the anchovies and cook, breaking them up with a wooden spoon, until they have disintegrated into the olive oil. Add the shallot, garlic, and crushed red pepper and cook, stirring, until they just begin to brown. Add the capers and olives and remove the pan from the heat.

In a bowl, combine the cherry tomatoes, plum tomatoes, parsley, and oregano, if using. Use a flexible spatula to scrape out all of the caper and olive mixture and add it to the bowl with the tomatoes. Let this mixture sit for a few minutes or up to an hour at room temperature for the combined flavors to develop. (Refrigerate it for any longer stretches and use it within 24 hours.)

When ready to serve, bring a large pot of salted water to a boil and cook the spaghetti until just shy of al dente. Before draining, reserve about $1/2$ cup of the cooking water. When the pasta is just about done, heat a large skillet over medium-high heat. Add a couple of tablespoons of the olive oil, and when hot, add the tomato mixture to the pan. (You want the tomatoes to have enough surface space so that when they hit the pan, the liquid that is released from them evaporates almost immediately.)

Drain the spaghetti, add it to the skillet, and use tongs to toss it with all of the ingredients. Add some of the pasta cooking liquid to the pan as necessary to keep the pasta moist. Transfer the spaghetti to warm bowls and drizzle with a little more of the remaining olive oil and some fresh chopped parsley, if you like.

WHICH WINE?

A **Greco di Tufo** (DOC) from Campania would really allow this dish to shine. A rich white wine made from Greco grapes, this wine offers a smokiness that's nicely tamed by the assertive flavors of the puttanesca.

RIGATONI WITH SAUSAGE, SPINACH, AND GOAT CHEESE

While this recipe is delicious as is, you can do a couple of things to give it even more flavor. Use a combination of spicy and sweet sausage instead of just sweet and—something I do almost every time I use goat cheese—use a fork to mix into it 1/2 teaspoon each of chopped fresh parsley, chives, and thyme.

MAKES **4** SERVINGS

2 tablespoons olive oil

1 medium onion, cut in half lengthwise and thinly sliced crosswise

3/4 pound sweet Italian sausage or a combination of sweet and spicy, casings removed

3/4 pound rigatoni

Salt to taste

4 ounces spinach, well washed and dried and coarsely chopped (about **2** cups)

1/2 pint cherry or grape tomatoes

2 tablespoons freshly grated Parmigiano-Reggiano

2 tablespoons fresh goat cheese

1 tablespoon chopped fresh parsley (optional)

BRING A LARGE POT OF SALTED WATER TO A BOIL. Heat the oil in a large sauté pan over medium-low heat. Add the onion and sauté until it is tender and begins to color, 10 minutes. Crumble the sausage into the pan, increase the heat to medium-high, and fully cook the sausage.

Cook the rigatoni until just shy of al dente. Before draining, reserve about 1 cup of the cooking water.

Add the spinach and tomatoes and some of the pasta cooking liquid to the sausage and cook, tossing, until the spinach has wilted. Add the pasta, half of the reserved cooking liquid, Parmigiano-Reggiano, and goat cheese. Toss well and lightly smash the tomatoes. Add a bit more of the cooking liquid if needed and serve sprinkled with parsley, if you like.

WHICH WINE?

A **Montepulciano d'Abruzzo** (DOC) transforms the widely cultivated Montepulciano into an enticing wine with warm, red fruit aromas, including ripe red cherries and currants. A good-quality bottle would be perfect with this hearty dish.

Pasta and Gnocchi

FARFALLE WITH FRESH CORN, ASPARAGUS, AND JALAPEÑO

> This is easy and quick to make yet it's so good—one of those pastas whose flavor intensifies with each bite. The fresh green heat of jalapeño makes the whole dish come alive.

MAKES **4** SERVINGS

1 large or **2** small ears of corn

1/2 pound asparagus

3/4 pound farfalle

1/4 cup extra virgin olive oil

1/2 medium red onion, chopped

1/2 jalapeño pepper, stemmed, seeded, and very finely chopped

Kosher salt and freshly ground black pepper to taste

1/4 cup pecorino Romano

BRING A LARGE POT OF SALTED WATER TO A BOIL. With a sharp knife, cut kernels off of the cob or cobs; you should have 1 cup of kernels. Snap the tough end off of the asparagus. Cut the asparagus into pieces the size of the corn kernels (more or less); you should have 1 cup.

Cook the penne until just shy of al dente. Before draining, reserve 1 cup of the cooking water.

Meanwhile, heat the olive oil in a large sauté pan over medium heat. Add the onion and jalapeño and cook until the onion is just tender, 5 minutes. Add the corn and asparagus and cook until the asparagus is crisp-tender. Add the pasta and the reserved cooking liquid and cook, tossing, until the pasta is fully cooked and has absorbed some of the flavor of the sauce. Season with salt and pepper to taste and top with grated pecorino.

WHICH WINE?

Try a Vermentino from Sardinia, such as a **Vermentino di Gallura** (DOC). The almondy and lemon notes bounce around well with the Pecorino and asparagus while its dryness is a welcome complement to the sweet corn.

Scott Conant's New Italian Cooking

ORECCHIETTE WITH CARAMELIZED CAULIFLOWER AND SHALLOTS, HERBED BREAD CRUMBS AND BOTTARGA

To give much-maligned cauliflower a greater depth of flavor, sear it until it is good and browned. While this dish is fine and filling without the shaved *bottarga* (dried, salted fish roe), it's this final touch that gives the dish its subtle brininess. I've been racking my brain to think of a substitute, but I don't know of anything that comes close to imitating *bottarga's* flavor. (To mail-order *bottarga*, which keeps just about forever, check out the Sources.) Finally, there are few cooking rules I follow steadfastly, but one of them is "no cheese with fish." The bread crumbs here take the place of that sprinkling of cheese we all reach for whenever pasta is involved. So even if you are leaving the *bottarga* off, try the bread crumbs; they add a pleasing texture and a fresh herb flavor.

MAKES **4** SERVINGS

1/2 cup dry, unseasoned, coarse bread crumbs, preferably *panko* (see Sources)

1 teaspoon finely chopped mint leaves

2 teaspoons finely chopped parsley leaves

1/4 teaspoon crushed red pepper

3 to **4** tablespoons extra virgin olive oil

1/2 head of cauliflower, stemmed and broken or cut into tiny florets (**4** cups), boiled in salted water until it just loses its crunch, and drained

1 heaping cup thinly sliced shallots (**6** shallots)

3/4 pound orecchiette

1$\frac{1}{2}$ tablespoons grated *bottarga*

(continued)

TO MAKE THE HERBED BREAD CRUMBS, pulse the bread crumbs, mint, parsley, and crushed red pepper in a food processor. Add a tablespoon of the olive oil and pulse again briefly.

Bring a large pot of salted water to a boil.

Heat 2 tablespoons of the olive oil in large sauté pan over medium-high heat. Add the blanched cauliflower, season with a little salt, and cook, stirring occasionally, until the cauliflower pieces are well browned, 8 to 10 minutes. Remove the cauliflower from the pan, add a little more oil to the pan, and then cook the shallots over medium-high heat, stirring, until tender and browned as well, 8 to 10 minutes.

Meanwhile, cook the orecchiette until al dente. Before draining, reserve about $1/2$ cup of the cooking water. Add the drained pasta to the pan with the shallots. Return the cauliflower to the pan, add some of the pasta cooking liquid, and toss the ingredients together for a few minutes; add more water to the pan as necessary to keep the pasta moist. Divide the pasta among four warm bowls. Sprinkle a tablespoon of the herbed bread crumbs over each bowl and finish with the *bottarga* shavings. Serve immediately.

WHICH WINE?

Pairing the intriguing flavor of *bottarga* with a wine is a bit of sport for me. In this dish, the added nuttiness of the caramelized cauliflower points me toward a **Vernacci di San Gimignano**, which has a pleasing chalkiness, a citrusy aroma, and enough acidity to keep the flavors going even as it meets up with such a full-flavored pasta. Its pale yellow color also looks nice in the glass when served with this golden brown dish.

✳ LINGUINE WITH MUSSELS AND KALE

MAKES **4** SERVINGS

Kosher salt

1/4 cup plus **2** tablespoons extra virgin olive oil

1 medium onion, halved and thinly sliced

2 garlic cloves, thinly sliced

1/4 to **1/2** teaspoon crushed red pepper

2 pounds mussels, scrubbed, if necessary, and debearded

1 pound linguine

6 large kale leaves, stems removed, and leaves coarsely chopped

BRING A LARGE POT OF SALTED WATER TO A BOIL. In a large sauté pan, heat $^1/_4$ cup olive oil over medium heat. Add the onion and cook until just soft, 5 minutes. Add the garlic and crushed red pepper and cook another 2 minutes. Increase the heat to medium-high, add the mussels, and cook, shaking the pan a bit, until about half the mussels open. Add the kale to the mussels and cook until it's wilted; in the few minutes this takes, the rest of the mussels should open.

Meanwhile, add the linguine to the boiling water. Reserve $^1/_2$ cup of the pasta cooking water. Drain the linguine while it is still shy of al dente. Add the pasta to the mussels along with the reserved cooking water. Cook, tossing the pasta, until the linguine is al dente and the sauce has thickened a bit. Season with additional salt. Divide the pasta among warm bowls, drizzle each with $^1/_2$ tablespoon olive oil, and serve immediately.

WHICH WINE?

Pale, straw yellow **Tocai Friulano** offers an enticing mixture of wildflowers and pears that go well with the slight bitterness of the kale and the briny sweetness of the mussels.

The bitterness of the kale plays off the briny sweetness of the mussels; you can substitute spinach, but the flavor of the greens will be much more mild.

SPAGHETTI WITH SPICY GARLIC SHRIMP, BABY TOMATOES, AND BREAD CRUMBS

> The shrimp obtain great depth and flavor from the short marinating time. If you like very spicy food, go with the whole amount of crushed red pepper.

MAKES **4** SERVINGS

1/2 pound medium shrimp, shelled, deveined, and cut into large chunks

1/2 pint small tomatoes, such as pear, grape, or currant tomatoes

1/4 cup plus **1** tablespoon extra virgin olive oil

2 cloves garlic, finely chopped

1^1/2 teaspoons finely chopped fresh rosemary

1^1/2 teaspoons chopped fresh parsley

1/2 to 3/4 teaspoon crushed red pepper

Kosher salt and freshly ground black pepper

1/4 cup dry, unseasoned, coarse bread crumbs, preferably *panko* (see Sources)

1 pound spaghetti

IN A LARGE SAUTÉ PAN, toss together the shrimp, tomatoes, ^{1}/4 cup olive oil, garlic, rosemary, parsley, and crushed red pepper. Season with salt and pepper and keep the pan off the heat for now. In a small sauté pan, heat the remaining 1 tablespoon olive oil over medium heat. Add the bread crumbs and cook, stirring occasionally, until browned and crisp, 3 minutes. Transfer the bread crumbs to a plate to keep the residual heat from the pan from burning them.

Bring a large pot of salted water to a boil and cook the spaghetti until just shy of al dente. Before draining, reserve about $1/2$ cup of the cooking water. When the pasta is done, put the waiting sauté pan on medium-high heat. Add the spaghetti and a little of the reserved cooking liquid, and cook, tossing the pasta and crushing the tomatoes lightly, until the shrimp just begin to turn pink, adding more liquid to the pan as necessary to keep the pasta moist. Season with additional salt and pepper to taste. Transfer the spaghetti to warm bowls and sprinkle the bread crumbs on top.

WHICH WINE?

For this spicy dish I would reach for a delicate white wine with a light finish, such as a **Cinqueterre** (DOC).

PENNE WITH ROASTED BUTTERNUT SQUASH, PANCETTA, AND SAGE

> Few flavors marry as well as butternut squash, sage, and pancetta. I love to serve this dish in the fall, when its autumnal personality will be most appreciated, and when I'm most in the mood to roast vegetables.

MAKES **4** SERVINGS

One medium (2^1/4 pounds) butternut squash, peeled and cut into **1/2**-inch dice (**3** cups)

1/4 cup olive oil

Kosher salt

1 pound penne

3 ounces pancetta, preferably thickly sliced (1/4 inch) and cut into small dice

2 shallots, thinly sliced

1/4 teaspoon crushed red pepper

10 fresh sage leaves, coarsely chopped or torn

1/2 teaspoon freshly grated black pepper

1/2 cup finely grated pecorino Romano, plus more for serving

HEAT THE OVEN to 400°F. On a rimmed baking sheet, toss the butternut squash with 1 tablespoon olive oil and season with salt. Roast until browned and tender, 15 minutes. Bring a large pot of salted water to a boil and cook the penne until al dente. Before draining, reserve about ^{1}/2 cup of the cooking water. Meanwhile, heat the remaining 3 tablespoons of olive oil in a large sauté pan over medium-low heat. Add the pancetta and cook until just crisp, 4 to 5 minutes. Add the shallots, crushed red pepper, and sage. Cook until the shallots are soft, 4 to 5 minutes. Add the penne and squash and toss gently, adding enough of the pasta liquid to moisten the dish without making it "saucy."

Add the black pepper and pecorino and cook, tossing gently, until the pasta and squash are heated through. Serve immediately with extra grated pecorino, if you like.

WHICH WINE?

Try a Sangiovese, particularly a **Sangiovese di Romagna** (DOC). It reminds me of dried fruit, a flavor I think goes well with butternut squash and sage.

SPAGHETTI WITH FRESH TOMATO SAUCE AND BASIL

This is a straightforward, traditional, fresh tomato sauce in which ripe tomatoes—and little else—get cooked quickly to retain their vibrant flavor. Why then is it such a hit? The key is in the finish. Here's how I put the dish together at the restaurant: I take a single portion of pasta cooked just shy of al dente and add it to a sauté pan that holds a single portion of hot, bubbling tomato sauce. To toss the pasta and sauce together I use that pan-jerking method we chefs are so fond of. I do this to look cool. Just kidding. The real reason is that this technique not only coats the pasta evenly with the sauce but it also introduces a little air into the process, making the dish feel lighter and brighter. To accomplish this aeration with larger portions and without fancy wrist work, cook the sauce in a pan with a lot of surface area. When you add the pasta to the sauce, gently toss the pasta with a couple of wooden spoons (tongs can bruise and break the strands), lifting the pasta high above the bottom of the pot. Finish the dish with some butter, cheese, and basil.

MAKES **4** SERVINGS

20 ripe plum tomatoes

1/3 cup extra virgin olive oil, plus more to finish the dish

Pinch of crushed red pepper

Kosher salt and freshly ground black pepper

1 pound spaghetti, either good-quality dried or homemade (page 116)

1 tablespoon unsalted butter

6 to **8** fresh basil leaves, well washed and dried, stacked and rolled into a cylinder and cut thinly crosswise into a chiffonade

1 ounce freshly grated Parmigiano-Reggiano (**1/2** cup)

TO PEEL THE TOMATOES: Bring a large pot of water to a boil. Have a large bowl of ice water nearby. Cut a small X on the bottom of each tomato. Ease about five tomatoes in the pot and let boil for about 15 seconds, then promptly move them to the waiting ice water. (Do this with the remaining tomatoes.) Pull off the skin with the tip of a paring knife. If the skin sticks, try a vegetable peeler using a gentle sawing motion. Cut the tomatoes in half and use your finger to flick out the seeds.

To cook the tomatoes: In a wide pan, heat the olive oil over medium-high heat until quite hot. Add the tomatoes, crushed red pepper, and season lightly with salt and pepper. (I always start with a light hand with salt and pepper because as the tomatoes reduce, the salt will become concentrated.) Let the tomatoes cook for a few minutes to soften. Then, using a potato masher, chop the tomatoes finely. Cook the tomatoes for 20 to 25 minutes, until the tomatoes are tender and the sauce has thickened. (You can make the sauce, which yields 3 cups, ahead of time. Refrigerate it for up to 2 days or freeze it for longer storage.)

To serve: Bring a large pot of amply salted water to a boil. Cook the spaghetti until just shy of al dente. Drain the pasta, reserving a little of the cooking water. Add the pasta to the sauce and cook over medium-high heat, gently tossing the pasta and sauce together with a couple of wooden spoons and a lot of exaggerated movement (you can even shake the pan) until the pasta is just tender and the sauce, if any oil has separated from it, now looks cohesive. (If the sauce seems too thick, add a little pasta cooking liquid to it.) Take the pan off the heat, toss the butter, basil, and cheese with the pasta in the same manner (the pasta should take on an orange hue), and serve immediately.

(continued)

WHICH WINE?

A **Vino Nobile di Montepulciano** (DOCG) is a pretty expensive wine, but since the dish itself came cheap and is so delicious, why not splurge a little? This red wine, which does not contain a bit of the Montepulciano grape, is instead named for the hilly area around the town of Montepulciano in Tuscany. Its raspberry and anise aroma, its full juicy flavor with hints of spice and black pepper, and its good finish are just perfect with my signature spaghetti. Another good bet, which you can find for a reasonable price, would be a **Chianti Classico** (DOCG).

Transforming Pantry Staples into Delicious Pasta Dishes

"WHAT DO YOU COOK FOR YOURSELF AT HOME?"

I get asked that question all of the time. The truth is that I almost never, ever cook at home. I'm at the restaurant fifteen hours a day, every day but Sunday. I'm not complaining, and this may change someday, but on Sundays, if I'm not cooking for a demo or a charity, I try my best not to cook at all. During my limited free time I would much rather go see the Yankees than go food shopping. And what good would perishables do me anyway? I'm telling you—I'm never home. But those times when I do get hungry and the restaurant is closed (whether it's a Sunday afternoon or three in the morning), I can almost always create a satisfying pasta dish out of stuff that even I always have on hand (and I'm not including the truffle trimmings I poach from the restaurant kitchen) in my barely used apartment kitchen. So can you.

Take a look at the food in your pantry and fridge and notice the things that are almost always there: olive oil and garlic, of course. Canned tuna, canned beans, canned tomatoes. Jars of capers, olives, roasted red peppers, and probably artichokes, too. If you do any kind of Italian cooking there's always a hunk of some grating cheese in the fridge, and likely some pancetta. You definitely have some dried herbs to use at will, but if you're lucky or smart you have some growing in the garden or on a windowsill. If not, at least get into the habit of regularly buying fresh parsley, which is cheap and which will last a while in the crisper. A sprinkling of chopped fresh parsley transforms the most humble pantry pasta—pasta tossed with olive oil and cheese—into something surprisingly tasty.

What follows are a few of my favorite pantry pastas. From experience I can tell you that the spaghetti with anchovies and garlic, with its lively yet comforting flavors, is a perfect way to cap off a late night out. You know those times when you're way too wired and a little too hungry to go right to sleep? This dish hits the spot whether you're rehashing the evening with friends, courting your date, or—more like my life when opening a new restaurant—you're standing at the counter eating alone and reading the early edition of the Sunday *Times*. In each of the recipes that follow, I've suggested amounts for a pound of pasta, which makes about 4 hearty servings. Adjust the dish (or your social life) accordingly.

✳ SPAGHETTI WITH GARLIC, OLIVE OIL, AND ANCHOVIES

PANTRY INGREDIENTS: *spaghetti, extra virgin olive oil, garlic, anchovies, crushed red pepper, and parsley*

Rinse 4 anchovy fillets and slice 3 cloves of garlic. Heat $1/2$ cup of extra virgin olive oil in a sauté pan. Add the garlic, anchovies, and a good pinch of crushed red pepper. Heat, shaking the pan, just until the edges of the garlic slices are golden brown. The anchovies will break up and become strewn throughout the oil. Cook a pound of spaghetti in boiling salted water until about three-quarters of the way cooked. Reserve a cup of the pasta cooking water. Drain the pasta and toss it with the olive oil, garlic, and anchovies. Turn the heat up to medium-high and continue to cook the pasta until al dente. Add some of the cooking liquid to the pan to loosen the pasta. Drizzle a little more olive oil onto the pasta and sprinkle with some chopped fresh parsley.

Which wine?
Yes, even pantry pastas deserve some wine. A **Falanghina**, a simple white wine from Campania, is happy to take the backseat to this simple but flavorful pasta.

✳ PENNE WITH CHICKPEAS, ROSEMARY, AND BLACK PEPPER

PANTRY INGREDIENTS: *penne (or similar-shaped pasta), extra virgin olive oil, one (15-ounce) can of chickpeas, rosemary (dried or fresh), chicken broth, canned tomatoes, crushed red pepper, Parmigiano-Reggiano*

Heat $^1/4$ cup of olive oil in a sauté pan. Add $^1/2$ teaspoon of dried rosemary or a couple teaspoons chopped fresh rosemary and heat until fragrant. Add the chickpeas with their liquid, 3 or 4 chopped canned tomatoes, a cup of chicken broth, and a pinch of crushed red pepper. Cook until the chickpeas are heated through. Puree about half of the pan's contents in a food processor and then return the puree to the pan. Season with salt to taste. Meanwhile, cook a pound of penne in boiling salted water until about three-quarters of the way cooked. Reserve about a cup of the pasta cooking liquid. Toss the drained pasta with the chickpeas. Turn the heat up to medium-high and cook, tossing, until the pasta is al dente. Add some of the pasta cooking liquid to thin the sauce, if necessary. Divide the pasta among bowls and top with grated Parmigiano-Reggiano and ample freshly ground black pepper.

Which wine?

How about a young **Chianti Classico** (DOCG)? Its velvety color and texture will draw you back to the glass even as the earthy chickpeas and resinous rosemary pull you back to the bowl—a tug of war I'm always game for!

LINGUINE WITH TUNA, OLIVES, AND TOMATOES

PANTRY INGREDIENTS: *linguine (or other pasta), canned tuna packed in oil, canned chopped tomatoes, black olives, crushed red pepper, fresh basil—if you have some—or fresh parsley*

Heat $1/4$ cup of extra virgin olive oil in a sauté pan. Add $1/2$ cup of the chopped tomatoes, a pinch of crushed red pepper, and a small handful of pitted, coarsely chopped olives to the pan. Meanwhile, cook a pound of linguine in boiling salted water until three-quarters of the way cooked. Reserve about a cup of the pasta cooking liquid. Toss the drained pasta with the olives and tomatoes. Add some chopped fresh basil or parsley. Turn the heat up to medium-high and cook, tossing, until the pasta is al dente. Add some of the pasta cooking liquid to moisten the pasta, if necessary. Divide the pasta among bowls, top with some of the canned tuna, and serve.

Which wine?

I like to drink a very approachable white wine from Le Marches with this salty, briny dish. A **Verdicchio di Matelica** (DOC) would be worth seeking.

✳ RIGATONI WITH PANCETTA (OR PROSCIUTTO) AND PEPPER

PANTRY INGREDIENTS: *rigatoni (or other pasta), extra virgin olive oil, garlic, pancetta or prosciutto, freshly ground black pepper, grana Padano or Parmigiano-Reggiano, chopped fresh parsley*

Slice a clove of garlic and chop $1/4$ pound pancetta or prosciutto into pieces. Heat a couple tablespoons of extra virgin olive oil in a sauté pan and add the garlic. If using pancetta, add it at this time and cook until it has rendered most of its fat. Meanwhile, cook a pound of rigatoni in boiling salted water until three-quarters of the way cooked. Reserve about a cup of the pasta cooking liquid. Toss the drained pasta with either the garlic and pancetta or just the garlic. Turn the heat up to medium-high and cook, tossing, until the pasta is al dente. Add some of the pasta cooking liquid to moisten the pasta, if necessary. Just before serving, toss in the parsley, and, if not using pancetta, the prosciutto. Divide the pasta among bowls, top with some grated Parmigiano-Reggiano, and serve.

Which wine?

The simplicity of this dish dictates something in the glass as simple and harmonious as the ingredients in the bowl. **Soave** (DOC), Italy's most popular white wine, would work really well, especially a good-quality Classico. Made from a combination of grapes, this elegant wine has a nice balance and offers sensations of honey and cream on the palate, which is really nice with the heat of the pepper and the salty sweetness of the prosciutto or pancetta.

FARFALLE WITH CRISPY SWEETBREADS, BITTER GREENS, AND CHANTERELLES

One night at the restaurant a little old lady caught my arm and told me just how much she enjoyed this pasta. "But where were the sweetbreads?" she asked. No, she wasn't senile. She was expecting the sweetbreads in a more traditional form: medallion sized, lightly breaded, and fried. But in this dish, I break the sweetbreads up into little pieces and brown them till crispy in olive oil so that you get a little of the sweetbreads, chanterelles, and kale in every bite. Words don't do justice to how wonderful a lineup these ingredients are. Even people who swear they hate sweetbreads rave about this dish once convinced to try a bite, making this the perfect recipe to try on the offal-shy people in your life. For best results, choose veal sweetbreads that are white, plump, and firm and plan to use them soon after buying them. They will need a soak of a couple of hours and a quick poach before the final sauté.

TO POACH THE SWEETBREADS: Remove the sweetbreads from the cold water, rinse them, and pat them dry. In a large saucepan, bring 6 cups of water, the onion, carrot, peppercorns, bay leaves, wine, and 2 tablespoons salt to a boil. Reduce to a gentle simmer and let the ingredients steep for 25 minutes. Add the sweetbreads and simmer until they are medium rare, 12 to 15 minutes. (The inside of the sweetbreads will be pinkish and milky.)

Remove the sweetbreads from the poaching liquid and let cool slightly. When you are able to handle them remove any membrane or blood vessels. You can do this quite easily as you tear them into small lobes to give you $3/4$ cup of

MAKES **4** SERVINGS

$1^1/2$ pounds sweetbreads, trimmed, outer membrane removed, and soaked in cold water in the refrigerator for a couple of hours

1/2 onion, sliced

1 carrot, chopped

1 tablespoon black peppercorns

2 bay leaves

1 cup white wine

2 tablespoons kosher salt

1 pound good-quality dried farfalle or homemade (page 116)

3 to **4** tablespoons olive oil

2 shallots, thinly sliced

3 ounces chanterelle mushrooms, tough stems removed and coarsely chopped to give you **1** cup

Kosher salt and freshly ground black pepper to taste

2 ounces kale, well washed and torn into bite-size pieces to give you **1** cup

1/2 cup homemade Chicken Reduction (page 15) or purchased chicken reduction diluted with water until a little thicker than chicken stock

2 tablespoons grated Parmigiano-Reggiano

1 teaspoon snipped fresh chives

sweetbread pieces. (You can poach and tear the sweetbreads a few hours before assembling the final dish; keep them covered and refrigerated.)

When you are ready to eat, bring a large pot of well-salted water to a boil. Cook the farfalle until al dente. Before draining, reserve about $1/2$ cup of the cooking water to moisten the pasta if needed.

While the pasta cooks, heat 3 tablespoons of the olive oil in a large sauté pan over medium-high heat. Have your ingredients handy, as you will be adding them to this pan in quick succession, adding more oil if needed.

Begin with the sweetbreads and cook, stirring occasionally, until the pieces are well browned and beginning to crisp. Add the sliced shallots and sauté until they begin to brown on the edges. Add the mushrooms, season with a little salt and pepper (use less salt if using purchased chicken reduction), and brown those well. Add the kale and stir it around to wilt it. Add the cooked pasta and the chicken reduction. Cook until the reduction has reduced just enough to glaze the pasta and sweetbreads without becoming overly sticky. Divide the pasta among four warm plates, sprinkle with the cheese and chives, and serve immediately.

WHICH WINE?

An older Barbaresco would taste great with this. Then again, an older Barbaresco always tastes great. For something more moderately priced, look to a **Chianti Colli Senesi** (DOCG); its firm tannins will be nicely muted by the rich sauce.

TAGLIATELLE WITH
BOLOGNESE SAUCE

I got this recipe from my good friend Dino Baldini, who owns a restaurant in Budrio, Italy, called Centro Storico. His mother taught him. Their version might be a little different from the Bolognese sauce you are used to. For starters, there is no milk in it (though I do add a little butter when tossing the sauce with pasta); there is also no garlic, no herbs, and no olive oil. The meat itself is the star. To coax the best flavor from the meat, the sauce cooks for a good amount of time, but it requires little attention. And for your effort, you get a lot of sauce, which means you can freeze some for when you have a craving for it—which I promise you will. Here's to Dino. I love this.

IF YOU HAVE A MEAT GRINDER, use a medium grinding disk and grind the celery, carrot, onion, and pancetta. (I use a medium grind, which means the holes are the size of my pinky fingernail.) Then grind the veal, beef, and pork.

If you don't have a grinder, chop the celery, carrot, onion, and pancetta by hand into small dice. (Don't use a food processor for the vegetables as it can too quickly turn them to mush.) Do use a food processor to grind the meat, but be very careful not to overprocess it. Use the blade and pulse the meat until it just begins to break apart, erring on the side of larger rather than smaller pieces. (Alternatively, chop the vegetables yourself, but have a butcher coarsely grind the meat.)

Heat the olive oil in a deep, heavy-based Dutch oven or similar pot over medium heat. Add the celery, carrot, onion, and pancetta to the pot and sauté the vegetables until they are lightly browned, 15 minutes. Season the ground meat with salt and pepper, add it to the pot, and cook it until browned, 8 to

MAKES **4** CUPS OF SAUCE,
ENOUGH FOR **8** TO **12**
SERVINGS

2 celery stalks

1 medium carrot

1 medium onion

2 ounces pancetta, cut into chunks

6 ounces veal stew meat,
such as shoulder

6 ounces beef stew meat,
such as chuck

6 ounces pork stew meat, such as
shoulder (also called butt)

1/4 cup olive oil

Kosher salt and freshly ground black
pepper

1 cup dry white wine

1 cup good-quality canned pureed
tomatoes

1 quart Chicken Broth, preferably
homemade (page 14), or purchased
low-salt chicken broth

Tagliatelle, preferably fresh (see page
116), or good-quality dried

Butter, vegetable oil,
and Parmigiano-Reggiano for serving

10 minutes. Add the wine and cook until the wine evaporates almost completely and the pan looks dry, 10 to 15 minutes. Add the tomatoes and cook until the mixture darkens considerably and begins to look dry, 10 to 12 minutes. Add the chicken stock and cook, uncovered, on very low heat until the meat is remarkably tender and full of flavor, $2^1/2$ to 3 hours. If not using the sauce right away, refrigerate it for up to three days in the refrigerator or portion it and freeze it.

To serve: I love this sauce over tagliatelle, preferably fresh, but it's also immensely satisfying with good-quality fusilli or farfalle. Use $1/3$ to $1/2$ cup of sauce per serving. Toss the sauce with cooked, drained pasta, adding about a teaspoon of butter and a drizzle of vegetable oil (grapeseed, canola, safflower, or soy, but *not* olive oil) per serving. Top with grated Parmigiano-Reggiano, but leave off the parsley for this one.

WHICH WINE?
Dino would probably pour a **Sangiovese Riserva** from his own Emilia-Romagna.

PASTA DOUGH

To roll out fresh pasta, you will need a pasta rolling machine. A hand crank machine feels nice and rustic and works well, but a motorized one—nowadays some stand mixers even have roller attachments—might compel you to make your own dough more often. To really enjoy the process, get your work space set up efficiently, put on some good music, and relax. If you plan on making a filled pasta, prepare the filling a day or two before making the dough.

MAKES 1^1/$_4$ POUNDS
OF DOUGH

4 large eggs

2 large egg yolks

1 teaspoon olive oil

2^1/$_4$ to **2**^{1}/$_2$ cups "00" or unbleached all-purpose flour, plus more regular flour or semolina flour as needed for the dough and for flouring surfaces

TO MIX AND KNEAD THE DOUGH: You can mix the dough entirely by hand, but I find it helpful to start it in a stand mixer fitted with a dough hook. If you are starting the dough in a stand mixer, combine the eggs, egg yolks, olive oil, and ^{1}/$_4$ cup water in the mixing bowl. Add the flour. With the machine on its lowest speed, begin to mix. Increase the speed to medium-low and mix-knead it for 10 minutes, occasionally stopping the mixer and pulling the dough off the hook. Add a little more flour if the dough seems sticky. You'll know you have added the right amount when the dough no longer sticks to a clean finger.

If you are starting the dough by hand, put the flour in a very large bowl and make a well in the center. In a separate bowl, combine the eggs, egg yolks, olive oil, and ^{1}/$_4$ cup water and whisk to combine. Add the liquid ingredients to the well of the flour and gradually mix in the flour with a fork, adding a little more flour if the dough feels sticky. You'll know you have added the right amount when the dough no longer sticks to a clean finger.

Flour your work surface. Dump the dough onto the surface and continue to knead it until it's smooth and resilient and an indent made with your finger bounces back. If the dough needs more flour to keep it from sticking to the work surface, go ahead and add a little more, but don't add too much or the dough will be difficult to work with and your finished product will lack tenderness. Wrap the dough well in plastic wrap and let it rest in the refrigerator for at least an hour before rolling it.

Prepare your work space: It's best to have everything you need at arm's length before you actually get started. If you are making a filled pasta, have the filling made and cooled before you begin to roll out the pasta. Take the pasta dough out of the refrigerator and let it warm up a bit. Set up your pasta rolling machine at one end of your work surface (a long counter or table) to allow room for the long ribbon of pasta to emerge from the roller and lie on the work surface. Flour the work surface. Line a sided baking sheet with parchment paper and flour the paper. If you are making filled pasta, choose the cutter you will use to shape the pasta based on what the recipe directs.

Fill a cup with water or mix a little water with a whole egg and have it as well as a pastry brush nearby. Have handy a sharp knife to cut long lengths of pasta, if necessary, and additional flour for re-flouring the work surface. Finally, clear out a space in your freezer so that you can initially freeze the pasta spread out on a baking sheet. (If your freezer won't accommodate a baking sheet, freeze the pasta in smaller batches on plates.)

To roll the pasta: Set the pasta machine on its widest setting. Cut the pasta dough into four pieces. Take one piece to roll and wrap the others in plastic wrap. Very lightly flour this piece and run it through the pasta machine two times. Fold it in half and run it through again. Do that two times.

Set the machine to the next level of thickness and run the piece of dough through again. As the pasta thins, it lengthens and can be unwieldy. As you make fresh pasta more often, you will create your own best way of handling the dough, but I find it helpful to rest the dough on the back of my hands, almost at my wrist, as it emerges from the rollers to help guide the sheet along. This keeps my fingers, which may poke through the dough, out of the way. The hand that "catches" the pasta as it comes through the machine gently turns clockwise to move the sheet away from the machine. (Don't pull on the pasta; let the machine do the work.) The back of the hand that's feeding the dough into the rollers also turns clockwise. If the sheet gets too long, simply cut it in half with a knife; just remember that each of these shorter sheets will need to run through each of the settings as you go.

Continue to roll the pasta until you can see the shape of your hand through the sheet (the actual setting will vary by machine). You may want to very lightly dust the sheet with flour as you near the final setting as it can get a little dicey at this point.

If you have enough work space, you can roll out all of the dough at one time. If you go that route, cover each sheet of dough with plastic wrap to prevent it from drying out. (Our pasta maker Yssac—he goes by one name like Cher— flours each sheet and stacks one on top of the other until he's got a thick stack of pasta sheets. It's a good system for him, and one you might want to try, but be sure to flour generously; if the sheets stick to each other, you're in trouble.)

If you don't have a lot of room (either on the work surface or in the freezer), roll, fill, and freeze one piece of dough before moving on to the other pieces.

If you are *not* filling the pasta, you actually want the pasta to dry out a bit for easier cutting. Leathery is the word most often used to describe the texture you're looking for, and that seems apt.

To fill and freeze stuffed pasta: Follow the filling and freezing directions that go with a particular pasta recipe.

To make and store unfilled pasta: Let the strips of dough air dry until they feel leathery.

For fettuccine and linguine: Cut the strips of pasta with the pasta roller designated for that shape. As the strands emerge from the rollers, hold them in the palm of one hand. Once released from the rollers, wrap the lengths around your hand to make a little nest. Put the nests on the lined and floured baking sheet and freeze. Once frozen, they can be stored in an airtight freezer container or freezer bag.

For tonarelli (spaghetti): We call this cut pasta spaghetti at the restaurant, but technically, that's wrong as spaghetti is an extruded pasta, which gives it its round shape. The pasta that's closest to spaghetti using cutters is called tonarelli. It's about the same thickness as spaghetti and feels very similar in the mouth, but if you look closely, you will see that it is actually square instead of round. You will need rollers designed for this shape (which may or may not have come with your pasta machine), and will need to have the sheet of pasta just a bit thicker than what you use to make fettuccine. Store these in nests as you would fettuccine.

For pappardelle: Use a pastry cutter or pizza wheel, fluted or otherwise, to cut long, 1/2-inch strips of pasta from the sheets of pasta. Store these in nests as you would fettuccine.

For tagliatelle: Make the strips the same way as for pappardelle but cut the strips 1/4-inch wide.

For farfalle: Cut fresh pasta into 1-inch strips with a pastry wheel or pizza cutter. Cut those strips into 1 1/2-inch rectangles. Pinch each rectangle in the middle of its long sides to bring the sides together. Freeze in a single layer on a floured baking sheet. Once hard, they can be transferred to an airtight freezer container or freezer bag.

MELTED TOMATOES

This sauce is so simple but so good. Paired with Ricotta Raviolini, it's a marriage made in heaven, but I also like it with spinach gnocchi or served over soft or baked polenta.

MAKES 1½ CUPS

2 tablespoons olive oil

1 pint cherry tomatoes, halved

1/2 teaspoon chopped fresh oregano

Kosher salt and freshly ground black pepper to taste

2 tablespoons Fresh Tomato Sauce (page 104) or other good-quality, lightly seasoned tomato sauce

HEAT THE OLIVE OIL in a large sauté pan over medium-high heat. Add the tomatoes, oregano, some salt, and a touch of pepper. Cook the tomatoes, adjusting the heat as necessary, until most of their juices have been released and reduced so that there is little liquid left in the pan, 10 minutes. Add the tomato sauce and bring to a boil. Reduce the heat and keep warm.

RICOTTA RAVIOLINI WITH

MELTED TOMATOES

Few foods are as soul-satisfying to me as a simple ricotta cheese ravioli. But what I don't like are those giant pucks you find at way too many Italian restaurants. I like to make cheese ravioli quite small (hence the "ini" in the name), shaping them into 1-inch squares so that they can be eaten in one delicate bite. Since the filling ingredients for this ravioli are so few, it's very important that they be of the best quality, especially the ricotta cheese. This may mean a trip to a good cheese store or an Italian market. Look for a delicate, not-too-wet curd. Melted Tomatoes would also work well with the potato gnocchi or the spinach-ricotta gnocchi in this chapter.

MAKES **4** SERVINGS

For the filling

8 ounces ricotta

2 egg yolks

1 ounce Parmigiano-Reggiano, finely grated

Kosher salt and freshly ground white pepper to taste

FOR THE FILLING: Combine well the ricotta, egg yolks, grated Parmigiano-Reggiano, salt, and pepper.

For the dough: Roll out the dough as directed on page 117.

To fill and freeze: I use a ravioli mold with tiny squares on it. If you have one of those, go ahead and use it—it makes filling the pasta really easy and efficient—following the manufacturer's directions. If you don't have a mold, you can make these tiny shapes by hand. Very lightly brush the sheet of pasta with water or egg wash. Place dots of filling ($^1/2$ teaspoon each) at one-inch intervals just below and just above the middle of the strip. (You can use a pastry bag to do this if that's easier for you; just be sure the opening is big enough to accommodate the filling.) *(continued)*

For the dough

1¼ pounds fresh Pasta Dough (page 116)

To serve

1 recipe Melted Tomatoes (page 120), warm on the stove

2 teaspoons unsalted butter

Parmigiano-Reggiano, shaved using the side of a box grater or vegetable peeler

Carefully lift the bottom edge of the sheet and bring it to meet the middle, letting it fall loosely over the bottom row of filling. Then bring the top edge of the dough down to meet the middle. Using the pinky side of each hand, gently pat the area close to each lump of filling to coax out any trapped air. Use a pastry cutter to cut out tiny squares around each dot of filling.

As you work, transfer the filled pasta to the parchment-lined baking sheet in a single layer. (Don't stack them or they will stick together.) An easy way to do this is to hold the baking sheet just below the edge of your work surface and use the cutter to flick and drop the pasta onto the baking sheet. The pasta should glide easily if the surface is well floured. Freeze the pasta on the baking sheet until they feel rock solid and then transfer them to freezer bags or some other airtight container for longer storage. (They'll keep, frozen, for up to two weeks.) If you prefer to cook the pasta right away, freeze them for as long as you can so they will be easier to handle.

Bring a large pot of amply salted water to a boil. Have the Melted Tomatoes warm on the stove in a large sauté pan. Cook the pasta until just tender. Gently drain the raviolini and add it and the butter to the pan with the tomatoes. Increase the heat to medium-high and toss gently.

To serve: Divide the raviolini and tomatoes among four wide bowls and top with some shavings of Parmigiano-Reggiano.

WHICH WINE?

For a dish that's as soft and simple as this raviolini, I choose a red wine that's also soft and simple—**Ruchè di Castagnole Monferrato** (DOC).

Scott Conant's New Italian Cooking

SHORT RIB AGNOLOTTI
WITH **HORSERADISH** AND
BROWN BUTTER

Is it unseemly for a chef to keep saying how much he likes his own dishes? Maybe. But I have to tell you that this dish makes me really happy. While contemplating what kind of sauce would go well with short rib–filled pasta, my mind wandered to the horseradish sauce often served with a standing rib roast. Could horseradish somehow work with pasta? I almost dismissed it as too odd, but I'm glad I didn't. The result is this rich, almost sweet meaty filling countered by the distinctive heat of horseradish. A drizzle of browned butter ties the dish together and makes the exceedingly quick-to-make "sauce" taste toasty and feel silky smooth.

MAKES **4** SERVINGS

For the filling

1 teaspoon olive oil

1 small onion, finely chopped

1 recipe Thyme and Rosemary Braised Short Ribs, prepared as directed in the Note accompanying the recipe (page 168)

HEAT THE OLIVE OIL in a large sauté pan over medium heat. Add the onion and cook until the onion is soft and lightly browned, 8 minutes. Add the shredded short ribs to the pan and toss to combine. Remove from the heat and let cool to room temperature. You want the meat filling for the pasta to be very moist, but if there are pools of liquid, drain the liquid away.

Roll out the dough as directed on page 117.

To fill and freeze: With the sheet of dough in front of you, very lightly brush the water or egg wash over the entire piece of dough. Place about a teaspoon of filling at 2-inch intervals just a little bit above the middle of the sheet. Carefully lift the

For the pasta

1 1/4 pounds fresh Pasta Dough (page 116)

Water or 1 large egg mixed with a little water to make an egg wash

To serve

6 tablespoons unsalted butter

3 tablespoons prepared horseradish (not the cream kind)

1 tablespoon snipped chives

Parmigiano-Reggiano, thinly shaved with a vegetable peeler

bottom edge and bring it to meet the top, letting it fall loosely over the filling. Using the pinky side of each hand, gently pat the area close to each lump of filling to coax out any trapped air.

Flour a 2-inch diamond-shaped cutter and stamp out triangle shapes by positioning the folded edge of the dough across the center of the diamond to result in a nice triangle with the filling approximately centered. (Alternatively, you can use a circular cookie cutter to create half-moon shapes or use a pastry cutter to cut the pasta into square ravioli.)

As you work, transfer the filled pasta to the parchment-lined baking sheet in a single layer. (Don't stack them or they will stick together.) An easy way to do this is to hold the baking sheet just below the edge of your work surface and use the cutter to flick and drop the pasta onto the baking sheet. The pasta should glide easily if the surface is well floured. Freeze the pasta on the baking sheet until it feels rock solid and then transfer to freezer bags or some other airtight container for longer storage. (It'll keep, frozen, for up to two weeks.) If you prefer to cook the pasta right away, freeze it for as long as you can so it will be easier to handle.

To serve: Warm four pasta bowls or plates. Bring a large pot of amply salted water to a boil. Reduce to a rapid simmer and cook the pasta until just tender. Meanwhile, in a large sauté pan, heat 2 tablespoons of butter over medium-low heat. Add the horseradish and stir to distribute it. In a smaller sauté pan, heat the remaining butter over medium heat.

Reserve a little of the pasta cooking water, and gently drain the pasta. Add the pasta to the pan with the butter and horseradish and toss gently to coat, adding a bit of the pasta cooking water to moisten the pasta, if necessary. Taste an agnolotti to be sure there is some good horseradish flavor present. (Horseradishes can vary in potency.) If not, add a bit more.

Divide the pasta among four hot bowls or plates. Increase the heat under the small pan of butter and cook until the butter turns brown, watching it carefully and taking it off the heat before it begins to burn. Drizzle the brown butter over the plated pasta. Sprinkle with some chives and top with some shavings of cheese. Serve immediately.

WHICH WINE?

I would look for a nice **Bordeaux Blend** from the Trentino region. Bordeaux grapes that do well in this southern portion of Trentino–Alto Adige include Cabernet Sauvignon, Cabernet Franc, and Merlot.

PUMPKIN AND AMARETTO
COOKIE CAPPELLACCI

A good amount of crushed red pepper keeps this pasta from becoming cloyingly sweet. If you're not up to making your own dough, square gyoza (wonton) wrappers work perfectly.

MAKES **4** SERVINGS

For the filling

3 pounds pumpkin, such as cheese pumpkin or even your classic jack-o'-lantern pumpkin, peeled, seeded, and cut into **1**-inch pieces (**3** cups)

1/4 cup olive oil

Kosher salt and freshly ground black pepper

1/4 teaspoon crushed red pepper

1 tablespoon finely ground Amaretto cookies

For the pasta

11/4 pounds fresh Pasta Dough (page **116**) or purchased **3**-inch-square gyoza (wonton) wrappers

Water or **1** large egg mixed with a little water to make an egg wash

HEAT THE OVEN to 400°F. Toss the pumpkin with the olive oil and season with salt and pepper. Place in a sided pan and roast until the pumpkin is very tender, 1 1/2 hours. Halfway through the cooking, add the crushed red pepper and toss the pumpkin around so the pepper flakes don't burn. Cool. Puree the pumpkin in a food processor until smooth. Mix in the Amaretto cookies and refrigerate.

Roll out the dough as directed on page 117 or have the gyoza wrappers handy.

To fill and freeze: With the sheet of dough in front of you, cut the sheet into 3-inch squares and place a rounded teaspoon of the pumpkin mixture in the center of each. (You can use a pastry bag to do this if that's easier for you; just be sure that the opening is big enough to accommodate the filling.) Very lightly brush some water or the egg wash over the edges of each piece. Fold each square in half along the diagonal. Using the pinky side of each hand, gently pat the area close to each lump of filling to coax out any trapped air and then press the moistened edges together to form a triangle. Pull the two corners on the fold side together by holding one corner

For the sauce

1 tablespoon unsalted butter

1 tablespoon olive oil

Pinch of crushed red pepper

1 tablespoon ground Amaretto cookie

1 tablespoon grated Parmigiano-Reggiano

between your thumb and index finger and using the other hand to pull the opposite corner around the tip of the index finger. Use the index finger to gently make an indent where the filling is and then pinch the corners together where they join.

Transfer the filled pasta to a parchment-lined baking sheet in a single layer without touching. Freeze the pasta on the baking sheet until it feels rock solid and then transfer it to freezer bags or some other airtight container for longer storage. (It'll keep, frozen, for up to two weeks.) If you prefer to cook the pasta right away, freeze it for as long as you can so it will be easier to handle.

To serve: Bring a large pot of amply salted water to a boil. Reduce to a rapid simmer and cook the pasta until just tender. Meanwhile, heat the tablespoon of butter and olive oil with the crushed red pepper in a very large sauté pan over medium heat. Gently drain the pasta and add it to the pan with the butter. Increase the heat to medium-high and toss gently to coat. Sprinkle with the ground Amaretto cookie and cheese. Divide the pasta among warm bowls or plates and serve immediately.

WILD MUSHROOM RAVIOLI
WITH THYME, TRUFFLE OIL,
AND PANCETTA

You don't need a trained pig to find the mushrooms in this ravioli. A mix of wild mushrooms are found inside and out, plus there is a finish of truffle oil that gives this dish an intoxicating aroma, one that will make you want to sit for a moment to breathe it in. The amount of salt you want in the filling and the topping will vary depending on the saltiness of the pancetta, but for a balanced final flavor, you want the ravioli filling to be a little on the salty side.

MAKES **4** SERVINGS

For the ravioli filling

2 to **3** tablespoons extra virgin olive oil

2 shallots, sliced

3 ounces pancetta, chopped fine

4 sprigs fresh thyme, stems removed

1 pound mixed, preferably wild, mushrooms, trimmed, cleaned, and sliced

Kosher salt and freshly ground black pepper to taste

1¼ pounds fresh Pasta Dough (page 116)

TO MAKE THE RAVIOLI FILLING: Heat the olive oil in a large sauté pan over medium heat and sauté the shallots until just tender, 5 to 7 minutes. Add the chopped pancetta and thyme sprigs and cook until the pancetta starts to crisp and brown, another 5 minutes. Add the mixed mushrooms, season with salt and pepper, and sauté, increasing the heat if necessary, until tender and browned. Remove the pan from the heat and allow the mixture to cool to room temperature. Pulse the mushrooms in a food processor or blender until the mixture is the consistency of barley. Taste and add more salt if needed.

Roll out the dough as directed on page 117.

To fill and freeze: With the sheet of dough in front of you, very lightly brush some water or egg wash over the entire piece of dough. Place about a teaspoon of filling at 2-inch intervals just a little bit above the middle of the sheet. (You can use a pastry

To accompany the ravioli

2 tablespoons extra virgin olive oil

1 ounce pancetta, diced

Pinch of fresh thyme leaves

1 shallot, thinly sliced

4 chanterelle mushrooms, quartered

4 oyster mushrooms, broken into pieces

1 tablespoon grated Parmigiano-Reggiano, more to taste

1 teaspoon finely chopped fresh chives, more to taste

1 teaspoon truffle oil

bag to do this if that's easier for you; just be sure the opening is big enough to accommodate the filling.)

Carefully lift the bottom edge of the sheet of dough and bring it to meet the top, letting it fall loosely over the filling. Using the pinky side of each hand, gently pat the area close to each lump of filling to coax out any trapped air.

Using a pastry wheel or pizza cutter, cut the sheet into squares around the mounds of filling, trimming the rough edge for a neater appearance.

As you work, transfer the filled pasta to a parchment-lined baking sheet in a single layer. (Don't stack it or it will stick together.) An easy way to do this is to hold the baking sheet just below the edge of your work surface and use the cutter to flick and drop the pasta onto the baking sheet. (The pasta should glide easily if the surface is well floured.) Freeze the pasta on the baking sheet until it feels rock solid and then transfer it to freezer bags or some other airtight container for longer storage. (It'll keep, frozen, for up to two weeks.) If you prefer to cook the pasta right away, freeze it for as long as you can so it will be easier to handle.

To serve: Bring a large pot of amply salted water to a boil. Meanwhile, heat a large sauté pan over medium-high heat. Add the oil, diced pancetta, and thyme leaves and cook until the pancetta just begins to crisp. Add the shallot and cook until it wilts in the heat. Add the chanterelles and oyster mushrooms and allow them to brown and crisp slightly, then lower the heat to just keep the mushrooms warm.

Reduce the water to a rapid simmer and cook the pasta until just tender.

Reserve $1/4$ cup of the pasta cooking water and then gently drain the pasta. Add it to the pan with the mushrooms along with a few tablespoons of the pasta water. Increase the heat to medium-high and toss gently to coat. Sprinkle with the grated cheese and chives. Divide the pasta among warm bowls or plates. Top each with a tiny drizzle of the truffle oil and a little more cheese and chives, if you like.

WHICH WINE?
This dish, typical of Emilia-Romagna, would do well with a wine from that region, such as a **Sangiovese di Romagna** (DOC).

YUKON GOLD POTATO

GNOCCHETTI

The tiny size of these "little gnocchi" makes a dish featuring them more refined than the same dish served with their bigger sibling. Use this recipe for Potato Gnocchetti with Shrimp, Peas, and Scallion (page 134). For other preparations—they're delicious simply tossed with some brown butter and fresh sage—you can add up to $1/4$ cup finely grated cheese, such as Parmigiano-Reggiano or grana Padano. You can cook the gnocchetti right away, if you can't stand the wait. But, as with my fresh pasta, I think gnocchetti only benefits from a deep freeze; they absorb less water during cooking and turn out meltingly tender yet sturdy enough to toss in your sauce without the risk of becoming a heap of mush. For the best texture, you'll need a ricer to mash the potatoes.

MAKES **7** CUPS GNOCCHETTI;
8 SERVINGS TOTAL

2 pounds Yukon gold potatoes
(**4** large)

1 large egg

1 large egg yolk

1 teaspoon salt

1$1/2$ to **2** cups "00" or all-purpose flour, plus more for rolling and shaping

BOIL THE POTATOES, whole and in their jackets, in well-salted water until just tender when pierced with a paring knife, 30 to 35 minutes. Do not overcook the potatoes; they should still hold their shape. Drain the potatoes, send them through a ricer into a bowl, and let them cool to room temperature. Add the egg, egg yolk, and salt to the potatoes and mix to combine well.

Generously flour your work surface. Dump the potatoes out and lightly knead in 1 cup of the flour. Add additional flour until the mixture just begins to hold together and feels like your earlobe. Try not to overmix the dough and don't be tempted to add too much flour at once; you can always add more flour if the dough needs it.

Before shaping all of the dough, make a few gnocchetti and cook them to be sure the texture is right: Bring a small pot of salted water to a boil. Roll a small piece of the potato dough into a rope $1/4$ inch thick. Using a sharp knife, cut the rope on a diagonal at intervals of $1/2$ inch. Cook the sample gnocchetti for a couple of minutes after they float on top of the water. Drain and taste. The gnocchetti should hold together during cooking and their texture should feel light and tender. Don't worry if they taste bland; the flavor comes mostly from the sauce. If the gnocchetti fall apart, add a bit more flour to the remaining dough before you roll and shape the rest of it.

To finish shaping the gnocchetti, line a sided baking sheet (one that will fit into your freezer) with parchment paper and lightly flour it. Once the gnocchetti dough is made to your liking, continue rolling the rest of the dough on a well-floured surface into $1/4$-inch-thick ropes. As you roll, be aware that too much pressure will flatten the tender dough, so use light hands. Using a sharp knife, cut the rope into $1/2$-inch lengths on a slight diagonal. As you slice the rope, keep the knife blade on your work surface after the cut and gently push the cut gnocchetti out of the way of the rope so it doesn't stick to the next slice.

After you cut each rope, transfer the gnocchetti to the prepared baking sheet in one layer. An easy way to do this is to hold the baking sheet just below the edge of your work surface and use the knife to flick and drop the gnocchetti onto the sheet. Freeze the gnocchetti until they feel rock solid and then transfer them to freezer bags or some other airtight container for longer freezer storage.

When preparing the gnocchetti, send them straight from the freezer to a pot of boiling, well-salted water. Cook until they are tender with no raw flour taste; this usually takes a minute or two after the gnocchetti begin to float.

POTATO GNOCCHETTI WITH

SHRIMP, PEAS, AND SCALLION

A lot of people think frozen peas taste just as good as fresh peas. A lot of people are wrong. Make this dish only when you can buy fresh peas to shell yourself. I'm not asking you to do much work here; the recipe calls for just a quarter cup of peas. You'll also have better flavor if you seek out the best shrimp; my favorite comes from the deep waters off the coast of Maine. I also like spot prawns from Alaska.

MAKES **4** SERVINGS

1 pound large shrimp (**16**), shelled and deveined

2 teaspoons chopped fresh rosemary

1 teaspoon chopped fresh parsley

1/4 teaspoon crushed red pepper

1 garlic clove, finely chopped

1/3 cup plus **2** tablespoons extra virgin olive oil

1/4 cup fresh peas

1 tablespoon thinly sliced scallion

3 to 3^{1}/2 cups frozen Yukon Gold Potato Gnocchetti (page 132)

TOSS THE SHRIMP with the rosemary, parsley, crushed red pepper, garlic, and 2 tablespoons olive oil. Refrigerate the shrimp and allow it to soak up the flavors of the marinade for at least 3 hours and up to a day.

Bring a large pot of well-salted water to a boil.

Pour the ^{1}/3 cup of olive oil into a large sauté pan and add the shrimp, peas, and scallion. Season with salt and fresh pepper but keep the pan off the heat for now.

Drop the frozen gnocchetti into the boiling water and cook, adjusting the heat so that the water is a gentle boil (not a rollicking one), just until the gnocchetti no longer taste of raw flour. This usually takes a couple of minutes from the time the gnocchetti have begun to float.

When the gnocchetti are done, put the waiting sauté pan on high heat. Using a slotted spoon or Chinese skimmer, gently transfer the gnocchetti to the sauté pan. Add ^{1}/4 cup of the

pasta cooking liquid to the pan and cook the shrimp until they are just barely cooked through. I take them off the heat when they are just starting to turn pink but are still gray in places, 3 to 5 minutes, depending on how quickly your stove heats the pan. By this time the sauce should have reduced slightly so that you end up with a concentrated flavor of shrimp, peas, and scallion. Season with additional salt and pepper to taste but skip the cheese!

WHICH WINE?

Go with a white wine, preferably one that's been stainless steel aged as too much wood would ruin the flavor combination. I like an **Orvieto Classico** (DOC).

SPINACH AND RICOTTA GNOCCHI

While spinach and ricotta gnocchi may not seem like "new" Italian cooking, I do tweak this classic by adding bread crumbs to the mixture. Bread crumbs, especially light Japanese *panko*, add body to the dumplings, making then easier to shape without weighing them down, as excessive flour can do. Exactly how much flour you do use will vary every time you make the gnocchi, depending on the water content of your cheese and spinach. (If the ricotta is very liquidy, pour off the excess before combining the cheese with the rest of the ingredients.) At the restaurant we serve this with fava beans, tomatoes, and *guanciale*, which you can do by following the directions on page 140. But both fava beans and *guanciale* are a little tough to come by, so you should feel free to enjoy these with the tomato sauce on page 104 or the Melted Tomatoes on page 120.

MAKES **4** TO **6** SERVINGS

3 tablespoons olive oil

1 large shallot, sliced

1 clove garlic, sliced

1/4 teaspoon crushed red pepper

1 bunch spinach, tough stems trimmed, well washed and dried (to yield **8** ounces), **6** cups, packed

1 teaspoon kosher salt

3 large egg yolks

15 to **16** ounces fresh ricotta cheese (**2** cups)

1/2 cup finely grated Parmigiano-Reggiano

3/4 cup fine, dry unseasoned bread crumbs, preferably *panko* (see Sources)

Freshly ground black pepper

1 cup "00" or all-purpose flour, plus more if needed, and more for rolling

HEAT THE OLIVE OIL in a medium sauté pan over high heat. Add the shallot, garlic, and crushed red pepper and cook, stirring constantly, until the shallot is lightly browned on the edges, 2 minutes. Remove the pan from the heat, add the spinach and $^1/_2$ teaspoon salt and toss until wilted. (Put the pan back on the burner over medium heat if the heat in the pan is not enough to wilt it.) Drain the spinach in a colander, pressing on it lightly to get rid of any excessive moisture. Chop the spinach finely by pulsing it in a food processor or using a large chef's knife.

In a large bowl, combine the egg yolks, ricotta cheese, Parmigiano-Reggiano, bread crumbs, and another $^1/_2$ teaspoon salt. Season with a little black pepper. Add the spinach, mixing it in well to distribute it more or less evenly. Add 1 cup of the flour to the mixture and combine well. Continue to add more flour, a little at a time, until the mixture no longer sticks to your hands. Try not to overmix the dough and don't be tempted to add too much flour at once; you can always add more flour if the dough needs it.

Line a sided baking sheet (one that will fit into your freezer) with parchment paper, lightly flour it, and set it aside.

Before shaping all of the dough, make a few gnocchi and cook them to be sure the texture is right. To do this, bring a small pot of salted water to a boil. Flour your work surface and your hands. Roll a small piece of the dough into a rope between $^1/_2$ inch and $^3/_4$ inch thick. Using a sharp knife, cut the rope on a diagonal at $^1/_2$-inch intervals. Cook the gnocchi at a gentle boil for a couple of minutes after they float on top of the water. Drain and taste. The gnocchi should hold together during cooking and their texture should feel light and tender. If the gnocchi fall apart, add a bit more flour to the remaining dough before you roll and shape the rest of it.

Once the gnocchi dough is made to your liking, continue rolling the rest of the dough on a well-floured surface into $^1/_2$-inch-thick ropes. As you roll, be aware that too much pressure will flatten the tender dough, so use light hands. Using a sharp knife, cut the rope at $^1/2$-inch intervals on the diagonal to create gnocchi that measure an inch from point to point. As you slice the rope, keep the knife blade on your work surface after the cut and gently push the cut gnocchi out of the way of the rope so it doesn't stick to the next slice.

After you cut each rope, transfer the gnocchi to the prepared baking sheet in one layer. An easy way to do this is to hold the baking sheet just below the edge of your work surface and use the knife to flick and drop the gnocchi onto the pan. Freeze the gnocchi until they feel hard and then transfer them to freezer bags or some other airtight container for longer storage.

Send the frozen gnocchi straight from the freezer into a pot of boiling, well-salted water. Cook until they are tender with no raw flour taste; this usually takes a minute or two after the gnocchi begin to float; your best bet is to taste. Add the drained gnocchi right to the pan in which you are heating your sauce and serve.

SPINACH AND RICOTTA GNOCCHI WITH FAVA BEANS, TOMATOES, AND GUANCIALE

> This is my favorite accompaniment to Spinach and Ricotta Gnocchi. The saltiness of the *guanciale*, the sweetness of the tomatoes, and the earthy flavor and texture of the fava beans really complement the light, green-specked gnocchi.

MAKES **4** TO **6** SERVINGS

3/4 pound fresh fava beans, shelled

1 to **2** tablespoons extra virgin olive oil

8 slices *guanciale* (see page 9), sliced thinly crosswise

1 shallot, thinly sliced

1/2 cup halved cherry tomatoes

1 recipe Spinach and Ricotta Gnocchi (page 137)

1 to **2** tablespoons finely grated Parmigiano-Reggiano

BLANCH THE SHELLED FAVA BEANS to loosen their skin by boiling them for a minute and then plunging them in cool water. Drain and slip off their skin by cutting the skin with your thumbnail and then popping the bean out of its skin with a pinch. (If it's early in the season, and the favas are very small, you can skip the skinning step.) You should have about 2/3 cup of beans.

Bring a large pot of well-salted water to a boil.

In a large sauté pan, heat a teaspoon of olive oil over medium heat. Add the *guanciale* and cook, stirring occasionally, until cooked through and just beginning to crisp. With a slotted spoon, remove the *guanciale* from the pan.

Add enough olive oil so there is 2 tablespoons of fat in the pan and heat it over medium to medium-high heat. Add the shallot and cook, stirring, until tender. Add the tomatoes and cook until they release most of their liquid. Add the *guanciale*, cook another minute, and remove from the heat.

Meanwhile, drop the frozen gnocchi into the boiling water and cook, adjusting the heat so that the water is a gentle boil (not a rollicking one), just until the gnocchi no longer taste of raw flour. This usually takes a couple of minutes from the time the gnocchi have begun to float.

Reserve $1/2$ cup of the gnocchi cooking water. Return the sauté pan to medium-high heat. Add the blanched fava beans to the sauté pan and, using a slotted spoon or Chinese skimmer, gently transfer the gnocchi to the sauté pan. Don't worry if some of the cooking water joins the sauce. In fact, you can add up to $1/4$ cup of the gnocchi cooking liquid to the pan to help loosen the sauce. Gently toss all of the ingredients in the pan together, adding additional cooking liquid if the gnocchi look dry, until heated through. Sprinkle 1 tablespoon of the cheese over the gnocchi and divide it among four hot plates or shallow bowls. Serve with additional grated cheese, if you like.

WHICH WINE?

One of the best glasses of rosé I have ever had was in Apulia, where I was loving the food, the company, and the countryside. To replicate that warm feeling in the middle of New York City is tough; the best I can do is pour the exact wine I enjoyed, which is from the **Rosa del Golfo** winery in Apulia. Buy some of this reasonably priced wine yourself—it's much cheaper than a flight to Italy. Then make the gnocchi and imagine yourself in Apulia.

Risotto

* Basic Risotto
* Spinach Risotto with Fontina
* Risotto with Broccoli Rabe,
  Raisins, and Pine Nuts
* Clam and Zucchini Risotto
  with Melted Scallions
  Crabmeat Risotto with Spicy Red Peppers
  Farro and Vegetable Risotto
  Seared Foie Gras and Green Apple Risotto

IF THERE IS ONE "NEW" THING you should take away from this book regarding Italian cooking, it's how you approach risotto. I'm not talking only about technique here. I'm talking about how you view this dish in your general cooking repertoire. Risotto does not have to be reserved for special occasions. It is not difficult to make. (In fact, it's very forgiving.) It does not take very long at all to cook. And you don't have to stir it constantly! There. I'm done. Now go make some risotto.

You'll need a wide saucepan, one that's a few inches high and has a heavy bottom, and a wooden spoon. (I prefer a squared-off spoon that allows me to efficiently scrape the bottom of the pot as I stir.) You'll also need starchy, medium-grain rice.

Arborio rice is often used for risotto, but I prefer an Italian rice called Vialone Nano. I find that sometimes in risotto, you get too much damn starch and the rice grains become barely distinguishable. Now, some people really like that style, but I prefer a looser risotto, one in which each rice grain is distinct even while the overall impression of the dish is smooth and supple. Vialone Nano helps ensure you get the latter style of risotto (see Sources).

The reason for the differing results is the ratio of starches each rice contains. The main starch in Arborio (amylopectin for you food-science types) more readily dissolves during cooking, which makes a stickier risotto. Vialone Nano has more amylose starch, which does not soften as easily. Carnaroli, yet another option, has less amylopectin than Arborio, but is still a bit too starchy for my taste. If Arborio is your only choice, you may want to up the fat called for in the dish to counter the high levels of starch release.

Vialone Nano, aside from creating a risotto I like, is also a practical choice for restaurant cooking and even the home cook who entertains a lot. Because its starch does not dissolve so easily, you can cook the risotto halfway, let it cool, and then quickly finish the dish just before serving. (For exactly how to do that, see page 149.)

All rice absorbs liquid, but risotto rice (all styles of it) absorbs a *lot* of liquid (five times its weight compared to three times its weight for most other rice). This may seem obvious, but it's very important for that liquid to taste good. (Or as in the case of some seafood risottos, to taste neutral.) The absolute best choice is a light, homemade broth, such as the one on page 14. If that's not an option, choose the best-tasting store-bought broth you can find.

Finally, if you already make risotto, you may be surprised by the amount of olive oil I use. The idea is to create an emulsion between the olive oil and starch released by the rice. The result is a dish so smooth and unctuous that it's almost hard to believe it started as hard little grains of rice.

BASIC RISOTTO

> This risotto recipe acts as the base for almost all of the other risotto recipes in the book. To call it "basic" is a bit of an understatement since it's so good.

MAKES **4** FIRST-COURSE SERVINGS

5 tablespoons extra virgin olive oil

1 small shallot, finely chopped (1 tablespoon)

Pinch of crushed red pepper

1 cup Vialone Nano or Arborio rice

1/2 cup dry white wine, such as Sauvignon Blanc

4 cups homemade Chicken Broth (page 14) or purchased low-salt chicken broth, kept at a simmer

1 tablespoon unsalted butter

2 tablespoons grated Parmigiano-Reggiano

Kosher salt to taste

IN A WIDE, HEAVY-BASED SAUCEPAN, heat 3 tablespoons of the olive oil over medium-high heat until very hot. Add the shallot and red pepper and stir until the shallot is barely browned, 1 to 2 minutes. (Take the pan off the heat if the shallot starts to scorch.) Add the rice and cook over medium-high heat, stirring with long strokes, until you see that each grain has been coated with the oil, another 1 to 2 minutes. Pour in $1/4$ cup of the wine and boil until the wine is almost completely absorbed (but do not let the pot become completely dry).

Add a couple ladlefuls of the hot broth to the rice and stir well every minute or so until almost all of the liquid has been absorbed. (On medium-high heat, the risotto bubbles away throughout, which is fine.) To see if it's time to add more liquid, drag the spoon through the rice; if the liquid doesn't immediately fill in the space, it's time to add more. Add another ladleful of stock, the remaining wine, and a tablespoon of olive oil. Continue to cook, adding more stock as needed and stirring, until the risotto looks creamy but is still al dente, 20 to 25 minutes.

How to gauge the final amount of liquid left in the pan takes a little practice. My risotto looks quite fluid but does not feel "wet." I strive to create an emulsion that suspends the perfectly

Risotto

cooked and separate grains of rice evenly within it; the addition of the olive oil helps to create this emulsion. If the risotto seems too dry, add a bit more broth. If there's too much broth in the pan, but the rice is done, crank up the heat to evaporate the liquid. Bear in mind that the risotto will thicken a bit as you add the cheese and as it cools.

Remove the rice from the heat and let the risotto stand for 30 seconds. Add a final drizzle of olive oil, butter, and cheese, and stir with a wooden spoon until well combined and cohesive. Season to taste with salt, if needed (it might not be, if you used purchased broth). Serve immediately.

SAFFRON VARIATION
Crumble a pinch of saffron threads into the chicken broth before adding it to the rice.

WHITE TRUFFLE VARIATION
Swirl in 2 tablespoons of white truffle butter (see Sources) at the end of cooking along with the butter and cheese.

SPINACH RISOTTO WITH FONTINA

The speckled green color of this risotto belies the richness the fontina adds. You can make the spinach puree ahead of cooking the risotto or, because it goes in at the end of the risotto, you can make it while you are cooking the rice—whichever is easiest for you.

MAKES **4** FIRST-COURSE SERVINGS

1 pound spinach, tough stems removed, well washed and dried

5 to **6** tablespoons extra virgin olive oil

2 shallots, one thinly sliced, the other finely chopped

Pinch of crushed red pepper

1 cup Vialone Nano or Arborio rice

1/2 cup dry white wine, such as Sauvignon Blanc

4 cups homemade Chicken Broth (page 14) or purchased low-salt chicken broth, kept at a simmer

1 tablespoon unsalted butter

1 tablespoon grated Parmigiano-Reggiano

1/2 cup shredded fontina cheese

Kosher salt to taste

CHOP THE SPINACH COARSELY. Heat a tablespoon of olive oil in a large sauté pan over medium heat. Add the sliced shallot and cook until the shallot is soft and lightly browned. Add the spinach and cook, tossing, until the spinach is well wilted. Take the pan off the heat and allow the spinach to cool a bit before pureeing it.

In a wide, heavy-based saucepan, heat 3 tablespoons of the olive oil over medium-high heat until very hot. Add the chopped shallot and crushed red pepper and stir until the shallot is barely browned, 2 minutes. (Take the pan off the heat if the shallot starts to scorch.) Add the rice and cook over medium-high heat, stirring with long strokes, until you see that each grain has been coated with the oil and looks separate, another 1 to 2 minutes. Pour in $^1/4$ cup of the wine and boil until the wine is almost completely absorbed (but do not let the pot become completely dry).

Add a couple ladlefuls of the hot broth to the rice and stir well every minute or so until almost all of the liquid has been absorbed. (On medium-high heat, the risotto bubbles away throughout, which is fine.) To see if it's time to add more liquid, drag the spoon through the rice; if the liquid doesn't

Risotto

immediately fill in the space, it's time to add more. Add another ladleful of stock, the remaining wine, and a tablespoon of olive oil. Continue to cook, adding more stock as needed and stirring, until the risotto looks creamy but is still al dente, 20 to 25 minutes.

Meanwhile, puree the cooked spinach in a blender or food processor.

When the rice is fully cooked, remove it from the heat. Add a final drizzle of olive oil, butter, pureed spinach, and both cheeses. Stir with a wooden spoon until well combined and cohesive. Season to taste with salt, if needed (it might not be, if you used purchased broth). Serve immediately.

WHICH WINE?
A **Chianti Classico** (DOCG) would be just great with this.

Make-Ahead Risotto

IT'S THE RARE RESTAURANT that can make every risotto to order. There just isn't the time, manpower, or stove space to devote to it. Instead, the rice is cooked halfway earlier in the day. When an order comes in, a portion is heated, stock is added, and any finishing touches are given. The time it takes to get an order out when the rice is parcooked this way is about a third of the time it takes to cook the rice from start to finish.

You may not have as much reason to start risotto ahead, but there are times when it might come in handy to know this trick. If you are making risotto for a dinner party, you can better time the doneness of the dish and be away from your guests for ten minutes as opposed to thirty-five.

To make risotto ahead, very lightly brush a baking sheet with some olive oil. Cook the rice, sautéing the aromatics, toasting the rice, adding the wine and then some broth, until it has absorbed 1 1/2 cups of stock and is almost halfway cooked through. Spread the risotto out on the baking sheet—the spreading helps cool the rice quickly and evenly—and cover the rice loosely with parchment paper or wax paper. If you are going to get back to cooking the rice in an hour or so, you can leave it out; otherwise refrigerate it for up to 24 hours.

When ready to cook the rice, return it to the saucepan along with a cup of broth and heat it over low heat, stirring gently to break up any clumps of rice. Increase the heat and finish cooking the rice as directed, adding more broth and any other finishing ingredients.

RISOTTO WITH BROCCOLI RABE, RAISINS, AND PINE NUTS

Spinach, currants, and pine nuts (called *pignoli* in Italian) are a classic flavor combination in Sicily and elsewhere in the Mediterranean. I prefer countering the sweetness of the dried fruit, in this case raisins, with the more bitter flavor of broccoli rabe.

MAKES **6** FIRST-COURSE SERVINGS

1 bunch broccoli rabe

1/3 cup pine nuts *(pignoli)*

2 tablespoons olive oil

1 to 2 cloves garlic, thinly sliced

Pinch of crushed red pepper

1/3 cup raisins

Basic Risotto (page 145)

BRING A LARGE POT OF WATER TO A BOIL. Discard any bruised broccoli rabe leaves and trim the tough bottoms off the stems. Wash well. Boil the broccoli rabe for 2 minutes (it will finish cooking in the sauté pan). Drain the broccoli rabe and, when cool enough to handle, chop it into pieces 2 inches long.

Heat the pine nuts in a large, dry sauté pan over medium heat, stirring occasionally, until lightly browned. Remove the pine nuts from the pan. In the same pan, heat the olive oil over medium-high heat. Add the sliced garlic and red pepper and cook, stirring, until the garlic just begins to color. (Remove the pan from the heat for a minute if necessary to keep the garlic from burning.) Add the broccoli rabe, raisins, and pine nuts and toss to combine. Divide the risotto among four heated bowls and top with the broccoli rabe mixture.

WHICH WINE?

A **Nero d'Avola**, a deep red wine *(nero* means black in Italian), has a strong enough personality to deal with the bitter broccoli rabe, the sweet raisins, and the toasted *pignoli*.

Scott Conant's New Italian Cooking

CLAM AND ZUCCHINI RISOTTO
WITH MELTED SCALLIONS

I make a version of this dish for the restaurant using braised eels. But since most people are a bit squeamish handling eels (I can't blame them), I decided to try it with clams. The results are a little different but just as good.

MAKES **6** FIRST-COURSE SERVINGS

7 tablespoons extra virgin olive oil

2 cloves garlic, coarsely chopped

2 pounds small clams, such as Manila clams, tiny littlenecks, or even cockles

2 shallots, finely chopped

1 cup Vialone Nano or Arborio rice

1/2 small zucchini julienned to yield **1/2** cup

1/4 cup dry white wine

2 cups homemade Chicken Broth (page 14) or low-salt purchased chicken or vegetable broth, kept at a simmer

2 tablespoons very finely chopped scallions (1 scallion)

IN A LARGE, HEAVY-BASED SAUCEPAN, heat 3 tablespoons of olive oil over medium-high heat. Add the garlic and sauté it until fragrant. Add the clams and 1 cup of water. Cover the pan and cook the clams for a minute or two after they open. Drain the clams in a colander set over a bowl to catch the cooking liquid. Remove the clams from their shells and discard the shells. Carefully strain the liquid through your finest strainer, leaving any sediment behind.

In a wide, heavy-based saucepan, heat another 3 tablespoons of olive oil over medium-high heat until very hot. Add the shallots and cook, stirring, until the shallots are barely browned, 2 minutes. (Take the pan off the heat if the shallots start to scorch.) Add the rice and cook over medium-high heat, stirring with long strokes, until you see that each grain has been coated with the oil and looks separate, another minute. Add the zucchini and wine and cook, stirring occasionally, until the wine is almost completely absorbed (but do not let the pot become completely dry).

Add a ladleful of the hot broth and a ladleful of the reserved clam cooking liquid to the rice; stir well every minute or so until almost all of the liquid has been absorbed. To see if it's time to add more liquid, drag the spoon through the rice; if the liquid doesn't immediately fill in the space, it's time to add more. Add another ladleful of broth and clam liquid and a tablespoon of olive oil. Continue to cook, adding more broth and clam liquid, until the risotto looks creamy but is still al dente, 20 to 25 minutes. Stir the clams and the scallions into the risotto and continue cooking, adding more liquid if necessary, until the clams are heated through and the scallions are tender. Serve immediately.

WHICH WINE?

For this risotto, I turn to a dry white **Fiano di Avellino** (DOC), which has a complex bouquet and a refined flavor.

CRABMEAT RISOTTO WITH
SPICY RED PEPPERS

I usually have no problem substituting chicken broth for fish broth in most fish-based recipes, especially when the fish itself will give up a lot of juices to add flavor. This particular risotto would probably taste okay made with chicken broth, but after spending all that money on lump crabmeat, you want more than just okay. The Lobster-Tomato Broth, which you can make ahead and freeze, brings this dish to a whole other dimension of flavor. Because the risotto contains no butter or cheese, you will need to finesse the technique a little to have it turn out as good and creamy as you'd expect risotto to be. Keep reading and you will see how this is done.

MAKES **4** TO **6** SERVINGS

For the peppers

1 tablespoon olive oil

2 shallots, sliced

2 red bell peppers, stemmed, seeded, and julienned very thin

1/4 teaspoon crushed red pepper

2 tablespoons red wine vinegar

TO MAKE THE PEPPERS: In a small sauté pan over medium heat, heat the tablespoon of olive oil and sauté the sliced shallots until tender. Add the bell peppers and crushed red pepper and cook until the peppers are limp and releasing liquid. Add the vinegar, cover, and cook until the peppers have absorbed most of the liquid, 15 minutes. (You can make the peppers a day or two ahead; reheat them gently just before serving.)

To make the risotto: In a wide, heavy-based saucepan, heat 3 tablespoons of the olive oil over medium-high heat until very hot. Add the shallots and stir until they are barely browned, 2 minutes. (Take the pan off the heat if the shallots start to scorch.) Add the rice and cook over medium-high heat, stirring with long strokes, until you see that each grain has been

For the risotto

4 tablespoons olive oil

2 finely chopped shallots

1 cup Vialone Nano or Arborio rice

1/4 cup dry white wine

3 cups Lobster-Tomato Broth (page 13), simmering on the stove

1/4 cup Fresh Tomato Sauce (page 104) or good-quality canned tomato sauce

6 ounces lump crabmeat, picked over for any stray bits of shell

1 tablespoon snipped fresh chives

Kosher salt and freshly ground black pepper to taste

coated with the oil and looks separate, another 1 to 2 minutes. Pour in the wine and boil until the wine is almost completely absorbed (but do not let the pot become completely dry).

Add a ladleful of the hot broth to the rice and stir well every minute or so until almost all of the liquid has been absorbed. (On medium-high heat, the risotto bubbles away throughout, which is fine.) To see if it's time to add more liquid, drag the spoon through the rice; if the liquid doesn't immediately fill in the space, it's time to add more. Add another ladleful of stock and a tablespoon of olive oil. Continue to cook, adding more stock as needed and stirring.

If it seems, after 15 minutes of cooking, that the liquid is not thickening properly, remove the pot from the heat and stir vigorously off the fire. Continue cooking and adding broth a little at a time until the risotto looks creamy but is still al dente, 20 to 25 minutes.

Add the tomato sauce, crabmeat, and a tablespoon of olive oil. Stir like crazy! Adjust the consistency of the risotto with more broth if needed, and season the risotto with salt and pepper. Add the chives and stir again.

Divide the risotto among warm bowls and top with the spicy red peppers.

WHICH WINE?

Look for a **Kerner** from Alto Adige. This grape, a hybrid of a red wine grape native to the region (called Schiava) and the white Riesling grape, makes wonderful Riesling-like wines that are a bit floral with a nice level of acidity that would go well with this risotto.

FARRO AND VEGETABLE RISOTTO

Farro is an ancient cousin of wheat cultivated in Italy. It has a firm, nutty texture and is available at Italian groceries, gourmet markets, and through mail order (see Sources). You can substitute spelt, found in most health food stores. Although technically a different grain, spelt cooks up and tastes almost exactly like farro. It's also cheaper than farro, which has suddenly become quite trendy. Just don't call this "spelt risotto" when you serve it; it just doesn't sound as appetizing, does it? This tastes great with the short ribs on page 168.

MAKES **4** SERVINGS

3/4 cup farro or spelt

Kosher salt and freshly ground black pepper to taste

2 tablespoons olive oil

2 cups homemade vegetable or Chicken Broth (page 14) or purchased low-salt broth, kept at a simmer

1/2 cup diced zucchini

1/2 cup diced yellow squash

1/2 cup sliced asparagus (optional)

1/2 pint small tomatoes, such as pear, grape, or currant tomatoes (larger ones cut in half)

2 teaspoons butter

1 to **2** tablespoons grated grana Padano or Parmigiano-Reggiano

BRING A MEDIUM SAUCEPAN FULL OF SALTED WATER TO A BOIL. (Farro will expand to about three times the volume you started with, so be sure your pot is big enough to accommodate the finished amount.) Add the farro, reduce the heat to a gentle boil, and cook until chewy but no longer hard, 15 to 20 minutes. Drain and reserve.

Heat the olive oil in a medium pot over medium-high heat. Add the farro and $1/4$ cup of the broth and bring to a boil, stirring, until the broth is almost completely absorbed (but do not let the pot become completely dry).

Add the vegetables to the pot along with another $1/2$ cup or so of broth, season with a little salt and pepper, and cook, stirring well every minute or so, until almost all of the liquid has been absorbed. Add another ladleful of broth and continue to cook, adding more broth as needed and stirring until the farro has thickened considerably and the vegetables are tender, 20 minutes. Remove the pot from the heat, stir in the butter and cheese, season with additional salt and pepper, and serve immediately.

WHICH WINE?

When serving this risotto with the short ribs on page 168, a **Barbera d'Alba** (DOC) is just the ticket. Otherwise, you could choose a light red or even a full-bodied white wine.

SEARED FOIE GRAS AND
GREEN APPLE RISOTTO

I remember playing around with the elements of this dish, the rich, luxurious flavor and texture of the foie gras, the tartness of the green apple, the creamy risotto. The act of creating a new dish is not unlike a painter approaching a blank canvas. If the painter is not in the mood to paint, he's often better off just putting the brush down. I had made similar dishes to this one quite a few times and got no reaction at all. I left it alone for a while and came back to it when I was literally in a better place in my life, personally and professionally. I went at the risotto again and created the version you have here. People loved it. That's when I realized that the energy you project can really affect your cooking. When I approached this dish not in a forced way but with an easy confidence and trust in the people I was making it for, I could be receptive to the "soul" of the dish. But that's just how I feel about it. Make this dish and see if you agree.

MAKES **4** SERVINGS

For the risotto

5 tablespoons extra virgin olive oil

1 small shallot, finely chopped
(1 tablespoon)

Pinch of crushed red pepper

1 cup Vialone Nano or Arborio rice

1/2 cup dry white wine,
such as Sauvignon Blanc

4 cups homemade Chicken Broth
(page 14) or purchased low-salt chicken
broth, kept at a simmer

1 cup peeled and diced Granny Smith apple

For the foie gras

4 slices foie gras (see Note), each **3/4** inch thick

Kosher salt and freshly ground black pepper

1 shallot, finely chopped

8 sprigs fresh thyme

To serve

1 tablespoon unsalted butter

2 tablespoons grated Parmigiano-Reggiano

Kosher salt to taste

1/3 cup Vinegar Reduction (page 17), using balsamic vinegar

IN A WIDE, HEAVY-BASED SAUCEPAN, heat 3 tablespoons of the olive oil over medium-high heat until very hot. Add the shallot and crushed red pepper and stir until the shallot is barely browned, 2 minutes. (Take the pan off the heat if the shallot starts to scorch.) Add the rice and cook over medium-high heat, stirring with long strokes, until you see that each grain has been coated with the oil, another 1 to 2 minutes. Pour in $1/4$ cup of the wine and boil until the wine is almost completely absorbed (but do not let the pot become completely dry).

Add a couple ladlefuls of the hot broth to the rice and stir well every minute or so until almost all of the liquid has been absorbed. (On medium-high heat, the risotto bubbles away throughout, which is fine.) To see if it's time to add more liquid, drag the spoon through the rice; if the liquid doesn't immediately fill in the space, it's time to add more. Fifteen minutes into the cooking, add the diced apple to the pan. Add another ladleful of stock, the remaining wine, and a tablespoon of olive oil. Continue to cook, adding more stock as needed and stirring, until the risotto looks creamy but is still al dente, 20 to 25 minutes.

Meanwhile, heat the oven to 250°F. Heat a large, ovenproof sauté pan over high heat. Season the foie gras well on both sides with salt and pepper. When the pan is very hot, add the foie gras slices and sear them well on one side. This will take just a couple of minutes and will render much fat. Add the shallot and thyme sprigs to the pan once you see some of that fat. Turn the foie gras over and let it finish cooking in the low oven for a few minutes while you finish the risotto.

Remove the rice from the heat and let the risotto stand for 30 seconds. Add a final drizzle of olive oil, butter, and cheese and stir with a wooden spoon until well combined and cohesive. Season to taste with salt, if needed (it might not be, if you used purchased broth).

To serve: Divide the risotto among four warm rimmed plates or shallow wide bowls. Drizzle the vinegar reduction around the perimeter of the risotto. Top each with a slice of foie gras. Drizzle just a little of the fat from the pan over the foie gras and top with a crispy thyme sprig. Serve immediately.

> NOTE Foie gras, goose or duck liver from specially raised fowl, is available at some gourmet grocery stores. A whole foie gras weighs 1 1/2 pounds, and you often need to purchase a whole one, even if you are not using all of it. Foie gras will keep for about five days in the refrigerator; it can also be frozen, although its texture may suffer a little for it.
> *To slice foie gras:* Divide the lobe into its two naturally forming pieces. Remove any obvious connective matter and large veins (but don't break up the foie gras; you won't notice the smaller veins once the foie gras is seared). Rub a thin, flexible knife under hot water, quickly wipe it dry, and slice the foie gras, rinsing and drying the knife between each slice. If you are not searing the foie gras right away, arrange the slices on a piece of wax paper and chill the slices, loosely covered in plastic wrap, for up to a day.

WHICH WINE?

You're already going all out with the foie gras, so why not go all out with the wine, too? Look for a **Valpolicella Classico** (DOC) made by the *ripasso* process, which adds body and fullness, making the wine almost portlike. (Since it won't say *ripasso* on the label, you will need to talk to a knowledgeable wine merchant to find a producer making the wine in this style.) You could also go with a **Moscato Frizzante**, which is sweet and lightly sparkling and always a good match for foie gras.

Main Courses

✳ Seared and Slow-Roasted Sirloin of Beef
Thyme and Rosemary Braised Short Ribs
✳ Sear-Roasted Beef Tenderloin
with a Bread and Herb Crust
"Boneless" Osso Buco
Stewed Tripe in Spicy Tomato Sauce
Pork Chops with Wilted Scallions and Radicchio
✳ Pan-Roasted Pork Tenderloin with Sage and Pancetta
Braised Pork Belly with Aromatic Spices
✳ Spice-Crusted Lamb
Oven-Braised Lamb Shanks with Red Wine Vinegar
Moist Roasted Baby Goat (Capretto)
with Peas, Fingerling Potatoes, and Shallots
✳ Pancetta-Wrapped Chicken Legs
✳ Chicken Breast Topped with Peas, Asparagus,
Tarragon, and Melted Fontina Cheese
✳ Herbed Paillard of Chicken
✳ Sicilian-Spiced Boneless Chicken Breast Medallions
with a Citrus and Radish Salad

Sear-Roasted Chicken Thighs with Garlic, Thyme,
and Juniper Berries
Spicy Whole Roasted Chicken with Orange
and Rosemary
Cumin-Spiced Roast Chicken with
Currant-Fegato Sauce, Toasted Almonds, and Chives
Braised Chicken Thighs with Parsnips and Mint
Cacciucco (Italian Fish Stew)
Moist-Roasted Whole Fish
with Cherry Tomatoes and Scallions
∗ Grilled Shrimp with Mint, Orange,
and Fennel Couscous
∗ Seared Branzino and Sliced Lemon
∗ Salmon with Thyme and Fresh Juniper Berries
∗ Tuna Poached in Olive Oil Infused with Thyme,
Rosemary, and Lemon

MY APPROACH TO COOKING MEAT AND FISH is generally either/or: It's either cooked pretty quickly or very, very slowly. On the quicker side, I use a method that is easily replicated at home: a quick sear for color and flavor and then a finish in a very, very low oven. When I describe this method to food critics, I often get a raised eyebrow. But I think once you try this method with, say, the Seared and Slow-Roasted Sirloin of Beef, you may not cook steak any other way. The slow cooking relaxes the muscle so it cooks up tenderly. Instead of a charred exterior with only a rawish center, the inside of this steak is a beautiful rosy red from center to edge. The juices from the meat mingle with the extra virgin olive oil that I add to the pan (which I can do since the oven is so low the oil won't burn) to create the most tasty, most easy-to-prepare pan sauce. An added benefit is that you can get the rest of the meal together in the 15 minutes or so the meat spends in the oven.

When I think of really relaxed cooking, however, I think of braises, stews, and roasts, those dishes that once you get them going practically cook themselves. Braises, especially, get me excited as an eater and a businessman.

With a braise, you cook cheaper cuts of meat (the muscles in the animal that actually did some work) in a flavorful liquid, and the meat ends up tasting better than the most expensive cuts ever could. I also cook large pieces of meat and fish, using a method that's really a hybrid of roasting and braising in which I brown a large piece of meat in a little oil and then cook it uncovered in a little liquid in a pretty hot (400°F) oven. I call this moist roasting because the moisture in the oven cooks the meat very tenderly, but the high temperature also continues to brown the exposed meat, which adds a depth of flavor.

Roast chicken is another pleasurable dish to make when you have a couple of hours on a Sunday. I roast mine at a super-high temperature (it's about the only thing I cook so hot). The bird's water content keeps the meat moist while the hot oven crisps the skin beautifully. I also like to bone the bird before roasting it; the meat cooks evenly, it looks inviting on the plate, and it's much more pleasant to eat. On page 210, you will find friendly, detailed instructions on how to bone a bird—a task that's not too difficult once you've done it a couple of times. But if you're not up to the task, I've also included a whole roast chicken on page 206 that takes barely 5 minutes of prep time; this juicy, fragrant bird is perfect on a night when you're lacking more for energy than time.

Finally, don't forget fish and shellfish when you want something delicious to eat in a hurry. Especially if you are only cooking for one or two, the cost of fish is not prohibitive. Be sure to buy the freshest and best you can find.

SEARED AND SLOW-ROASTED SIRLOIN OF BEEF

To get the most tender, juicy, perfectly cooked steaks, I use the sear-then-slow-roasted cooking method described on the opposite page. At the restaurant, we cut the sirloin double thick and then in half the short way to get two portions the same size and shape as a filet mignon. If your butcher will do that for you, great: The thick pieces cook up beautifully, and the even, square slices look good on the plate. Otherwise, use very thick sirloin and take a few minutes off the cooking time. Because the meat finishes at such a low temperature, it leaves the oven less than piping hot. For this reason, heat your plates as hot as you can handle them. Serve the steak with the pan-fried potatoes on page 241 or the roasted baby vegetables on page 248.

MAKES **2** SERVINGS

1/4 cup extra virgin olive oil

Pinch of crushed red pepper

3 cloves garlic, one clove sliced, the other two cut in half

3 sprigs rosemary

2 sirloin steaks, preferably portioned as described above, **9** ounces each

Kosher salt and freshly ground black pepper to taste

Coarse sea salt to finish

1 ounce Parmigiano-Reggiano, shaved into paper-thin slices

IN A SHALLOW PLATE OR ZIP-TOP BAG, combine 2 tablespoons of the olive oil, the crushed red pepper, sliced garlic, and a sprig of rosemary. Add the sirloin and coat well with the marinade. Allow it to sit at room temperature for 20 to 30 minutes or up to 8 hours in the refrigerator. Heat the oven to 250°F. Add the remaining 2 tablespoons of olive oil, the halved garlic cloves, and the remaining rosemary to a sauté pan just large enough to hold the steaks.

Remove the meat from the marinade and season it with salt and pepper. If you have a grill on your stove, grill the steaks just so the exterior of the meat is nicely browned (brown all sides if using a thick square of meat). If you don't have a grill, sear the meat in a heavy-based sauté pan (not the prepared

one) over medium-high heat. Take the meat off the grill or out of the pan before the interior starts to cook. The entire browning process should last about 4 minutes for a thick cut of beef and a little less for thinner cuts.

Transfer the meat to the prepared sauté pan and cook in the oven, basting the meat with the olive oil every 4 minutes or so, until the meat is cooked to your liking. We serve ours medium rare (about 130°F on a meat thermometer), and it usually takes 18 minutes. A thinner cut will take less time; begin checking at 12 minutes. Transfer the steaks to a cutting board and stir together the meat juices and olive oil that remain in the pan.

Let the meat rest for a couple of minutes to allow the interior juices to redistribute and then slice the steaks across the grain $1/4$ inch thick. Arrange the slices on the heated plates. Drizzle some of the juices from the pan over the slices, sprinkle with a pinch of sea salt, and top with shavings of Parmigiano-Reggiano.

WHICH WINE?

Go ahead and open a **Super Tuscan**. These are the wines made by winemakers who disavowed the traditional Chianti formula and went on to create their own breed of wine that flouted the DOCG laws. Generally bold in flavor, they are usually made with either Sangiovese or Cabernet Sauvignon as the primary grape and can have a tannic edge rounded out by some oak barrel aging. Technically classed in the lowly *vino da tavola* ranking, these wines can be of exceptional quality with a price tag to match. Since the nickname Super Tuscan is a marketing moniker and not an official term, it will not be on the bottle. Ask someone knowledgeable at your favorite wine store to point you in the right direction. A less expensive wine that would also make a nice pairing is a **Montepulciano** from Le Marche. This new style is very fleshy with young tannins, and it goes great with steak.

THYME AND ROSEMARY
BRAISED SHORT RIBS

I cook short ribs long and low to get the most tender and flavorful results. I like to remove the meat from the bone, let it cool, and then slice it to serve with a little of the reduced cooking liquid over the Farro and Vegetable Risotto on page 156 (pictured on page 170) or the Basic Risotto on page 145 or the Creamy Polenta on page 234. If you are making the ribs to use in the Short Rib Agnolotti with Horseradish and Brown Butter on page 124, you will have enough meat for a light dinner for two after setting aside the amount needed for the pasta. Follow the instructions in the Note for how to handle the cooked short ribs for use as a filling for pasta.

MAKES **4** SERVINGS

3$\frac{1}{2}$ pounds beef short ribs (choose the largest, meatiest ribs available)

Kosher salt and freshly ground black pepper to taste

2 tablespoons olive oil

1 small carrot, cut into small dice

1 stalk celery, cut into small dice

1 medium onion, chopped

4 cloves garlic, coarsely chopped

1/2 cup balsamic or red wine vinegar

3/4 cup red wine

6 ripe plum tomatoes, seeded and cut into quarters

2 cups homemade Chicken Reduction (page 15) or purchased chicken reduction diluted with water until a little thicker than chicken stock

3 sprigs fresh thyme

3 sprigs fresh rosemary

HEAT THE OVEN to 300°F. Season the short ribs all over with salt and pepper. Heat a couple of tablespoons of olive oil in a deep, heavy-based Dutch oven or similar pot over medium-high heat. Sear the ribs—in two batches if they don't fit in the pot in a single layer—until they are well browned all over.

Remove the ribs and add the carrot, celery, onion, and garlic to the pot with more olive oil, if necessary. Sauté the vegetables until they are browned. Add the vinegar and red wine to the pan and, using a wooden spoon, scrape up the bits stuck to the bottom of the pan. Continue to cook the wine and vinegar until reduced by one-third. Add the tomatoes, chicken reduction, and herbs. Return the short ribs to the pot, bring the liquid to a boil, cover the pot, and put it in the oven. Cook, turning the ribs once or twice during the cooking, until they are fork tender and the meat is just barely clinging to the bone, 3 1/2 to 4 hours.

Remove the ribs from the pot and strain and reserve the cooking liquid. If you are serving the ribs right away, keep them warm. Use a large spoon or ladle to remove as much of the clear fat floating on top of the cooking liquid as possible and then cook the defatted sauce over medium-high heat until it has reduced somewhat, becoming thicker and more flavorful. (The ribs can be made up to two days before serving them and only taste better for being made in advance. If you are making them ahead, you can also wait to remove the fat from the cooking liquid. Refrigerate the ribs in their cooking liquid and then remove the hardened fat on top. Reheat the ribs in a 300°F oven in the cooking liquid. This reheating may reduce the sauce enough; if not, remove the ribs and cook it down further until thicker and more flavorful.)

(continued)

To serve: Slice the meat from the ribs across the grain into pieces $^1/3$ inch thick and serve with some of the reduced sauce. (Alternatively, serve the ribs whole.) If you are serving the ribs with polenta or risotto, go ahead and arrange them—sliced or whole—right on top and drizzle the sauce over all.

NOTE If you are using the short ribs as a stuffing for the agnolotti, let the meat cool so you can work with it. Remove the meat from the bone and chop enough of it into small pieces to give you 3 cups. (Serve the rest for dinner with some polenta or risotto, save it for an amazing sandwich, or add it to a tomato sauce.) Strain the sauce, defat it, and reduce it as directed above. Store the meat in the reduced sauce tightly covered in the refrigerator for up to two days.

WHICH WINE?

The answer here is simple: **Chianti Classico** (DOCG) **Riserva**.

Seasoning with Salt:
When, Why, and How Much?

JUST HOW DELICIOUS A RECIPE TURNS OUT is due in no small part to how well seasoned it is. By seasoned, I primarily mean how well it is salted. The goal in salting foods before and during cooking is not to make them taste salty; it's to bring out the full flavors of the food. While no one knows exactly how salt makes this happen, we know that it does. Pasta cooked in water without salt tastes flat, and a little salt added to sweet things brings out their sweetness. But I think one of the most convincing arguments in favor of cooking with salt comes with the cooking of meat, chicken, and fish. Try this little experiment for yourself. Cook a steak seasoned well with kosher salt and one without the salt and taste the difference.

To get into the habit of salting as you cook, get rid of your saltshaker. For one thing, table salt only adds a sharp, salty flavor to foods. (This is due to how it's mined and how tiny its crystals are.)

Get some kosher salt, which is sold in boxes near the table salt. Next, keep the salt near the stove in a container that is easy to reach into with your fingers. You can get one of those cute ceramic salt cellars, if you're looking for something decorative. For the more practical minded, you might want to buy a condiment holder. You know that compartmentalized metal box that bars use to store olives for martinis and lemons for gin and tonics? With its three or four removable plastic containers and clear plastic lid, such a box, left out and near the stove, allows you to keep not only your kosher salt handy but also any other ingredients you use often and by the pinch, teaspoon, or tablespoon, such as flour, sugar, or crushed red pepper.

But back to the salt. I use about a pinch (a little less than 1/4 teaspoon) per serving. Keep in mind this would mean a few pinches for a larger cut of meat, such as a boneless leg of lamb or a whole chicken.

When salting, do as we chefs do, and salt from on high. Take some salt between your thumb and first two fingers and release it onto your food or over your pot by rubbing your fingers back and forth and moving your hand so that the crystals fall evenly. You don't want the piece of meat to turn completely white, but you do want to see grains of salt scattered about on every inch of it. (If I'm seasoning with pepper as well, I use freshly ground and use about half as much as the salt.) This seasoning with salt (and often pepper) does not apply just to meat, chicken, and fish, but to vegetables as well. And just as important as salting foods *before* you cook is to salt *as* you are cooking. Not a lot—remember it's easy to add more salt but impossible to take it out—but do add a little bit in stages as you cook a dish with multiple steps, such as in a ragu or a topping for pasta. That way the full flavor of all of the ingredients is brought to the fore and the salt has plenty of time to work its magic. If you add all of the salt at the end of the cooking, the dish will just taste salty.

A big caveat: Keep in mind the salt content of some of your salty foods, the obvious and the less obvious. Anchovies, capers, and olives are obviously salty, as are bacon, pancetta, *guanciale,* and prosciutto; use restraint when salting dishes that include these ingredients. A less obvious ingredient is store-bought chicken broth, which can be quite salty. Also know that any salt that you add at the beginning of a long-cooking dish will be intensified as it cooks. The same is true for a sauce that you are reducing; as the liquid evaporates, all of the flavors, including the salt, will intensify.

Finally, I rarely give exact amounts for salt content in my recipes, instead suggesting you season something well or lightly, depending on the other ingredients and the cooking method. This is partly because the perception of salt will vary from person to person and partly because the salt content in various ingredients will vary. Just remember to keep tasting and adding a little salt now and again to discover just what level works best for you.

✳ SEAR-ROASTED BEEF TENDERLOIN
WITH A **BREAD** AND **HERB CRUST**

MAKES **4** SERVINGS

2 to **4** tablespoons olive oil

2 slices Italian or country-style bread, cut into **1/4**-inch cubes to yield **1** cup

11/2 to **2** pounds trimmed beef tenderloin, cut into **8** medallions

Kosher salt and freshly ground black pepper

2 tablespoons finely chopped scallions

1 tablespoon chopped fresh thyme

1 teaspoon finely chopped fresh parsley

1 egg, lightly beaten

HEAT THE OVEN to 350°F. In a medium sauté pan, heat 2 tablespoons olive oil. Add the bread cubes and cook until lightly browned on all sides. Remove from the heat and drain on paper towels.

Coat the beef medallions lightly with olive oil and season both sides with salt and pepper. Heat a large ovenproof sauté pan or grill pan over medium-high heat and sear the medallions lightly on both sides. Take the meat off the heat before it starts to cook through and reserve it at room temperature.

Toss the toasted bread with the scallions, thyme, parsley, and enough of the beaten egg to bind the ingredients (you may not need it all). Season with a little salt and pepper.

Return the beef to the sauté or grill pan. Top the medallions with the bread crumb mixture and finish cooking the meat and browning the bread crumbs in the oven, 8 minutes for rare.

WHICH WINE?
A **Cabernet Sauvignon** from Sicily would offer a perfect mouthfeel with the beef.

What really makes this dish is the contrast between the tender interior of the beef and this very rustic bread coating. The Artichoke, Pancetta, and Potato Torta on page 229 would make a delicious accompaniment.

"BONELESS" OSSO BUCO

Here I am having fun with the traditional alla Milanese way of serving osso buco by serving the "bone with a hole"—the literal translation of osso buco—on the side. Instead of buying the veal shank cut into slices of meat surrounding the bone, ask the butcher to remove the bone altogether and give you the boneless shank, which you will stuff with gremolata (a mixture of parsley, garlic, and lemon peel), roll, and tie at home, a process that is easier than it sounds. Traditionally, the gremolata gets sprinkled on the cooked veal as a final flourish; in this version, it releases its flavor deep within the meat as it slowly braises.

As for the bone marrow, which for many people is the whole reason for making (or ordering) osso buco, it is not forgotten. Ask the butcher to cut the bone he removed into pieces $1\frac{1}{2}$ inches long and give those to you, too. These bones will get cooked separately in a little of the braising liquid and be served alongside the sliced, boneless veal. Not only is this a dramatic presentation but it also pleases those who like their bone marrow pure in flavor. If, on the other hand, you don't feel like dealing with the marrow bones at all, you can use a boneless veal breast in place of the shank. Serve this nontraditional osso buco with its traditional accompaniment: saffron risotto (page 146).

HEAT THE OVEN to 300°F. Lay the shank "bone" side up and season the meat with salt and pepper. Sprinkle the lemon zest, parsley, chopped rosemary, half of the garlic, and the crushed red pepper evenly over the surface. Roll the shank around the filling and tie it at intervals using butcher twine.

Heat a couple of tablespoons of olive oil in a deep, heavy-based Dutch oven or similar pot over medium-high heat. Sear the rolled veal on all sides until browned. Remove the meat and add the carrot, celery, onion, and the remaining garlic to the pot with more olive oil if necessary. Sauté the vegetables until they are tender and browned, 7 minutes. Add the wine to the pan and,

MAKES **4** SERVINGS

One large hind veal shank
(**3** to **4** pounds) boned by your
butcher, and the bone cut by your
butcher into $1^1/2$-inch pieces

Kosher salt and freshly ground black
pepper to taste

1 tablespoon grated lemon zest
(from $1^1/2$ lemons)

1 tablespoon chopped fresh parsley

1 tablespoon chopped fresh rosemary

1 tablespoon chopped garlic
(**2** cloves)

1/4 teaspoon crushed red pepper

2 tablespoons olive oil

1 small carrot, cut into small dice

1 stalk celery, cut into small dice

1 medium onion, chopped

3/4 cup dry white wine

3 ripe plum tomatoes, seeded
and cut into quarters

2 cups homemade Chicken Reduction
(page 15) or purchased chicken
reduction diluted with water until a little
thicker than chicken stock

Sprig fresh thyme

Sprig fresh rosemary

using a wooden spoon, scrape up the bits stuck to the bottom of
the pot. Continue to cook the wine until reduced by about one-
third. Add the tomatoes, chicken reduction, thyme, and rosemary.
Return the veal to the pot, bring the liquid to a boil, cover the
pot, and put it in the oven. Cook, turning the veal once or twice,
until the meat feels fork tender, $2^1/2$ to 3 hours. (The osso buco
can be made up to two days before serving. Refrigerate the veal
in its cooking liquid. Remove any hardened fat before reheating
the meat in a 300°F oven in the cooking liquid. This reheating
may reduce the sauce enough; if not, remove the meat and cook
it down further until thicker and more flavorful.)

If you are serving the veal right away, remove the veal from the
pot and keep it warm. Strain and reserve the cooking liquid.
Use a large spoon or ladle to remove as much of the clear fat
floating on top of the liquid as possible and then cook the sauce
over medium-high heat until thicker and more flavorful.

About a half hour before the veal is to be served, put the veal
bones, hole side up, in a large ovenproof skillet or small
roasting pan. Transfer $2/3$ cup of the braising liquid from the
rolled veal into the pan with the marrow bones. Sprinkle the
bones with some salt and pepper and pop them into the oven to
liquefy and heat up the marrow.

Remove the twine and slice the shank in four pieces. Divide the
veal and marrow bones among warm plates. Pour some of the
braising liquid over the slices and serve immediately.

WHICH WINE?

An Italian **Cabernet Sauvignon** would be an obvious choice
here. Cabernets from Latium (Lazio) are a good choice for
lighter meat dishes.

STEWED TRIPE IN

SPICY TOMATO SAUCE

I know that this is not exactly the idea of a good meal for most people. I grew up eating tripe, called by its Italian name, *trippa,* in my house. My mother would make it for my grandfather after my grandmother died. My own mother hated the stuff, and my father would leave the house because he couldn't take the smell. But I loved its chewy texture, and its acrid flavor and spiciness became something that I would think about days after the pot was gone. (I was admittedly not your average child, in more ways than that I can assure you.) Nowadays, cooking tripe to appeal to a restaurant clientele has become a challenge that I have undertaken with pride. With the following recipe, which has ardent fans, I think that I've succeeded. I like to serve this tripe simply with some grilled ciabatta. It's also really good the next day tossed with rigatoni and some chopped parsley.

MAKES **4** SERVINGS

2 pounds honeycomb tripe

1/4 cup olive oil

1 onion, thinly sliced

4 sprigs rosemary

1 cup Fresh Tomato Sauce (page 104) or good-quality canned tomato sauce

1/2 teaspoon crushed red pepper

1 cup cooked or canned white beans or chickpeas

3 tablespoons Parmigiano-Reggiano

HEAT THE OVEN to 300°F. Rinse the tripe in cold water. Put the tripe in a pot of well-salted water and bring the water to a boil. Reduce to a roiling simmer and cook the tripe for 25 minutes. Drain the water, rinse the tripe under cold water, and simmer it again in fresh salted water for 25 minutes. Drain and repeat a third time. Give the tripe a final rinse and when cool, slice it into "sticks" 1 1/2 inches long and 1/4 inch thick. (You can do this a day ahead of finishing the dish; wrap the sliced tripe in plastic wrap and refrigerate until ready to proceed.)

In a large ovenproof sauté pan, heat the olive oil over medium heat. Add the onion and rosemary and cook until the onion is sweet and lightly browned, 15 minutes. Add the tripe and sauté together and allow the natural moisture of the tripe to be released and reduced, 20 minutes. Add the tomato sauce and crushed red pepper, cover, and bake for 40 minutes. Remove from the oven and add the beans. Bring to a boil and add the cheese and some more olive oil. Remove the rosemary stems; if there is some rosemary still on the tripe, that's fine. Stir well and serve.

WHICH WINE?

Try a good-quality **Sangiovese** from Emilia-Romagna with this.

PORK CHOPS WITH WILTED
SCALLIONS AND RADICCHIO

> This dish takes a bit longer to prepare than most of the quick-cooking main courses, but it includes a vegetable side along with the meat and some of the time is unattended. If you're not a fan of bitter radicchio, cook only the pork and serve it with your own favorite accompaniment.

MAKES **4** SERVINGS

6 tablespoons olive oil

2 shallots, thinly sliced

1/4 teaspoon crushed red pepper, more to taste

4 thick, bone-in pork chops, either rib or loin chops

2 small heads of radicchio, trimmed and cut into quarters

8 scallions, trimmed and cut into **3**-inch pieces

Kosher salt and freshly ground black pepper

1¹/₂ tablespoons balsamic vinegar, preferably one aged at least five years

IN A SHALLOW PLATE OR ZIP-TOP BAG, combine 2 tablespoons of the olive oil, the sliced shallots, and the crushed red pepper. Add the pork chops and coat well with the marinade. Allow them to sit at room temperature for 20 to 30 minutes or up to 8 hours in the refrigerator.

Heat the oven to 250°F. In a large skillet, heat 2 tablespoons of olive oil over medium-high heat. Add the radicchio to the pan and brown it on all sides. Add the scallions, cover the pan, and cook the vegetables in the oven until wilted and tender, 25 minutes. Season with salt and pepper to taste.

Meanwhile, in a separate skillet large enough to hold the four pork chops with space between each, heat another 2 tablespoons of olive oil over medium-high heat. Remove the pork chops from the marinade and season them well with salt. Sear the chops on one side until well browned, then turn the chops over and sear the other side until well browned. (This should take a total of 4 minutes.) Put the pan in the oven and cook the chops until medium rare to medium, 145°F. The time will vary, depending on the thickness of the chops, but figure on 20 minutes for a medium-rare 1^1/2-inch chop. A thinner cut will take less time; begin checking at 12 minutes.

Transfer the pork chops to a plate, but leave any juices and oil behind in the pan. Let the meat rest for a couple of minutes to allow the interior juices to redistribute. Add the balsamic vinegar to the pan the pork chops cooked in and heat it over low. Add any juices that have collected on the plate to the pan as well.

Divide the radicchio and scallions among four plates and rest a pork chop against each portion. Drizzle the pan juices and a little extra virgin olive oil over all and serve.

WHICH WINE?
A **Cabernet Sauvignon** from Friuli would work well with the bitterness of the radicchio.

PAN-ROASTED PORK TENDERLOIN
WITH **SAGE** AND **PANCETTA**

Maybe you haven't heard the good news yet, but pork no longer has to be cooked until it's white and tough. In fact, we serve it medium-rare, as we would beef or lamb. You cannot believe what a difference it makes; a piece of pork with a pinkish-red center feels completely different in your mouth, and there's not all that endless chewing involved. But, you might well ask, what about the dreaded trichinosis? I'm not looking for any lawsuits, but even the new edition of *The Joy of Cooking* notes that modern farming has greatly diminished that risk. At any rate, the trichinosis can't survive at temperatures greater than 137°F, and I'm not asking you to eat raw pork for crying out loud. This easy yet flavorful dish can be ready in less than a half hour. The ragout of leeks, peas, and asparagus (page 230) would go smashingly well with the flavors of the pork, sage, and pancetta.

MAKES **4** SERVINGS

2 to **3** tablespoons olive oil

1/4 cup diced pancetta

10 sage leaves

2 whole pork tenderloins, **2**¹/**2** pounds total, trimmed

Kosher salt and freshly ground black pepper

1/4 cup sliced shallot

IN A SMALL SAUTÉ PAN, heat a teaspoon of olive oil over medium heat. Add the pancetta and sage and cook until the pancetta has rendered most of its fat and is just starting to crisp. Remove from the heat and reserve.

Heat the oven to 350°F. Season the tenderloins all over with salt and pepper. Heat a large, ovenproof sauté pan over medium-high heat. Add a couple tablespoons of olive oil and when hot, add the pork loin and brown it on all sides.

Remove the pork and add the sliced shallot to the pan, plus a little more olive oil, if needed. Sauté the shallot over medium heat until it is transparent, 5 minutes.

Return the pork to the pan on top of the shallot and top the tenderloins with the sage and pancetta. Put the pan in the oven and cook the pork until it registers 145°F on a meat thermometer, 15 to 18 minutes.

Remove the pan from the oven and put it on a cool burner on the stove. Transfer the tenderloins to a cutting board with a trough to collect any juices (or put a flat cutting board onto a sided baking sheet to collect the juices). Let the pork sit, untouched, for 5 minutes.

Slice the loins. (Don't worry about the sage and pancetta falling off as you cut; you will collect these bits in a minute.) Divide the slices among four warm plates. Pour any juices from the cutting board back into the sauté pan, scraping into the pan any pancetta and sage that may have fallen off the pork during slicing. Heat the juices briefly, drizzle them over the pork slices, and serve immediately.

WHICH WINE?
An **Aglianico del Vulture** (DOC) from Basilicata, a dark *rosso rubino* made from Aglianico grapes, would go well with this pork dish.

BRAISED PORK BELLY
WITH **AROMATIC SPICES**

Until you have had braised pork belly—pork belly being the cut that's famously made into bacon—you have not tasted the most tender, succulent pork there is. Here I have to give credit to my chef de cuisine Kevin Sipple, whose idea it was to switch from pork shoulder to pork belly in a similar dish we were making. Deeply flavored with a wonderfully balanced spice mix and then cooked in a full-bodied chicken reduction, both cuts of pork taste delicious. It's the texture of the pork belly that makes people swoon; it is braised until achingly tender and then seared to crispy perfection just before serving. Take a bite and you first experience a satisfying crunch before the meat and fat melt away in your mouth. You'll want to moan it's so good.

The pork needs a day to marinate and then cooks for a long time, so you need to start it two or three days before the day you actually plan to serve it. The pork, as well as its recommended accompaniment, Cabbage Braised with Bacon (yes, bacon!) on page 240, can also be made a day or two ahead and gently reheated in the oven or on the stove; the cooked pork can also be frozen with great results.

MAKES **8** TO **10** SERVINGS

For the spice mix

2 teaspoons cumin seeds

1/2 teaspoon whole cloves

1/2 teaspoon whole black peppercorns

1/2 teaspoon whole mustard seeds

1/2 teaspoon ground cinnamon

2 teaspoons paprika

4 teaspoons salt

For the pork

One **5**- to **5**^{1}/**2**-pound piece skin-on whole pork belly (see Sources)

5 to **6** tablespoons extra virgin olive oil

1 onion, chopped

1 quart homemade Chicken Broth (page 14) or purchased low-salt chicken broth

1 quart homemade Chicken Reduction (page 15) or purchased chicken reduction diluted with water until a little thicker than chicken stock

FOR THE SPICE MIX: In a small sauté pan, heat the whole spices (cumin, cloves, peppercorns, and mustard seeds) over low heat, occasionally stirring the spices with a wooden spoon to prevent them from scorching, until quite fragrant, 5 to 8 minutes. Add the cinnamon and paprika and cook the spices for an additional minute. Allow the spices to cool for a few minutes and then grind them coarsely in a spice grinder or coffee grinder dedicated to spices. Mix in the salt. The spice mix, which makes ^{1}/2 cup, will keep for at least a month if tightly covered.

To marinate the pork: Rub the pork all over with olive oil. Sprinkle the spice mix evenly over it on all sides. Wrap it well in plastic wrap and let it marinate in the refrigerator for at least 24 hours and up to 36 hours.

To cook the pork: Heat the oven to 325°F. Place the pork, skin side down, in a heavy-based roasting pan and cook for one hour.

Meanwhile, heat a couple of tablespoons of olive oil in a medium sauté pan over medium-low to low heat. Add the onion and cook, stirring occasionally, until it is soft and thoroughly browned, 25 minutes. Turn the pork over and add the onion, chicken broth, and chicken reduction to the pan. Reduce the heat of the oven to 300°F and cook the pork until it is very, very tender, another 6 to 7 hours. When the pork is fully and tenderly cooked, you will be able to easily pull any bones right out. If there are no bones, poke in a fork and take a taste of the meat to determine tenderness.

Remove the belly to a sided sheet pan and gently pull out any bones and any tough cartilage you see (there is not much) without disturbing the layers of meat and fat.

Using a ladle or large spoon, spoon off the thick layer of clear liquid fat floating on top of the broth and pan juices. You should be able to remove a few cups of fat easily this way. Strain the mostly defatted braising liquid into a large sauté pan or clean roasting pan. Continue to remove as much fat as you can with the ladle (there is plenty of liquid here so don't worry about spooning off some of it). Or, if you are making this dish ahead and chilling the liquid, simply spoon off any hardened fat after the liquid has chilled.

When the meat is cool enough to handle, use a sharp flexible knife to remove just the skin, leaving the layer of fat below intact. Refrigerate the meat and the sauce separately for up to two days.

Heat the oven to 350°F. Using a large chef's knife, cut the meat into serving pieces 1 1/2 to 2 inches square, between 3 and 4 ounces each. (This dish is so rich that smaller portions work best.)

Remove any remaining fat from the surface of the braising liquid and pour about two-thirds of the liquid into a roasting pan. (At this point you can freeze portions of the pork belly and sauce if you like. Put the portions on a plate or small sheet pan, wrap them well in plastic wrap, and freeze; freeze the braising liquid separately. Defrost in the refrigerator for at least 24 hours before cooking.)

Heat a couple of tablespoons of olive oil in a large sauté pan over high heat. Season the fat side of the pork belly with salt and pepper and put the pork pieces in the pan fat side down. Cook them undisturbed until well browned, a few minutes at least. You are not trying to render all of the fat here, just to create a crisp top. Place the pork pieces seared side up in the roasting pan with enough of the strained braising liquid to come halfway up the side of the pork pieces. (Be sure the crisp top of the pork pieces stays above the level of the liquid.) Heat the meat and braising liquid together in the oven for 15 minutes. If the pieces of pork have lost some of their crispness due to the moisture in the oven, recrisp them in a dry hot sauté pan immediately before serving.

Serve the pork, ideally atop the cabbage on page 240, and spoon some sauce around the meat and cabbage.

WHICH WINE?

The richness of the pork calls for a wine with enough tannin to provide some backbone in the glass. A **Montefalco Rosso** (DOC) would fulfill that need, plus add a richness of flavor that will hold up against the subtle but intriguing spices used on the pork. The best-quality wines of this region are generally the **Sagrantino di Montefalco** (DOCG) wines.

SPICE-CRUSTED LAMB

> If your butcher carries boneless lamb loin, you're in for a treat. Lamb loin is less gamey and more tender than other parts of the lamb, yet it still has enough going on flavorwise to stand up to this kickin' spice mix. (Lamb loin chops work well, too.) Toasting spices intensifies their flavor and is a very simple thing to do. An electric coffee grinder devoted to spices makes grinding them quick work; you can also smash them in a mortar and pestle. There is so much flavor here that a sauce is gilding the lily, but if you are making this for a special occasion, serve the lamb with some Vinegar Reduction (page 17) drizzled over it. I don't usually serve pasta as a side dish, but this lamb tastes really good with the Fettuccine with Escarole and Wild Mushrooms on page 90.

MAKES **4** SERVINGS

1/4 cup fennel seeds

1 tablespoon coriander seeds

1 tablespoon sweet paprika

1 teaspoon crushed red pepper

1 teaspoon cayenne pepper

2 whole boneless lamb loins (1 1/2 pounds) or **8** thick lamb loin chops (**3** pounds)

1 to **2** tablespoons extra virgin olive oil

Kosher salt and freshly ground black pepper

2 tablespoons vegetable oil, such as canola, corn, or grapeseed oil

IN A SMALL SAUTÉ PAN, heat the fennel seeds, coriander seeds, paprika, crushed red pepper, and cayenne pepper over low heat, occasionally stirring the spices with a wooden spoon to prevent them from scorching. Heat until the spices are quite fragrant, 5 to 7 minutes. Allow the spices to cool for a few minutes and then grind them in a spice grinder. The spice mix, which makes 1/2 cup, will keep for at least a month if tightly covered.

Rub the lamb all over with the olive oil. Rub the spice mixture over the lamb in a heavy coat. Let the lamb sit at room temperature for 20 minutes to soak up the flavors of the rub or refrigerate the lamb for up to 24 hours before cooking it.

Just before cooking, season the lamb with salt and pepper. Heat the oven to 300°F. In a large sauté pan, heat the vegetable oil over medium-high heat. If cooking lamb loins, add

them to the pan and sear them on both sides, 1 to 2 minutes per side. If
cooking loin chops, sear them on both sides, 3 to 4 minutes per side. Transfer
the pan to the oven to finish cooking to medium rare (5 minutes for the boneless
loins, and 10 minutes for the chops). Let the lamb rest briefly. Slice and divide
the slices among four plates, or serve two chops to a plate.

WHICH WINE?

Ripe plums and spice characterize **Sagrantino di Montefalco** (DOCG), making
this a perfect pour with the spicy lamb.

OVEN-BRAISED LAMB SHANKS
WITH RED WINE VINEGAR

I almost never serve lamb shanks on the bone at the restaurant simply because the look of that giant hunk on the plate just doesn't match the refined elegance of the room. At home, however, a great big lamb shank looks (and tastes) eminently gratifying, so it's up to you. Serve the ragu over Creamy Polenta (page 234) or homemade pappardelle (page 116).

MAKES **4** SERVINGS

4 lamb shanks

Kosher salt and freshly ground black pepper

2 to **4** tablespoons olive oil

1 carrot, chopped

1 celery rib, chopped

1/2 medium onion, chopped

3 cloves garlic, chopped

1/2 cup red wine vinegar

1/3 cup red wine

3 canned plum tomatoes (**3** ounces), chopped

2 cups homemade Chicken Reduction (page 15) or purchased chicken reduction diluted with water until a little thicker than chicken stock

HEAT THE OVEN to 300°F. Season the lamb shanks all over with salt and pepper. Heat a couple of tablespoons of olive oil in a deep, heavy-based Dutch oven or similar pot over medium-high heat. Sear the lamb shanks—in two batches if they don't fit in the pot in a single layer—until they're well browned all over, 5 minutes.

Remove the lamb shanks and add the carrot, celery, onion, and garlic to the pot with more olive oil if necessary. Sauté the vegetables until they are browned. Add the vinegar and red wine to the pan and, using a wooden spoon, scrape up the bits stuck to the bottom of the pan. Continue to cook the vinegar and wine until it's reduced by one-third. Add the tomatoes and the Chicken Reduction. Return the lamb shanks to the pot, bring the liquid to a boil, cover the pot, and put it in the oven. Cook, turning the lamb shanks once or twice during the cooking, until they are fork tender and the meat is just barely clinging to the bone, $3^1/2$ to 4 hours.

Remove the lamb from the sauce and strain and reserve the cooking liquid. If you are serving the lamb shanks right away, keep them warm. Use a large spoon or ladle to remove as much of the clear fat floating on top of the cooking liquid as possible; then cook the defatted sauce over medium-high heat until it has reduced somewhat, becoming thicker and more flavorful.

The lamb shanks can be made up to two days before serving them and only taste better for being made in advance. If you are making them ahead, you can also wait to remove the fat from the cooking liquid. Refrigerate the lamb shanks in their cooking liquid and then remove the hardened fat on top. Reheat the lamb in a 300°F oven in the cooking liquid. This reheating may reduce the sauce enough; if not, remove the lamb shanks and cook it down further until thicker and more flavorful.

Serve the shanks with some of the sauce spooned over them.

WHICH WINE?
Look for a **Rosso di Montalcino** (DOC) for a good red-wine match.

MOIST ROASTED BABY GOAT (CAPRETTO) WITH PEAS, FINGERLING POTATOES, AND SHALLOTS

Compared to lamb, goat—especially baby goat—has a much milder, less gamey flavor. Yet, while hugely popular in the Mediterranean, South America, and the Middle East, goat hasn't really caught on in America. Maybe it's because of our location (we're a block from the U.N.), but this dish flies out of L'Impero. I get my goat—more than two hundred pounds a week of it—from a farm in Vermont. You can usually find good-quality goat at gourmet grocers, but ethnic markets—Italian, Greek, West Indian, Hispanic, and Middle Eastern—are also a potential source for it, especially around Easter. You can easily use lamb—a 5-pound leg works well—in place of the goat. It changes the tenor of the dish, but it is still delicious. If you do use lamb, substitute a comparably sized small leg of lamb or lamb shoulder.

SERVES **4** TO **6**

For the goat

1 baby goat (also called kid, capretto, and chevron) leg and shoulder, about **5** pounds

1/2 cup extra virgin olive oil

3 sprigs fresh rosemary

6 to **8** whole garlic cloves

Pinch of crushed red pepper

Kosher salt and freshly ground black pepper

2 to **3** tablespoons vegetable oil, such as canola, corn, or grapeseed oil

6 to **8** cups Chicken Broth (page 14)

For the vegetables

2 to **3** tablespoons vegetable oil, such as canola, corn, or grapeseed oil

5 medium fingerling potatoes, boiled until just tender and cut into medium dice

2 small shallots or **1** large, thinly sliced

1/2 cup fresh or frozen peas

1 tablespoon chopped fresh parsley

TO COOK THE GOAT: Trim any fat off the goat and remove any silverskin. Combine the olive oil, rosemary, garlic, crushed red pepper, a teaspoon of salt, and a teaspoon of pepper. Marinate the goat meat overnight in this mixture.

Heat the oven to 400°F. In a large, heavy-based braising pan (a pan with sides about 4 inches high), heat a few tablespoons of vegetable oil over medium-high heat. Remove the goat from the marinade but reserve the marinade ingredients. Season the goat lightly all over with kosher salt. Sear the goat on all sides until golden brown; this should take 12 to 15 minutes. Add enough broth to cover the bottom of the pan by 1 inch, and add the reserved marinade ingredients to the pan as well. Roast the goat, basting it every 15 to 20 minutes, adding more broth as needed, until the meat is tender and falling off the bone, 2 to 2$\frac{1}{2}$ hours. Check on the shoulder earlier in the cooking time as it will take a little less time to cook; take the shoulder out earlier if necessary.

Reserve the goat separately from the sauce. Strain the sauce and let the goat cool. When the goat is cool enough to work with, cut the meat off the bone and slice it into pieces that are a little larger than bite size.

If serving the goat right away, degrease the sauce by repeatedly dipping a large spoon or ladle just beneath its surface until the spoon fills with mostly clear fat; discard the fat. If you are cooking the goat ahead of serving it—it can be prepared a day or two ahead up to this point—refrigerate the goat and the strained sauce separately (moisten the meat with a little of the sauce). Before reheating, remove any hardened fat on top of the sauce.

(continued)

Cook the degreased sauce at a rapid simmer until reduced by a third. (The sauce will be thin but very gelatinous. Too much reduction and the sauce will become sticky and unappealing.)

Reheat the meat in the sauce in a low (225°F) oven until heated through.

To cook the vegetables: Heat 2 tablespoons vegetable oil in a large sauté pan over medium-high heat. Cook the potatoes until crispy and lightly browned. A few minutes into the cooking, add the shallots and peas so that they cook together. Season with salt and pepper. Sprinkle with the chopped parsley.

To serve: Heap the potatoes and peas to one side of the plate. Lay the slices of goat near them and top with the sauce.

WHICH WINE?

A wonderful wine in winter, especially for hearty game-style dishes, is a **Carema Riserva** (DOC). Made with 100 percent Nebbiolo, and harking from northern Piedmont, it has all of the characteristics of a good Barolo but is more tannic and austere with a tarry, truffle finish.

PANCETTA-WRAPPED

CHICKEN LEGS

At the restaurant, I make this with whole boned chicken legs. If you feel like boning the legs yourself (see page 210) or have a butcher who will do it for you, it makes an appealing presentation. Buying boneless, skinless chicken thighs is an easier, time-saving option, and the flavor is just as delicious. If the thighs are very small, you may want to cook a few extra. Serve this with the ragout of leeks, peas, and asparagus on page 230 or the baby artichoke and potato torta on page 229.

MAKES **4** SERVINGS

16 to **20** thin and very cold pancetta slices

8 to **10** boneless and skinless chicken thighs or **8** boned and skinned whole chicken legs

2 tablespoons chopped fresh thyme

1 teaspoon sweet paprika

Kosher salt and freshly ground black pepper

2 tablespoons olive oil

HEAT THE OVEN to 350°F. For each piece of chicken lay 2 to 3 slices of the pancetta, slightly overlapping, on a sheet of wax paper or a cutting board. Lay the chicken piece on the pancetta. Season with a little of the thyme, paprika, salt, and pepper. Wrap the chicken completely with the pancetta. Secure with some butcher twine or toothpicks, if necessary.

Heat a large, ovenproof sauté pan over medium-high heat. Coat the bottom of the pan with olive oil and sear the chicken lightly on all sides, in batches. Finish the chicken in the oven, 25 to 30 minutes—check by seeing if the juices that result from pricking the thigh run clear—and serve.

WHICH WINE?

A **Negroamaro** from Apulia made from the eponymous grape that grows abundantly there would go well.

CHICKEN BREAST TOPPED WITH PEAS, ASPARAGUS, TARRAGON, AND MELTED FONTINA CHEESE

In this pretty dish, the tender vegetables top the seared chicken breasts and get covered with the cheese to make a pleasing package. But because it's a very thin layer of cheese, the green of the peas and asparagus still comes through, adding brightness to the plate. Finally, the flavors all meld together perfectly, making the chicken taste exciting while still allowing the flavor of the bird itself to shine. Since you've already got the vegetables, all you need to serve with the chicken would be some plain risotto or some steamed new potatoes.

MAKES **4** SERVINGS

4 boneless, skinless chicken breast halves (1^1/2 pounds)

Kosher salt and freshly ground black pepper

3 to **4** tablespoons olive oil

1/2 medium onion, sliced thinly

1 bunch asparagus (**3/4** pound), trimmed and chopped into 1-inch pieces

1/2 cup fresh or defrosted frozen peas

1 teaspoon chopped fresh tarragon

4 to **8** thin slices of fontina cheese

POUND EACH CHICKEN BREAST lightly with a meat pounder at its thickest end to make the breast an even thickness. Season both sides of each breast with salt and pepper.

Heat the oven to 300°F. Have ready two sauté pans. Heat 1 tablespoon of olive oil in one of them over medium heat. Add the onion and cook, stirring occasionally, until soft and lightly browned, 8 to 10 minutes. Increase the heat a little and add the asparagus, peas, and tarragon, adding up to another tablespoon of olive oil if necessary. Season with salt and a little pepper. Cook, stirring occasionally, until the asparagus is tender, 8 to 10 minutes.

Meanwhile, heat 1 to 2 tablespoons of olive oil in another large ovenproof sauté pan over medium-high heat. Add the

chicken breasts, lower the heat a little, and cook, turning the breasts once, until nicely browned on both sides, 10 minutes total. Remove the pan from the heat, but keep the chicken in the pan.

Spoon the vegetable mixture on top of the four breasts. (Don't worry if some of the vegetables fall into the pan, and add any extra vegetables to the pan, too.) Top the vegetables with a single layer of cheese to cover. Put the pan in the oven to melt the cheese and finish cooking the chicken, 5 minutes. Serve on warm plates with any extra vegetables scattered about and any juices from the pan poured over the chicken.

WHICH WINE?

A **Sauvignon Blanc** from Friuli would be a wonderfully refreshing pour with this brightly flavored chicken.

HERBED PAILLARD OF CHICKEN

A few of the benefits of this chicken recipe: It's quick to make, feels light and summery, and features the herbs you are likely growing, including rosemary. In fact, because rosemary grows just about everywhere in Italy and much of the Mediterranean, most stores and farmers' markets there don't even bother selling it—most people either have some growing at home or can just stop the car on the way home and snip some from shrubs growing on the side of the road. Serve this as we do at the restaurant, with some Concentrated Tomatoes (page 244) on the side. If you don't have any on hand, you might want to serve the tomato salad on page 65 with it instead.

MAKES **4** SERVINGS

4 skinless, boneless chicken breast halves (**1**^{1}/**2** pounds)

Kosher salt and freshly ground black pepper

1 to **2** tablespoons extra virgin olive oil

2 teaspoons chopped fresh parsley

2 teaspoons chopped fresh rosemary

2 teaspoons chopped fresh thyme

2 teaspoons chopped fresh chives

Pinch of crushed red pepper

POUND EACH BREAST WITH A MEAT POUNDER between layers of plastic wrap until ^{1}/4 inch thick. Season the breasts with ample salt and pepper. Drizzle the olive oil over both sides of the breasts and sprinkle both sides with the herbs and crushed red pepper.

Prepare the grill of your choice to high heat. Grill the breasts until just firm to the touch; this will take just 1 to 2 minutes of cooking per side. Serve with another drizzle of olive oil.

WHICH WINE?

For a wine with a moderate body to complement this light but flavorful dish, look for a **Dolcetto di Dogliani** (DOC). The Dolcetto grape, which translates as "little sweet one," produces purplish wine, which, despite its literal meaning, is dry.

SICILIAN-SPICED BONELESS CHICKEN BREAST MEDALLIONS WITH A **CITRUS** AND RADISH SALAD

Like most of Italy, the island of Sicily—which was the first official Roman province—has been invaded throughout its history. The Arabs, who took hold in the ninth century, contributed a legacy of intensely flavored dishes to the cuisine, and, more concretely, citrus trees. This abbreviated history lesson explains why you will find a few orange-accented recipes throughout the book. In this particular recipe, there is a lot going on flavorwise; you've got some heat and spice with the chicken, the refreshing crispness of the radishes, and the tart tang of the citrus. Yet it's very simple and quick to pull together.

TO MAKE THE MARINADE: In a small sauté pan, heat the fennel seeds and crushed red pepper over medium heat until fragrant. Let cool briefly and then grind them in a spice grinder.

Meanwhile, zest half of the orange and half of the lemon to get $1/2$ teaspoon finely grated zest from each. Combine the ground spices, citrus zest, and garlic clove. Add the $1/4$ cup extra virgin olive oil and reserve. (The marinade will keep, refrigerated in an airtight container, for up to a week.)

At least a half hour before cooking, cut the chicken breasts on the bias into three equal medallions. (Pound lightly, if need be, to make them all the same thickness.) Coat the pieces with the marinade, season with salt and pepper,

MAKES **4** SERVINGS

2 tablespoons fennel seeds

1 teaspoon crushed red pepper

1 orange

1 lemon

1 garlic clove, smashed

1/4 cup extra virgin olive oil, plus a tablespoon or two for the salad

4 boneless, skinless chicken breast halves (1$\frac{1}{2}$ pounds)

2 handfuls greens, preferably baby greens

8 radishes, trimmed and thinly sliced

and let sit at room temperature for about a half hour, or in the refrigerator for up to a day.

Heat the oven to 350°F. Heat a large ovenproof, nonstick sauté pan over medium heat. Add the seasoned chicken medallions and gently heat them to begin the cooking process. Turn them over and continue cooking them in the oven until cooked through, 10 to 12 minutes.

While the chicken finishes cooking, cut eight segments from the lemon and four segments from the orange (see page 28 for how to segment citrus). Cut these segments into smaller pieces and reserve.

Toss the greens with the citrus pieces and radish slices, moistening the greens with a little bit of extra virgin olive oil. Season the salad with salt and pepper. Place three medallions on each plate, top with some of the salad, and serve.

WHICH WINE?
A great food wine, for this dish and many others, is a **Cannonau di Sardegna** (DOC). A medium body, tart fruit, and crisp acids work well with the spices and texture in this dish.

SEAR-ROASTED CHICKEN THIGHS WITH GARLIC, THYME, AND JUNIPER BERRIES

Maybe featuring two recipes with juniper berries in a cookbook is a little weird (see the salmon recipe on page 223). But the way I figure it is that unless you already cook a fair amount of game—or you make your own gin—you had to go out and buy juniper berries for one of these recipes. Now that you've got them, you might as well use them. So here is an easy chicken dish that shows off the unique flavor of juniper berries. You could certainly substitute rabbit legs, guinea hen, or other game birds in place of the chicken. Serve whichever bird or beast you decide on with some roasted baby vegetables.

MAKES **4** SERVINGS

8 chicken thighs, bone-in or boneless, skin on but excess skin and fat removed

Kosher salt and freshly ground black pepper

1/4 cup extra virgin olive oil, plus a little more for cooking

2 tablespoons fresh juniper berries or 1 1/2 tablespoons dried, crushed

8 sprigs fresh thyme

8 cloves garlic, peeled and smashed

SEASON THE THIGHS WITH SALT AND PEPPER. Combine the 1/4 cup olive oil, juniper berries, thyme, and garlic in a large bowl. Add the chicken thighs and toss to coat. The chicken tastes better the longer it marinates. If you want to cook it right away, let it sit at room temperature for up to 45 minutes. Otherwise, marinate it in the refrigerator for up to 24 hours.

Heat the oven to 325°F. Heat one large or two medium sauté pans over medium-high heat. Add the thighs, skin side down, leaving room around each, and cook until the skin is a deep brown. Turn the thighs over and finish cooking them in the oven, 25 minutes for boneless thighs, longer for bone-in thighs. (When cooked through, the juices will run clear when the thigh is pricked.)

WHICH WINE?

While a very tannic wine would be too much with the thyme and juniper berries, the fresh fruit flavors of a **Santa Maddalena** (DOC), made from Schiava grapes, work well with this chicken. The wine's slightly smoky flavor adds to this pairing's allure.

SPICY WHOLE ROASTED CHICKEN
WITH **ORANGE** AND **ROSEMARY**

For this roast chicken, the work involved is inversely proportional to how delicious it is: The littlest bit of preparation yields loads of flavor, a perfect balance of sweet and spicy with a fragrant herbal undertone. Chili paste is an Asian condiment made mostly of pureed chiles balanced by a bit of vinegar; it's becoming more available here as western cooks exploit its ability to add nuanced heat to just about any dish (see Sources). I also like it because it's easy to spread evenly all over the chicken. If you can't find it (a popular brand has a rooster on the label), substitute about $1/2$ teaspoon of crushed red pepper in its place (which is the way the chicken was made for me when I was in Sicily). The pan juices that this bird creates are irresistible. Degrease them—a gravy separator does this quickly—and drizzle them over some rice or couscous as well as the chicken. Some sautéed broccoli rabe (page 233) would complete the plate nicely.

MAKES **2** TO **3** SERVINGS

1 whole $3^1/2$- to **4**-pound chicken

$1^1/2$ to **2** teaspoons Asian chili paste

1 small onion, quartered

1 orange, sliced

3 sprigs rosemary

Kosher salt and freshly ground black pepper

REMOVE THE CHICKEN'S GIBLETS, rinse the bird inside and out, and pat it dry.

Heat the oven to 350°F. Rub about half of the chili paste over the inside of the bird and half over the outside. Stuff the cavity of the bird with the onion, orange, and rosemary. Season the whole chicken with salt and pepper.

In a large sauté pan or in a small roasting pan (with or without a rack), roast the bird, periodically basting it with the fragrant juices that accumulate, 1 to $1^1/2$ hours, depending on the size of the bird. (Check by seeing if the juices that result from pricking the thigh run clear.) Let the bird sit for 10 minutes before carving and serving it. Degrease the pan juices and pass the juices on the side.

WHICH WINE?

A **Nero d'Avola-Cabernet** blend is a good match for the sweetness of the orange and the heat of the chili paste.

CUMIN-SPICED ROAST CHICKEN WITH CURRANT-FEGATO SAUCE, TOASTED ALMONDS, AND CHIVES

The spices in the rub, which include nutmeg, cloves, and star anise, give the chicken an undeniably autumnal feeling. A light hand with these spices makes the dish intriguing without overwhelming its intrinsic roast chicken nature, and a deeply flavored sauce also adds to its wonderful fragrance. (I strongly recommend taking a moment to savor the aroma that wafts upward from the plate.) Ah, but what is *fegato* you ask? It's Italian for liver (in this case, chicken liver). I kept the American word out of the title so that people who don't like chicken liver would not immediately turn the page. But while the liver adds richness, there's no "livery" flavor here at all. Even if you think you don't like chicken liver, try the sauce. The ingredients are inexpensive, and it doesn't take long to make, so there's no big investment of time and money. I probably should have added "and Creamy Polenta" to this recipe's already long title because the polenta on page 234 goes so well with this crisp skinned chicken, crunchy almonds, and wonderful (trust me) sauce.

MAKES **2** TO **3** SERVINGS

For the spice rub

5 pieces star anise

1 1/2 teaspoons ground nutmeg

1 teaspoon whole cloves

1 teaspoon whole cumin seeds

IN A SMALL SAUTÉ PAN, heat the star anise, nutmeg, cloves, and cumin seeds over medium-low heat, occasionally stirring the spices with a wooden spoon to prevent them from scorching, until the spices are fragrant, 8 minutes. Allow the spices to cool for a few minutes and then grind them in a spice grinder or a coffee grinder dedicated to spices.

Heat the oven to 450°F.

Scott Conant's New Italian Cooking

For the chicken and the sauce

1 whole 3^1/2- to 4-pound chicken, split and boned by you or your butcher as described on page 210

1 teaspoon plus 2 tablespoons olive oil

Kosher salt

3/4 cup homemade Chicken Reduction (page 15) or purchased chicken reduction diluted with water until a little thicker than chicken stock

1 tablespoon dried currants

1/4 cup finely chopped chicken livers (4 livers)

1 teaspoon snipped fresh chives

1 tablespoon sliced almonds, toasted

On each chicken half, rub a teaspoon of olive oil and a teaspoon of the spice mixture. (You can store any remaining spice mix for at least a month if tightly covered.) Season lightly with salt.

Heat 2 tablespoons olive oil in a sauté pan large enough to hold both halves of the bird. (Or divide the oil among 2 smaller pans.) Sear the chicken, skin side down, until well browned. Pop the pan (or pans) into the hot oven to finish cooking, about 15 minutes. (Check by seeing if the juices that result from pricking the thigh run clear.)

To make the sauce: Ten minutes before the chicken is done, heat the chicken reduction in a saucepan over medium heat. Add the currants and cook for a few minutes. Add the chicken livers and bring to a boil, stirring gently the entire time. Reduce the heat to a simmer while you finish the chicken.

Remove the chicken from the oven and let it rest in the pan for about a minute. Separate the breast from the leg and slice the breast through the skin into a few pieces. Place a leg and the sliced breast on each of two plates, ideally over some polenta, or divide the chicken among three plates. Add the chives to the sauce and drizzle the sauce over the chicken. Sprinkle almonds over all and serve.

WHICH WINE?
Choose one of the south of Italy's most famous wines: a **Taurasi** (DOC). Even better, go with the older Taurasi Reserve (DOCG), which is almost black and features aromas and flavors as intriguing as this dish.

How (and Why) to Bone a Chicken

THE ROAST CHICKEN RECIPE on page 208 calls for a split and boned chicken. Yeah, right, you might think. Save it for the restaurant. But I'm telling you that once you get the hang of boning a chicken (or know a good butcher who will do it for you), you will like the results immensely. A bird prepared this way cooks up more quickly and more evenly with lots of crisp skin. Once it's on the plate, you can put the knife anywhere, cut through with ease, and get right to the enjoyment of the tender meat and crisp skin. While cutting out the bones of a whole chicken might give the cook a little more work, the payoff for the effort is huge, which is not always the case in cooking—or in life for that matter. Keep in mind that the results from your first try won't look as good as the second, which won't look as good as the third. The trickiest part is the leg. But don't worry if it looks a bit ragged when raw; the meat will come together in a more attractive and compact way as the bird cooks.

Here's how to do it:

You will need a whole chicken (obviously), a cutting surface, and a sharp knife. A flexible boning knife is ideal, but a good paring knife will also do the trick. Sharpness is the key, and a smaller knife will give you more control. Remove the giblets from inside the chicken's cavity and rinse and dry the bird with paper towels both inside and out.

Keep in mind that you are trying to keep the leg and breast attached so that the whole bird is essentially cut down the middle into two large pieces. If the breast and thigh come apart, it is not the end of the world. Just throw them out and start again. (I'm kidding! I'm kidding!) Simply cook the breast and thigh as directed, but in two pieces.

To begin: With the breast side up, and the head opening away from you, find the breast plate. Run the knife along one side, keeping it as close as possible to the breast plate. But don't remove the actual breast meat from the bird yet.

When the knife reaches the leg, be careful not to cut the skin connecting the breast and the leg but do cut away the excess skin connecting the leg and tail. Turn the bird over, move the knife to the backside of the bird, and press the tip of the knife just behind the thigh joint. As you cut the leg from the carcass, be sure to include the little nugget of meat often referred to as the oyster.

Slice through the leg skin from the tip of the oyster to the opposite corner of the thigh to more or less detach the thigh.

Now you can carefully slice the rest of the breast away from the backbone. I hold the loose breast meat in one hand and let gravity help as I gently peel it back away from the ribcage, using small, fluid strokes of the knife to remove as much of the meat as possible from one side of the chicken. Cut around the shoulder bones attached to the breastbone, keeping the wing intact.

Snip any remaining pieces of skin holding the breast and thigh to the bird. You should now have half a bird lying in front of you. Cut off the wing tip to the wing's first joint and trim any excess skin of fat. Repeat the process on the other side of the bird.

After congratulating yourself on completing that task, get ready to bone the legs. If you lay the leg skin side down, where to cut out the thighbone should be apparent. Run the knife down the seams on either side of the thighbone. With the tip of the knife, gently cut around the top of the thighbone until that end is released. Wrestle the other bone free by using small strokes of the knife to cut away any flesh, tendons, or cartilage connecting it to the thigh. Use your fingers and the knife to loosen the bone from the meat. When that joint is more or less freed, leave that area for a minute. Position the knife blade perpendicular to the leg bone, about an inch away from the tip. Cut all the way around the bone, through any skin, flesh, and tendons. (This action is not unlike slicing the foil from a bottle of wine.) You should now be able to pull the leg bone free. It will be a bit of a struggle, and you may wind up temporarily turning the thigh inside out as you continue to use small knife strokes and cutting close to the bone to get most of the meat. If the final removal of this bone is giving you grief, return to the thigh and cut out any obstacles (bone or cartilage) keeping the bone from being liberated and try again.

There. You did it. When you smooth the thigh skin down, it even looks pretty good, doesn't it? Now do the same to the other thigh; it will be even easier, I swear.

BRAISED CHICKEN THIGHS WITH

PARSNIPS AND MINT

I especially enjoy this dish in early spring when I am getting a little tired of eating the heavier meat braises that so excited me back in November, but still want to be comforted by meltingly tender meat and long-cooked flavors. The chicken itself is very lean and the mint added at the end gives the stew a bright finish. Try it with the ragout of leeks and peas on page 230. By the way, if you love rabbit, you can make this same dish using rabbit legs instead.

MAKES **4** SERVINGS

3 pounds boneless, skinless chicken thighs

Kosher salt and freshly ground black pepper

3 to **4** tablespoons olive oil

1/2 cup dry white wine

1 medium parsnip, trimmed and peeled, and cut into **1/2**-inch dice to yield **1** cup

3 shallots, sliced

2 sprigs rosemary

Pinch of crushed red pepper

1 plum tomato, seeded and diced

2 cups homemade Chicken Reduction (page 15) or purchased chicken reduction diluted with water until a little thicker than chicken stock

10 whole mint leaves, stacked, rolled, and thinly cut crosswise into a chiffonade

HEAT THE OVEN to 325°F. Season the thighs with salt and pepper. Heat a couple of tablespoons of olive oil in a large sauté pan over medium-high heat and brown the thighs on both sides. Transfer them to another large sauté pan or wide Dutch oven and pour off any excess oil in the original sauté pan. Add the white wine to the pan in which the thighs were seared, put the pan over high heat, and bring to a boil, scraping up any browned bits stuck to the bottom of the pan. Continue cooking until the wine is reduced by half. Pour the reduced wine over the thighs.

In the now empty sauté pan, heat another 1 to 2 tablespoons of olive oil over medium-high heat. Add the parsnip and cook, stirring occasionally, until it begins to turn golden brown, 5 minutes. Add the shallots, rosemary, and crushed red pepper, plus additional oil, if needed, and cook, stirring occasionally, until the shallots have softened and have begun to brown. Add the tomato, stir, and cook for another minute or so. Add the chicken reduction, bring to a boil, and pour everything over the thighs; the mixture should cover the thighs about halfway. Cook in the oven until the chicken is fork tender, 50 minutes to an hour.

Remove the thighs from the sauce and divide them among four warm plates. Add the mint to the sauce and stir. Season with additional salt and pepper, if needed, pour the sauce over the thighs, and serve.

WHICH WINE?
A **Nebbiolo d'Alba** (DOC) is really an easy red wine to drink with this light braised dish.

CACCIUCCO (ITALIAN FISH STEW)

This is a very soothing, very flavorful stew. I suggest using a mix of clams and mussels, but you could easily go with all clams. Or replace the shrimp with squid or lobster. The key to the best texture is to undercook the fish initially. It will continue to cook with the residual heat and will get a final blast of heat when you pour the hot broth over it. You definitely want to serve this with plenty of good bread.

MAKES **4** SERVINGS

3 to **4** tablespoons extra virgin olive oil

1 medium zucchini, cut into small dice

1 medium yellow squash, cut into small dice

1 russet potato, peeled and cut into small dice

Kosher salt

2 cloves garlic, sliced very thin

1/4 teaspoon crushed red pepper

16 clams, preferably cockles or manila

16 mussels, cleaned and debearded

2 cups Lobster-Tomato Broth (page 13)

16 large shrimp, shelled (you can leave the tail ends on) and deveined

3/4 pound sea bass, monkfish, halibut, or other meaty white fish, cut into **12** pieces and lightly seasoned with salt and pepper

1 plum tomato, seeded and finely diced

2 teaspoons chopped fresh parsley

12 fresh basil leaves, stacked and sliced thinly crosswise into a chiffonade

Slices of Italian bread or ciabatta, preferably drizzled with a little olive oil and grilled or broiled

IN A MEDIUM SAUCEPAN, heat 1 to 2 tablespoons of the olive oil over medium-high heat. Add the zucchini, squash, and potato, season lightly with salt, and cook the vegetables until they are lightly browned and just tender, 5 to 8 minutes. Remove them from the heat and divide the vegetables among four wide bowls.

In a very wide and large saucepan or in a large, deep skillet, heat the remaining two tablespoons of olive oil over medium-

low heat. Add the garlic and crushed red pepper and allow the garlic to cook in the oil for 5 minutes, adjusting the heat to keep it from browning, to flavor the oil. Add the clams, mussels, and broth to the pan. Increase the heat to medium-high, cover the pan, and cook until the shellfish are just beginning to open, 5 minutes. Add the shrimp and fish fillets, and cook until the clams are fully opened, the shrimp has just started to turn pink in places, and the fish is beginning to firm up a bit, another few minutes.

Using a slotted spoon, divide the fish and shellfish among the bowls holding the vegetables. (The fish will be reheated by the broth in a few minutes.) Strain the broth into a saucepan. Add the diced tomato, parsley, and basil to the saucepan, bring the broth to a boil, and cook until it has reduced by between a third and a half; this will take between 5 and 10 minutes. Pour the hot broth over the fish and vegetables and serve immediately with the toasted bread.

WHICH WINE?

A Tuscan white for a Tuscan classic: Try a **Vernaccia di San Gimignano** (DOCG).

MOIST-ROASTED WHOLE FISH
WITH CHERRY TOMATOES
AND SCALLIONS

I love fish cooked whole. I'm one of those guys you see in restaurants eating fish with their hands, pulling the fish apart, and sucking on the bones. Not very attractive perhaps, but so good. Some people get a little squeamish when they see the head of the fish at the table. You can remove the head if you want, but please don't do it until after cooking it. The head adds flavor and body to the pan sauce. Herbed couscous would make a nice bed for the fish.

MAKES **2** SERVINGS

1 whole **2**-pound fish, such as *branzino* (also called European sea bass), gutted and scaled (see Note)

Kosher salt and freshly ground black pepper

2 tablespoons olive oil

3/4 cup halved cherry tomatoes

3/4 cup Lobster-Tomato Broth (page 13) or homemade Chicken Broth (page 14) or purchased low-salt chicken broth

1/4 cup thinly sliced scallions

2 teaspoons chopped fresh parsley

HEAT THE OVEN to 325°F. Season the fish both inside and outside with salt and pepper. Using a very large (14-inch) ovenproof sauté pan or even a small roasting pan, heat 2 tablespoons olive oil over medium-high heat. Add the cherry tomatoes and cook, stirring, until the tomatoes begin to release their liquid. Add the broth and the fish and cook it in the oven until done, 15 to 20 minutes. (To check for doneness, push the head down gently in the area between the nose and the top of the head; when the head easily moves away from the back of the neck, it is ready.)

Remove the fish from the oven but leave it in the pan while you heat the broiler. Put the pan under the broiler for a minute or so just to crisp the skin of the fish. Transfer the fish to a plate (crispy side up) and keep it warm.

Add the scallions to the liquid in the pan and bring to a boil. Reduce the heat a little and cook the sauce for a minute or two to reduce it slightly. Add the parsley and any additional salt and pepper. Drizzle the sauce over the fish and serve.

NOTE If you can't find *branzino*, you can substitute another small whole fish, such as snapper, wild striped bass, black bass, or Mediterranean orata.

WHICH WINE?

Try a **Costa d'Amalfi** (DOC). This white wine, made from indigenous grapes, such as Biancolella and Falanghina, is dry with a fruity quality reminiscent of fresh peaches. Because of the vineyard's close proximity to the sea, there is also a touch of salinity, which makes it a wonderful match for fish.

✳ GRILLED SHRIMP WITH MINT, ORANGE, AND FENNEL COUSCOUS

A lot of cooks like to blast fish and shellfish at excessively high temperatures. I strongly recommend against that. While it is a bit of a rush to see the flames that result when some of the fat from the item you are grilling causes a flare-up, it really is not so good for the shrimp, which can overcook in an instant. If you're cooking on a charcoal grill, stack the coals to one side and position the shrimp opposite the coals. On a gas grill, keep the heat on medium. Serve the shrimp and couscous with some greens tossed in a balsamic vinaigrette (page 61).

MAKES **4** SERVINGS

For the grilled shrimp

1 pound large shrimp (**20**), shelled and deveined

2 tablespoons extra virgin olive oil

2 teaspoons chopped fresh rosemary

1 teaspoon chopped fresh parsley

1/4 teaspoon crushed red pepper

1 garlic clove, finely chopped

Salt and freshly ground black pepper to taste

FOR THE SHRIMP: Toss the shrimp with the 2 tablespoons of extra virgin olive oil, the rosemary, parsley, crushed red pepper, and garlic. Allow the shrimp to sit at room temperature for a half hour to soak up the flavors of the marinade or refrigerate the shrimp in the marinade for up to a day.

For the couscous: In a broad, 2-inch-deep pan, heat 2 tablespoons of olive oil over medium heat. Add the fennel and onion and cook, stirring, until tender, 5 minutes.

Take a look at the directions for cooking that came with your couscous. Check to see that the liquid ratio recommended for the style of couscous you are using comes close to the amount I'm suggesting to use here. If not, err on the side of the couscous directions.

(continued)

For the couscous

2 tablespoons olive oil

1/2 cup finely diced fennel

1/4 cup finely diced onion

1$\frac{1}{4}$ to **1**$\frac{1}{2}$ cups homemade Chicken Broth (page 14) or purchased low-salt chicken broth

3/4 cup couscous

2 orange segments (see page 28) for how to segment an orange), diced

1 plum tomato, peeled, seeded, and diced

1$\frac{1}{2}$ teaspoons snipped fresh chives

12 fresh mint leaves, finely chopped

4 fresh basil leaves, cut into a chiffonade (optional)

Kosher salt and freshly ground black pepper

Add the stock and bring it to a boil. Add the couscous and cook, stirring with a fork, for 10 seconds. Remove the pan from the heat and cover the pan. The heat of the stock will cook the couscous in 5 minutes.

Fluff the grains with a fork. Add the diced orange and tomato as well as the chives, mint, and basil and toss gently. Drizzle the couscous with a touch of olive oil, season with salt and pepper, and keep it warm while you grill the shrimp.

To serve: Prepare the grill of your choice (or a grill pan if you are cooking indoors) so that the heat is at medium. Season the shrimp with salt and pepper. Grill the shrimp, brushing any extra marinade over them, until just cooked through, 2 minutes on each side. Put the couscous on a large platter or divide it among four plates. Set the shrimp on top of the couscous and serve.

WHICH WINE?

Fennel, like artichokes, is notoriously difficult to pair with wine. A **Lacryma Christi del Vesuvio Bianco** (DOC), dry and balanced with a persistent mineral finish, works really well when paired with this dish.

SEARED BRANZINO AND SLICED LEMON

Branzino, also known as Mediterranean sea bass, is fast becoming my favorite fish. Relatively new to the American market, this striped bass has long been caught in the waters outside Venice. Although you can substitute sea bass or striped bass for *branzino* if you can't find it (it also goes by the French name *loup de mer*), *branzino* cooks up sweeter and creamier than its more meaty cousins. In this very simple sauté, the lemon gets slightly caramelized, adding a flavor that's both tart and smoky-sweet. It's delicious with the Rosemary-Scented Lentils on page 243, but would also be quite tasty paired with some Stewed Tomatoes (page 249) and risotto. The flavors—the lemon, thyme, oil, and the juices from the fish—would also go well with the shaved asparagus on page 231.

MAKES **4** SERVINGS

4 *branzino* fillets, each one
6 to **8** ounces, scaled and boned
but with its skin still on

Kosher salt and freshly ground black
pepper

1 tablespoon flour, preferably Wondra

1 lemon, sliced very, very thin
(seeds removed)

4 sprigs thyme

2 tablespoons olive oil

SEASON THE *BRANZINO* with salt and pepper. Sprinkle the skin side of each fillet with a little flour. Lay two or three lemon slices on each fillet. Sprinkle with additional flour (it's acting like the glue here) and lay the thyme on top.

Heat a large sauté pan over medium-high heat and add the olive oil. When the oil is hot, use a spatula (preferably a thin, metal, flexible one) to help you flip the *branzino* over and into the pan so that it begins cooking with the lemon side down. Cook for 3 minutes. Once again using the spatula, flip the fish over and continue cooking for another 2 to 3 minutes, depending on the thickness of the fillet. Be careful not to overcook it, as it will continue to cook off the heat. I usually take it off when I can feel a slight separation of the flesh. If

you want to take a peek, look for the flesh to be just about opaque but not quite flaking yet. Serve immediately, drizzled with any of the juices that have accumulated in the pan.

WHICH WINE?

A **Pigato** from Riviera Ligure di Ponente is an intense white wine with a strong structure and slightly bitter finish. It's just what's called for when considering the fat content of the fish and the dish's overtly lemon flavor. The thought of this pairing makes my mouth water with anticipation.

SALMON WITH THYME AND FRESH JUNIPER BERRIES

I don't generally like to serve salmon as an entrée. I find that a big chunk of this fish can get very boring very quickly. This is one preparation, however, that I like a lot. Because the fish is thinly sliced and just barely cooked, you wind up with something that feels both unctuous and light. At the restaurant, the salmon does not even go into the oven; it gets cooked by the heat of heat lamps. The fricassee of fava beans on page 245 would make a perfect accompaniment, as would lightly dressed greens.

MAKES **4** SERVINGS

1¹/**2** pounds salmon fillet, preferably from the belly, pinbones removed

Kosher salt and freshly ground black pepper

20 fresh or **15** dried juniper berries, crushed

1 shallot, halved and sliced paper thin "with the grain"

2 teaspoons chopped fresh thyme leaves

Pinch of crushed red pepper

Sea salt and a drizzle of extra virgin olive oil to finish

HEAT THE OVEN to 200°F. Slice the salmon on a slight diagonal into 12 pieces ¹/2 inch thick; each piece should weigh 2 ounces. Lay the pieces on a baking sheet. Sprinkle with salt, pepper, the crushed juniper berries, shallot, thyme, and crushed red pepper. Cook the salmon in the oven for 8 to 10 minutes. Determining doneness is a bit tricky as the color of the fish won't change. Instead I look for a slight separation in the flesh and just a bit of the oil from the salmon to rise to the surface. Serve three pieces per plate with a tiny sprinkle of sea salt and a drizzle of olive oil.

WHICH WINE?

With this dish, I would pour a **Traminer Aromatico** from Alto Adige (DOC), a region with close ties to, no surprise here, Germany. (Traminer is the progenitor of the grape Gewürztraminer.) This wine's dry, pleasantly aromatic flavor blends nicely with the slight astringency of the juniper berries.

TUNA POACHED IN OLIVE OIL
INFUSED WITH THYME,
ROSEMARY, AND LEMON

The basic idea of this dish is to cook the tuna at a very low temperature so that its exterior gets cooked and the fish is warmed to the same temperature all the way through. As it warms, it absorbs the flavors of the oil, herbs, and lemon. Until you have prepared tuna this way a few times, it's a good idea to track the temperature of the oil with a thermometer. Serve the sliced tuna over Rosemary-Scented Lentils (page 243) and Spicy Sautéed Broccoli Rabe (page 233).

SERVES **4**

4 cubes of fresh sushi-grade tuna, each one weighing **5** ounces

Kosher salt and freshly ground black pepper

4 cups extra virgin olive oil

10 sprigs fresh thyme

5 sprigs fresh rosemary

1/2 lemon, sliced

2 shallots, sliced

3 cloves garlic, peeled and crushed

1 teaspoon crushed red pepper

Sea salt to taste

SEASON THE TUNA with salt and pepper and set it aside. Combine the olive oil, thyme, rosemary, lemon slices, shallots, garlic, and crushed red pepper in a saucepot and cook on medium heat until the olive oil reaches 130°F. Let the flavors steep at that temperature for 10 minutes. Submerge the tuna in the olive oil mixture and cook it at 130°F for 8 minutes, adjusting the heat as needed.

Remove the tuna from the oil to a cutting board and let any excess oil run off of it. (If you want to reuse some of the oil, strain it and refrigerate it to use in other fish-based dishes.)

Slice the tuna across the grain into pieces $1/4$ inch thick; ideally, the tuna will be quite rare inside. If serving the tuna with the rosemary lentils and broccoli rabe, stack the slices on a serving of the lentils and lay the broccoli rabe alongside it. Top the sliced tuna with a touch of sea salt and a drizzle of the olive oil poaching liquid and serve.

WHICH WINE?

A rosé (*rosato* in Italian) made from Nebbiolo with its wonderful mélange of flavors is just the right match for this tuna.

Vegetables and Side Dishes

✳ Artichoke, Pancetta, and Potato Torta

✳ Leeks, Peas, and Asparagus with Sliced Lemon

✳ Shaved Asparagus and Mushrooms

✳ Dandelion Greens with Anchovy and Lemon

✳ Spicy Sautéed Broccoli Rabe

Creamy Polenta

Polenta and Speck Canederli

✳ Silken Brussels Sprouts for Two

Grilled Eggplant with Potatoes, Capers,
and Tomatoes

Cabbage Braised with Bacon

∗ Herbed Pan-Fried Potatoes with Garlic
∗ Caramelized Carrots and
  Chanterelles with Fregola
∗ Rosemary-Scented Lentils
  Concentrated Tomatoes
  Fava Bean Fricassee
  Sweet Peperonata
∗ Grilled Zucchini with Mint and Pignoli
  Roasted Baby Root Vegetables
∗ Stewed Tomatoes

ITALIANS REVERE VEGETABLES. You have only to imagine a traditional antipasto, with plates of eggplant, artichokes, and peppers, to realize how true that is.

At home it's easy to give vegetables short shrift. You often think so much about the main thing that's going on the plate, the meat, chicken, or fish, that the vegetable then becomes an add-on, a must for a little color, maybe for some vitamins but not always for flavor. The recipes you'll find in this chapter strive to lift vegetables out of that rut. One way to do this is by simply combining vegetables in different ways: some eggplant, potato, and tomato, for example, or mushrooms and asparagus, or leeks with endive. Using different herbs also mixes things up a bit: some tarragon tossed with peas and asparagus or mint to top grilled zucchini.

Another easy way to add flavor is with little bits of intensely flavored ingredients, such as anchovy, capers, pancetta, and toasted pine nuts. (None of these notions, by the way, adds much to the time it takes to make these dishes or to their difficulty level.)

I have also included my signature Creamy Polenta (page 234) in this chapter because it tastes great with just about everything. Other versatile, delicious side dishes you'll find here include Rosemary-Scented Lentils (page 243) and a vegetable-laden fregola (page 242).

ARTICHOKE, PANCETTA, AND **POTATO TORTA**

This crisp and light torta pairs nicely with a hunk of meat, especially one with a bit of sauce for the potatoes and artichokes to drink up. Try it with the braised goat on page 194 or the Spice-Crusted Lamb on page 190. A larger piece of the torta, served with a salad, would also make a satisfying lunch or light dinner, especially if you include the pancetta. Don't worry about the artichoke oxidizing and darkening as you shred it since it gets browned anyway in the pan.

MAKES **4** SERVINGS

8 baby artichokes, trimmed, chokes removed

2 medium Yukon gold potatoes, peeled

3 to **4** tablespoons olive oil

1/4 cup thinly sliced onion

2 ounces pancetta, chopped (optional)

1/2 teaspoon chopped fresh thyme

Kosher salt and freshly ground black pepper

SHRED THE ARTICHOKES by using a mandoline, a food processor with the shredding blade, or by slicing them thinly with a very sharp knife.

Cook the potatoes in gently boiling water until they are just barely tender when poked with a fork. Let cool enough to handle and then shred.

Heat a 10-inch nonstick skillet over medium-high heat. Add a few tablespoons of olive oil and the artichokes and cook, stirring just occasionally, until the artichokes begin to brown. Reduce the heat to medium and add the onion, pancetta, and thyme. Cook until the onion and the pancetta begin to brown, about 10 minutes. Add the shredded potatoes and mix everything thoroughly. Lightly pat down the vegetables to form an evenly shaped, single cake. (It may not hold together completely.) Once the bottom is lightly browned, flip the torta by sliding it onto a plate, inverting it onto another plate, and then sliding it back into the pan to lightly brown the other side.

Vegetables and Side Dishes

LEEKS, PEAS, AND ASPARAGUS
WITH SLICED LEMON

It's impossible to make this recipe and not think, Spring! I would suggest specific dishes to try this with, but it goes with just about everything, and it looks pretty, too. Be sure to slice the lemon as thin as you possibly can so the skin can be eaten.

MAKES **4** SERVINGS

2 to **3** tablespoons extra virgin olive oil

1 cup diced leeks (white and light green parts only), rinsed very well (**2** medium)

Pinch of crushed red pepper, more to taste

Kosher salt

1 cup thinly sliced asparagus (1/2 pound)

1 cup fresh peas (from 1^1/2 pounds of whole pods), peas blanched if very large

1 lemon, preferably a thin-skinned one, **4** very thin slices cut into quarters

1 tablespoon fresh tarragon, chopped

Freshly ground black pepper to taste

HEAT THE OLIVE OIL in a large sauté pan over medium-high heat. Add the leeks and crushed red pepper and season with a little salt. Cook, stirring, until the leeks are tender and a bit browned, 8 to 10 minutes. Add the asparagus and peas and cook, tossing the mixture together, until the asparagus is crisp-tender, 3 to 4 minutes. Add the sliced lemon and cook, stirring occasionally, until the lemon has wilted, 2 minutes. Add the tarragon, stir to combine well, and remove the ragu from the heat. Squeeze a little lemon juice from the remaining lemon over all. Taste and season with additional salt, if needed, and a little black pepper.

SHAVED ASPARAGUS
AND MUSHROOMS

In an ideal world, you would make this crunchy, raw side dish with fresh porcini mushrooms. Do the best you can do with what's available in your world. The idea, no matter which mushrooms you use, is shavings dressed very lightly. I like to serve this with a piece of fish, such as the *branzino* with lemon on page 221, or even with a roasted chicken, including the orange-scented one on page 206.

MAKES **4** SERVINGS

12 stalks asparagus, trimmed

3 fresh porcini or other (preferably wild) mushrooms

1/4 to **1/2** teaspoon fresh lemon juice

1 to **2** teaspoons extra virgin olive oil

Kosher salt and freshly ground black pepper to taste

1 handful of baby greens

USING A MANDOLINE, slice the asparagus and mushrooms into very thin slices. In a medium bowl, toss the asparagus with the lemon juice and a teaspoon of the olive oil. Season with a little salt and pepper. Add the greens and divide among four plates. Top with the shaved mushrooms, a drizzle of olive oil, and more salt and pepper to taste.

DANDELION GREENS WITH

ANCHOVY AND LEMON

When I was a kid, my aunt would walk around our yard picking dandelion greens. I was hugely embarrassed by this, and I think I would have just died if my friends knew she was actually picking them for us to eat. But my aunt had the right idea: She was looking for tiny, tender dandelion leaves, which have a pleasantly bitter flavor. If you have a lawn untreated by chemicals, you won't need to go to the store either. But if you do buy dandelion leaves, avoid the big ones—if you make this dish with those, you will think I am nuts. The assertive nature of this dish makes it a good match for tender, almost sweet braises, such as the short ribs on page 168.

MAKES **4** SERVINGS

3 tablespoons extra virgin olive oil

1/4 cup thinly sliced scallions

4 anchovy fillets, rinsed (if oil-packed) or soaked in a couple of changes of water (if salt-packed) and coarsely chopped

2 to **3** teaspoons fresh lemon juice

4 cups baby dandelion greens, cleaned and rinsed

Kosher or sea salt and freshly ground black pepper to taste

IN A LARGE SAUTÉ PAN, heat the olive oil, scallions, and anchovy fillets over medium heat. Cook, stirring, until the anchovies melt into the oil. Add 2 teaspoons of the lemon juice. Toss the olive oil mixture with the dandelion greens; it will just barely wilt them. Add an additional bit of lemon juice or olive oil, if needed, season with salt and pepper, and serve.

✳ SPICY SAUTÉED BROCCOLI RABE

MAKES **4** SERVINGS

1 bunch broccoli rabe (about **1** pound), well washed, thick stem ends trimmed off

2 tablespoons extra virgin olive oil

2 cloves garlic, thinly sliced

1/4 to **1/2** teaspoon (I like it hot) crushed red pepper

Kosher salt and freshly ground black pepper to taste

BRING A LARGE POT OF SALTED WATER TO A BOIL. Add the broccoli rabe and cook it until just barely tender, 4 to 5 minutes. Drain it in a colander.

Meanwhile, heat the olive oil in a large sauté pan over low heat. Add the garlic and cook until it is fragrant and its edges just begin to turn golden. Sprinkle with the crushed red pepper and remove the pan from the heat. Toss the broccoli rabe with the warm oil until it warms the greens, putting the pan on low heat if necessary. Season with salt and pepper to taste, drizzle with a little more olive oil, and serve.

Also called *rapini*, broccoli rabe has an assertive, bitter flavor that nicely counters rich dishes. It also takes well to a little heat, which is why I like to add a healthy dose of crushed red pepper.

CREAMY POLENTA

If weight (my own) were no issue, I'd eat this polenta every single day. Although made with cream and milk, it doesn't feel heavy at all. This luscious, custardlike polenta gets that way by cooking it long and low in a rich mixture of milk and cream. I finish the polenta with a little freshly grated grana Padano. It's not that I'm cheap. (All right, maybe I am a little cheap since grana Padano is about a third of the price of that more esteemed Italian grating cheese, Parmigiano-Reggiano.) But I really believe that the grana's more muted flavor (it's aged for less time than Parmigiano) allows the flavor of the polenta itself to come through. But go ahead and finish the polenta with your favorite Parm if that's what you have on hand. This style of polenta goes well, in my opinion, with just about everything, including grilled and roasted meats, but I especially love it with a fricassee of wild mushrooms, which has become a signature appetizer at L'Impero. It's also fabulous with the Cumin-Spiced Roast Chicken on page 208. You can also use the polenta as a base for your favorite braise or stew.

MAKES **4** TO **6** SERVINGS

2 cups heavy cream

2 cups milk

1$\frac{1}{2}$ teaspoons kosher salt, more to taste

3 ounces (**2/3** cup) cornmeal, preferably coarse ground (see page 10)

1 tablespoon unsalted butter

2 tablespoons freshly grated grana Padano or Parmigiano-Reggiano

1 teaspoon chopped fresh chives (optional)

IN A HEAVY-BASED SAUCEPAN, combine the cream and milk and heat over medium-high heat just until small bubbles begin to appear on the surface. Add the salt and whisk the cream and milk until quite frothy. (I don't have a scientific explanation as to why this whisking step is important, but I know from experience that when I don't do it, my polenta just doesn't seem as delicious as usual. Since this initial whisk is easy and takes practically no time, I recommend you do it, too.)

Add the polenta and continue to whisk the mixture as it comes to a boil. Continue whisking for an additional 3 minutes. Reduce the heat to very low, cover the pan, and cook the polenta, stirring every 5 minutes or so, until the cornmeal is completely cooked and quite tender, 1 hour and 45 minutes. Be patient; even if the polenta has thickened and seems good after an hour, longer cooking will make it even better. As the polenta cooks, a skin will form on the bottom and sides of the pan (if you are not using a nonstick pan), which is proper and which gives the polenta a slightly toasty flavor.

Just before serving, stir in the butter, grana Padano, and chives, if using. The polenta should pour from the spoon as you serve it and will thicken as it cools. If necessary, you can thin the polenta with a little milk just before serving. Divide the polenta among heated bowls or plates.

POLENTA AND SPECK CANEDERLI

In the very north of Italy, a few miles from the Austrian border, is Trentino-Alto Adige. In the more northern Alto Adige, German is spoken first and the Tyrolean influence dominates. In both regions, you can get these wonderful fried dumplings. (Traditionally, canederli are made with day-old bread, but I make them here using cold polenta.) In the northern Trentino, they're called knödel while in the more southern Trentino, they're called canederli—the phonetic Italian spelling of the German. We can thank the region's nearby northern neighbor for speck, a smoked, dry-salted, and aged ham (see Sources). If you can't get speck, these dumplings are also delicious made with two slices of bacon fried until crisp and then crumbled. Reserve the fat from the bacon and add it to the oil for frying the canederli. Serve canederli tossed in butter if you like, as a first course, or as a side dish to braised or roasted meats.

MAKES **4** SERVINGS

2 cups cooked Creamy Polenta (page 234), cold

2 tablespoons finely chopped speck

1/2 cup finely chopped shallots

2 thyme sprigs, leaves finely chopped

1 cup dry bread crumbs, preferably *panko* (see page 6)

1/2 cup all-purpose flour

2 large egg yolks

2 tablespoons snipped fresh chives

Olive oil

HEAT THE OVEN to 200°F. Mix all of the ingredients together in a bowl. Pour enough olive oil into a large, heavy-based sauté pan to fill it by $1/4$ inch. Heat the oil over medium-high heat. When a bit of the canederli batter sizzles upon contact with the oil, begin dropping scant teaspoons of the batter into the oil. Fry the bits until browned on both sides, drain on paper towels, and season immediately with salt. Keep the fried canederli warm in the oven until all are fried and ready to sauce and serve.

SILKEN BRUSSELS SPROUTS
FOR **TWO**

This recipe is a little deceptive. Take a look at that ingredients list. Nice and short. But I can't lie: This dish is kind of a pain to make. I'm telling you this so that while you are cutting off each whole leaf of every single sprout you don't start waving the paring knife around and curse my name. I didn't create this recipe to torture you or my kitchen staff. I just think this is a wonderful way to enjoy Brussels sprouts. The leaves cook up tenderly and are barely adorned so that you get a pure flavor and a silky smooth texture. So consider this dish a labor of love and make it as part of a romantic dinner for two. Or make it just for yourself—you're worth it. Serve the leaves with Pancetta-Wrapped Chicken Legs (page 197) or the roasted whole fish on page 216.

Kosher salt (for blanching)

1 pint Brussels sprouts

2 tablespoons extra virgin olive oil

Sea salt and freshly ground black pepper

BRING A POT OF SALTED WATER TO A BOIL. Fill a medium bowl with ice and water and place it near the stove.

Meanwhile, peel each leaf off of every sprout by either holding a paring knife at the base of the sprout, cutting away the outermost leaf at its base, and working your way inward, or by cutting out the base of the core with a paring knife and pulling apart the leaves one by one.

Boil the leaves for 30 seconds. Transfer them to the ice bath with a mesh or slotted spoon. Once cool, drain them well in a colander and pat them dry with a paper towel.

Heat the olive oil in a sauté pan over medium-high heat. Add the leaves and toss until they are heated through. Season with sea salt and black pepper to taste. Serve immediately.

GRILLED EGGPLANT
WITH **POTATOES, CAPERS,**
AND **TOMATOES**

This side dish takes a little longer than most to assemble, but its longish baking time (25 minutes) gives you plenty of hands-free time to get the rest of the meal together. The slices of eggplant strewn with flavored diced potatoes and tomatoes would look and taste great alongside some slices of grilled lamb. This dish is also quite versatile: As is, the eggplant would be right at home as part of an antipasto; double the topping and you have a vegetarian main dish. And anchovy lovers out there should feel free to add a minced fillet along with the capers.

MAKES **4** SERVINGS

1 medium eggplant, cut into **12** rounds **1/4** inch thick (see Note)

Kosher salt

3 tablespoons extra virgin olive oil, divided

1 garlic clove

1 large russet potato, peeled, and cut into **1/4**-inch dice (**1** cup)

1 tablespoon capers, preferably salted Sicilian ones (if using salted, soak them in a couple of changes of water and then rinse them; brined capers need only to be drained and rinsed)

2 plum tomatoes, stemmed, seeded, and diced

3 whole basil leaves, stacked, rolled, and cut thinly crosswise into a chiffonade

1/2 teaspoon chopped fresh oregano

1 teaspoon chopped fresh parsley

HEAT THE OVEN to 350°F. Put the eggplant slices in a colander and toss with 1 teaspoon of kosher salt. Put the colander in a clean sink, weight the eggplant, and allow the salt to draw out the excess moisture for 20 to 30 minutes. Do not rinse the eggplant but do pat it dry with paper towels.

Heat 2 tablespoons of the olive oil in a sauté pan over medium-low heat; add the clove of garlic and allow it to brown slightly. Toss in the potato and capers, and cook until the potato is just tender, 5 minutes. Increase the heat to high, add the tomatoes, and cook for another minute. Add the basil, oregano, and parsley and remove the mixture from the heat.

Brush the eggplant slices with a little olive oil and lay them on a sided baking sheet. Remove the whole garlic from the potato and caper mixture and divide the mixture among the slices of eggplant, spooning 2 tablespoons of the mixture over each slice. Bake until the eggplant is tender, 25 minutes.

NOTE Leaving the skin on the eggplant makes it look a little nicer, but the skin can be tough. You can simply peel the eggplant, or try this trick: Run the tines of a fork down the length of the eggplant with enough pressure to peel away tine-width strips of the skin. Do this all the way around the outside of the eggplant. The resulting slices will still look "finished," but because the skin is no longer one continuous piece, it will be easier to eat.

CABBAGE BRAISED WITH BACON

The wine in this braised cabbage gives it an acidic edge that makes it a good match for rich foods. I always serve this with my Braised Pork Belly (page 186). If you're serving only four, cut the recipe in half and make it in a deep skillet. The cabbage needs a couple unattended hours in the oven, and is a great make-ahead dish.

MAKES **8** SERVINGS

1 head green cabbage

1 tablespoon olive oil

4 strips bacon

2 cups thinly sliced onion

2 cups dry white wine

1 cup homemade Chicken Broth (page 14) or purchased low-salt chicken broth

CUT THE CABBAGE head in half lengthwise. Cut again into quarters and remove the tough center core. Slice the cabbage quarters thinly to yield 9 to 10 cups shredded cabbage; you will have to shred $2^1/2$ to 3 of the quarters to get this amount.

Set your oven racks to accommodate a large pot and heat the oven to 350°F. In a large ovenproof pot, heat the olive oil over medium heat and sauté the whole strips of bacon until they render some of their fat, 5 minutes. Add the onion and cook until tender and beginning to brown, 10 to 15 minutes. Add the cabbage, increase the heat to medium-high and cook, tossing the cabbage with tongs, until it wilts and begins to take on some brown color, 8 to 10 minutes. Add the wine and broth and cook uncovered on the stove for 5 minutes. Cover the pot and cook the cabbage in the oven, stirring it occasionally, until very tender and flavorful, about 2 hours. Remove the bacon and serve or refrigerate the cabbage for up to 36 hours and reheat gently.

HERBED PAN-FRIED POTATOES
WITH GARLIC

These are like French fries, only better. Like French fries, they get good and crisp on the outside, but they offer more of the fluffy potato interior. Blanching the potatoes before pan-frying them helps the interior cook in the same time the exterior takes to get nicely browned. The parsley adds a nice fresh note to the potatoes, but they have plenty of flavor without it. Serve these with your favorite braise, the steak on page 165, or even a hamburger.

MAKES **4** SERVINGS

2 large or **3** small russet (Idaho) potatoes, peeled and cut into **3/4**-inch pieces (neat little cubes look nice, but you don't have to be that fussy)

1/4 cup olive oil

1 to **2** garlic cloves, finely chopped

2 sprigs fresh rosemary or thyme or both

Pinch of crushed red pepper

1 tablespoon chopped fresh parsley (optional)

Kosher salt and freshly ground black pepper

BRING A SAUCEPAN FULL OF SALTED WATER TO A BOIL and boil the potatoes for 5 minutes. Drain well.

Heat the olive oil in a large, high-sided sauté pan over medium-high heat. Add a potato, and if it sizzles right away, add the rest. (If it doesn't, allow the oil to heat up a little longer.) Cook the potatoes, stirring (more toward the end of cooking), until well browned and just tender, 10 to 15 minutes. Lower the heat and add the garlic, rosemary, and crushed red pepper. Cook, stirring, until fragrant, taking the pan off the heat if the garlic begins to brown. Add the parsley, if using, toss, and season to taste with salt and pepper.

CARAMELIZED CARROTS AND CHANTERELLES WITH FREGOLA

Fregola is a tiny toasted pasta similar to couscous. A Sardinian specialty, fregola is made by rubbing coarse semolina flour and water together to create little pellets. You can find fregola at specialty food stores and Italian markets (see Sources), but you can easily substitute regular couscous or, even better, the larger Israeli couscous for it in this recipe. I like to serve this earthy side with a simply seared fish, such as the *branzino* on page 221, or seared veal chops.

MAKES **4** SERVINGS

1 cup fregola (dry), Israeli couscous, or regular couscous, cooked until tender in salted water according to the package directions

1 to **2** tablespoons olive oil

2 cups baby carrots, halved lengthwise

2 shallots, thinly sliced

1 cup cleaned and trimmed chanterelles

1 teaspoon chopped fresh thyme

Kosher salt and freshly ground black pepper

HEAT A LARGE SAUTÉ PAN OVER MEDIUM-HIGH HEAT. Add a tablespoon of olive oil and cook the carrots, stirring occasionally, until tender and browned, 5 to 8 minutes. Add the shallots, mushrooms, thyme, additional oil if needed, and a little salt and pepper. Continue to cook, stirring, until the mushrooms and shallots are tender, another 5 to 8 minutes.

Toss the vegetables with the fregola, adding a bit more oil if it seems too dry. Season with more salt and pepper, if needed, and serve.

ROSEMARY-SCENTED LENTILS

In this humble dish a *soffrito* of shallot, garlic, and rosemary creates a wonderful foundation for the flavors that develop as the lentils cook. This fragrant, tender side dish is a staple of mine as the lentils pair effortlessly with any number of dishes. I especially like them with simply roasted or seared fish. Seek out tender green lentils, often called European lentils or lentils du Puy, for the best texture and flavor.

MAKES **4** SERVINGS

7 ounces French green lentils (**1** cup)

2 tablespoons extra virgin olive oil

1 medium shallot, finely chopped

1 tablespoon finely chopped fresh rosemary

1/4 teaspoon crushed red pepper

2 cloves garlic, finely chopped

1/4 cup canned tomato puree

PUT THE LENTILS IN A MEDIUM SAUCEPAN and cover with lightly salted water by 2 inches. Bring the water to a simmer and cook the lentils over medium-high heat until just al dente, 20 to 25 minutes, adding more water if necessary. Drain and reserve.

Meanwhile, in a medium sauté pan, heat the olive oil over medium heat. Add the shallot, rosemary, and crushed red pepper. Cook until the shallot is quite tender and well browned, 10 minutes. Add the garlic and cook until tender and just beginning to color, 2 minutes. Add the tomato puree and cook until it darkens and thickens somewhat, 7 to 10 minutes. Add the drained lentils and cook until they are tender but still hold their shape, 5 to 7 minutes.

CONCENTRATED TOMATOES

I'm always grabbing a couple of these tomatoes to add to a dish. They contribute deep, soulful flavor and color to green salads, sandwiches, bean dishes, and pasta. I always serve them with the Herbed Paillard of Chicken (page 201), and a few alongside some grilled lamb or steak would make a stellar summer dinner. Unlike most of the dishes in this chapter, these do need some time in the oven, so they're not exactly a "make it tonight" kind of thing. But they require very little effort on your part and they'll keep for almost a week.

MAKES **4** CUPS

3 pounds ripe plum tomatoes, halved and gently seeded

1/4 cup extra virgin olive oil

1 teaspoon chopped fresh oregano

1 teaspoon sugar

Kosher salt and freshly ground black pepper

HEAT THE OVEN to 300°F. Toss the tomatoes with enough olive oil to coat them liberally and lay them cut side down on a baking sheet with sides. Sprinkle over them just a touch of each of the remaining ingredients. Take into consideration that as the tomatoes cook, all the flavors will concentrate.

Cook the tomatoes until they are quite concentrated with a very deep red color; this will take $3\frac{1}{2}$ to 4 hours. Remember, you are not trying to dry the tomatoes completely; they should look quite dry on the outside but should retain some moisture within. Cool at room temperature, peel away the loose skins, and store in an airtight container in the refrigerator for up to 5 days. (You can also freeze the tomatoes, which will affect their texture only slightly.)

FAVA BEAN FRICASSEE

Fresh fava beans are one of the few truly seasonal foods left. Treat yourself to them in the spring and early summer. The beans themselves are easy enough to get out of their giant pods. The annoying part is removing the tough skin that surrounds each bean, but it's one of those cooking chores that's easy to do while carrying on a conversation, so don't be afraid of favas. This is an excellent, if homely, side dish to just about any grilled meat, especially lamb and beef. You can also make a delicious vegetable fricassee using fresh or frozen lima beans in place of the favas.

MAKES **4** SERVINGS

2^1/2 pounds fresh fava beans, shelled, or **2** cups thawed frozen lima beans

2 to 3 tablespoons olive oil

1 shallot, thinly sliced

1/2 cup homemade Chicken Broth (page 14) or low-salt purchased chicken broth

2 plum tomatoes, peeled, seeded, and finely chopped

1 tablespoon chopped fresh tarragon

Kosher salt and freshly ground black pepper to taste

1 teaspoon chopped fresh parsley

BLANCH THE SHELLED FAVA BEANS to loosen their skin by boiling them for about a minute and then plunging them in cool water. Drain and slip off their skin by cutting the skin with your thumbnail and then popping the bean out of its skin with a pinch. (If it's early in the season, and the favas are very small, you can skip the skinning step.)

In a sauté pan or saucepan, heat 2 tablespoons of the olive oil over medium-high heat. Add the shallot and cook until tender. Add the fava beans and the broth and cook until the beans are tender, 10 to 20 minutes, depending on the beans' size and age. Remove about half of the beans and puree them with a little olive oil with an immersion blender or in a food processor. Return the pureed beans to the pan along with the tomatoes and tarragon and cook until the tomatoes are warmed through. Season to taste with salt and pepper and serve sprinkled with the chopped parsley.

SWEET PEPERONATA

This classic pepper dish is hugely versatile. It makes a terrific accompaniment to grilled meats, fish, and chicken. You can also add it to an antipasto because it's delicious warm or at room temperature. I like it as a topping for both pizza and bruschetta or strewn over baked polenta. You could even toss it with pasta topped with some cheese.

MAKES **4** SERVINGS

2 ounces extra virgin olive oil

1 onion, cut into large dice (**1** cup)

2 cloves garlic, sliced very thin

2 tablespoons capers, preferably salted Sicilian

1/2 teaspoon crushed red pepper

2 red bell peppers, cut into large dice (**2** cups)

1/2 cup good-quality canned tomato puree

Up to **1/4** cup homemade Chicken Broth (page 14) or low-salt purchased chicken broth, if necessary

1 tablespoon chopped fresh parsley

HEAT THE OVEN to 350°F. Heat the olive oil in an oven-proof sauté pan over medium-low heat. Add the onion, garlic, capers, and crushed red pepper and cook, stirring occasionally, until the onion begins to turn light brown, 20 minutes. Add the red bell peppers and continue to cook until they begin to release their liquid, 10 minutes. Stir in the tomato puree, cover the pan, and bake until the peppers are very tender, 20 minutes. If the oil has begun to separate from the mixture, stir in a little of the chicken broth. Serve hot or at room temperature sprinkled with parsley.

GRILLED ZUCCHINI WITH
MINT AND PIGNOLI

Here's a simple, summery approach to zucchini. For the best flavor, choose zucchini that's on the smaller side. I like to salt the zucchini to draw out its moisture and intensify its flavor, but you could easily skip this step if you're pressed for time.

MAKES **4** SERVINGS

1 pound zucchini

Kosher salt

1/4 cup olive oil

3 cloves garlic, thinly sliced

1/4 teaspoon crushed red pepper

2 tablespoons pine nuts (*pignoli*), lightly toasted in a dry skillet

15 whole mint leaves, stacked, rolled tightly, and sliced thinly crosswise into a chiffonade

Freshly ground black pepper to taste

CUT THE ZUCCHINI LENGTHWISE into slices 1/4 inch thick. Put the slices in a colander and toss with a teaspoon of salt. Let them drain for 20 minutes.

Meanwhile, heat the olive oil over very low heat. Add the garlic and crushed red pepper and let cook in the oil just until the garlic takes on a golden hue. Be careful not to let either burn; if your stove has difficulty keeping a low simmer, you may need to turn it on and off.

Heat your grill to medium-high or a grill pan. Pat the zucchini dry with paper towels and brush both sides with the flavored oil. Grill until nicely marked and cooked through, 3 minutes on each side. Transfer the slices to plates or a platter, strew the pine nuts and the mint over them, and season with black pepper, if you like.

ROASTED BABY ROOT VEGETABLES

Do these have to be baby vegetables? Nah. You can cut larger vegetables into 1- and 2-inch pieces and cook them the same way. But the next time you are at the farmers' market seek out these little gems; they not only look beautiful on the plate but the young vegetables, especially in the case of turnips, have a sweeter flavor that only deepens with roasting. I like to toss the red beets separately, to keep the colors of the vegetables intact. These simple vegetables go with just about everything.

MAKES **4** SERVINGS

8 baby turnips, washed and dried

24 baby carrots, trimmed

8 purple potatoes or baby potatoes of any type, washed and dried

1 cup peeled pearl onions, preferably red ones

2 to **3** tablespoons olive oil

11/2 to **2** teaspoons kosher salt

2 sprigs fresh thyme

8 baby beets, red and golden, if available, trimmed

TOSS ALL BUT THE RED BEETS with 2 tablespoons of the olive oil, 1 1/2 teaspoons of salt, and the sprigs of thyme. In a small separate bowl, toss the beets with a little olive oil and sprinkle with salt. Place the vegetables (and the thyme) in a small roasting pan or large ovenproof sauté pan, giving the beets their own section in the pan. (You want a little space between the vegetables but not too much.) Roast the vegetables, stirring occasionally, until well browned in places and tender, 40 minutes. Serve hot or warm, mixing the red beets with the other vegetables just before serving.

STEWED TOMATOES

We all have those days (don't we?) when we can't decide what we feel like eating. On such days, I often reach for stewed tomatoes. I enjoy them as a side dish with steak or a piece of fish, but I have to tell you that I most often eat them with a loaf of good bread and some olive oil, especially on the days when I'm experiencing a little food burnout—a hazard of my occupation! This recipe is easily doubled and the tomatoes will keep for a few days in the refrigerator.

MAKES **3** TO **4** SERVINGS

2 tablespoons olive oil

1 clove garlic, thinly sliced

1/2 small red onion, thinly sliced

8 plum tomatoes, peeled (see page 105), seeded, and quartered

1 teaspoon chopped fresh oregano

1/2 to **3/4** cup homemade Chicken Broth (page 14) or low-salt purchased chicken broth

Kosher salt and freshly ground black pepper

IN A MEDIUM SAUCEPAN, heat the olive oil over medium heat. Add the garlic and onion and cook slowly until they are tender but have not taken on any color (adjust the heat as necessary). Add the tomatoes and cook, stirring occasionally but allowing the tomatoes to hold their shape, until most of their liquid is released and has evaporated, 10 minutes. Add the oregano and enough chicken broth to loosen up the tomatoes so that the texture looks stewlike but not soupy. Cook for another 10 minutes or so, stirring occasionally, and serve hot or warm. Season to taste with a little salt and pepper.

Sweets and Cheeses

Pineapple Chutney
Sweet Beet Compote
Black Pepper and Almond Taralle
Bittersweet Chocolate Truffle Cake
Chocolate Soup
Olive Oil Chocolate Mousse
Chocolate Salami
Chocolate Chip–Pecan Biscotti
Gianduia Truffles
Extra Virgin Olive Oil Cake
Whipped Lemon Cream
Crème Fraîche Panna Cotta with Caramel Sauce
Creamy Lemon Cheesecake
Walnut and Brown Butter Cake
Orange Cookies
Individual Apple Crostatas
Sesame Cannoli with Orange Mascarpone Mousse
Balsamic Marinated Berries
Warm Blackberries with Whiskey

MY DESSERTS TEND TO COMBINE SOME SAVORY ASPECT WITH THE SWEET, such as a "cannoli" made with sesame seeds or an apple pecorino crostata (a twist on apple pie with Cheddar). Even when I go all-out sweet, as in the chocolate desserts, I use bittersweet chocolate and often add a little coffee flavor to give these sweets a sophisticated edge. But I, like many Italians, would just as soon linger over some wonderfully chosen cheeses at the end of a meal.

The way we serve cheese at L'Impero was inspired by two things: a memorable cheese pairing and a less than memorable experience at a New York restaurant. I remember the first time I was served a little pecorino Romano along with a green tomato mostarda, a preservelike condiment usually served with boiled meats (insert the sound of harps strumming here). It was about nine years ago, in Italy, at a two-star Michelin restaurant in the north. The mostarda was somewhat sweet and lightly spicy, and I can still remember how it made my palate tingle when paired with the sharp, grassy flavor of the cheese. I found the pairing very compelling.

Fast forward a half dozen years, and I am sitting with my business partners Chris Cannon and Jane Epstein at a restaurant in New York engaged in an animated discussion about our plans for what would become L'Impero. Our conversation was interrupted midstream by the appearance of the restaurant's cheese guy (I'm sure he had a more formal title but you know the guy I mean), who proceeded to list and explain some thirty or so cheeses. The energy of our conversation, our train of thought, not to mention the first dozen cheeses he mentioned, were lost and forgotten as he droned on and on and on. When he left us (finally) we still had a lot to work out regarding L'Impero, but one thing we all agreed was that there would be no such lengthy interruption at our—as of then nonexistent—restaurant tables.

At L'Impero we offer customers nine different cheeses, each with its own specific accompaniment, and suggest ordering at least three. All of the cheeses are paired with a little something sweet: a cow's milk robiola from Lombardy paired with mixed berry preserves; a rich Taleggio served with a beet compote; some Gorgonzola topped with shaved bitter chocolate, surrounded by orange marmelatta (marmalade), and sprinkled with the tiniest bit of crushed red pepper. To say the cheese course has caused some commotion is an understatement. Although some cheese purists don't want anyone messing with their cheese—these people actually ask that the preserves or whatever be removed—the overwhelming majority of my customers appreciate and have fun with the flavor pairings.

What follows is a listing of some of the cheese pairings with which we have had the greatest success. For most of the composed plates, I use my favorite brands of marmalades and preserves, but we make our own pineapple chutney and sweet beet compote, so I have included those recipes here. With the cheeses, we serve small, hard, pretzellike biscuits called *taralle*. I got that idea after my friend Sergio received a box of homemade *taralle* from his Aunt Maria and I ate practically all of them. Sergio's aunt makes hers with black pepper and almonds. My grandmother used to make hers more traditionally, studding the *taralle* with fennel seeds. Both recipes are included here.

As for the cheeses themselves, maybe it sounds too obvious to say we look for the absolute best versions of each variety. You can do this yourself by seeking out gourmet grocers or cheese markets that have knowledgeable people behind the counter. Ask to taste a few different cheeses. Another possibility is to check out some of the cheeses available by mail order. Although you can't taste them beforehand, mail order might be your only option when seeking a specific type of cheese. In listing the cheeses we use, I have included where the cheese is from and often who makes it. The best cheeses are usually made by smaller, artisan cheesemakers; such cheeses will vary a little in flavor and texture from year to year and even month to month, so keep tasting and have fun.

Cheese and Sweet Pairings

WHEN SERVING THESE CHEESES, you can either serve each cheese on a small plate individually, or serve, say, three cheeses on a single larger plate with room between each cheese. When serving a cheese with a preserve or honey, I put a teaspoon of the preserve down first and then lay what would constitute a bite or two of the cheese on top of the preserve. Any crushed, grated, or ground garnish, such as red pepper or chocolate, gets sprinkled on top of the cheese. Obviously, I prefer creating these flavor vignettes, and would recommend you do this at home, too. But you could also present the cheese more casually, in hunks and chunks, with small dishes of the condiments and garnishes nearby. With a little direction from you, your guests can create their own plates. When choosing a few cheeses to feature, consider flavor and texture, serving a mix of hard and creamy cheeses, mild and full flavored. When you taste them, begin with the mildest first. For the best flavor and texture, serve the cheese close to room temperature.

Here are some of our favorite pairings:

STYLE/MAKER	MILK	ORIGIN	SERVE WITH
PIAVE	Cow	The Veneto	Preserved lemons
RICOTTO DI BUFULA	Water buffalo	Campania	Honey, preferably truffle
COACH FARM'S TRIPLE CREAM	Goat	New York	Pineapple Chutney (page 257)
ROBIOLA BOSINA "DUE LATTE"	Cow and sheep	Piedmont	Italian "Cogna" (mixed berry preserves)
TALEGGIO	Cow	Lombardy	Sweet Beet Compote (page 258) and pink peppercorns
PARMIGIANO "VACCA ROSSA"	Cow	Emilia-Romagna	12-year-old balsamic vinegar
PECORINO	Sheep	Vermont	Green tomato marmelatta
GORGONZOLA DOLCE	Cow	Lombardy	Orange marmelatta, crushed red pepper, shaved bitter chocolate

PINEAPPLE CHUTNEY

Serve a tiny bit of this flavorful chutney with a triple cream goat's milk cheese such as the one made by Coach Farm or a Chiabro d'Henry made with goat's milk from Piedmont. The chutney is composed of competitive ingredients: the sweet pineapple and dried currant, warm ginger and cinnamon, sour vinegar, and just a bit of hot cayenne. Somehow they all come together in a way that works, especially when paired with a very rich cheese. This makes quite a bit, so have it out when you're hosting a party. It also will keep for about a week in the refrigerator and would make an interesting accompaniment to pound cake, gingerbread, or ice cream.

YIELDS **2** CUPS

1/2 cup sugar

2 tablespoons water

2 tablespoons white wine vinegar

1 teaspoon grated fresh ginger

1$\frac{1}{2}$ teaspoons dry mustard

Pinch of ground cinnamon

Pinch of ground cloves

Pinch of cayenne

One **1**-inch sprig fresh rosemary

1 fresh pineapple, cored and cut into 1/4-inch dice

1 tablespoon currants

IN A MEDIUM SAUCEPAN bring all but the pineapple and currants to a boil. Reduce to low and cook until thick. Let come to room temperature and stir in the fruit. Keep chilled but don't serve the chutney straight out of the refrigerator or some of its flavor will be muted.

SWEET BEET COMPOTE

> You can keep the beets refrigerated for a few days, but allow them to come to room temperature before using. Also, taste the beets before serving to see if they need a bit more vinegar or honey. Trucioleto is a red wine vinegar made from the grape's first press and aged in oak wood that's softer than most red wine vinegars.

MAKES 1 CUP

2 medium red beets

2 teaspoons extra virgin olive oil

Pinch of kosher salt

2 tablespoons honey

2 tablespoons Trucioleto red wine vinegar (see page 12) or 1 tablespoon regular red wine vinegar and 1 tablespoon balsamic vinegar

HEAT THE OVEN to 350°F. Rinse the beets and dry them with a paper towel. Rub the beets all over with the olive oil and put them in a small ovenproof pan with $1/4$ inch of water on the bottom of the pan. Season them with just a little salt. Cover the pan with aluminum foil. (Alternatively, skip the pan and simply wrap the beets in heavy-gauge aluminum foil and place the wrapped beets on a baking sheet.) Bake until the beets are tender when pierced with a paring knife, 1 hour and 10 minutes.

Allow the beets to cool enough so that you can handle them. Peel the beets and cut them into tiny dice. Combine the still warm beets with the honey and vinegar in equal parts until the mixture binds together somewhat; you may not need to use all of the honey and vinegar.

Allow the beets to cool further to room temperature before serving with the cheese.

BLACK PEPPER AND
ALMOND TARALLE

Kind of a cross between a pretzel and a cracker, *taralle* are wonderful to nibble on with cheese. The yeast is used here in part as a leavening agent, but also to give the *taralle* their warm, comforting, breadlike flavor. The *taralle* will keep for a few days stored airtight, and you can freeze them as well.

MAKES **30**

One **2**-ounce package cake yeast (also called fresh or compressed yeast) or **3** envelopes dry yeast

1 cup warm water

14 ounces (**3** cups plus **2** tablespoons) unbleached bread flour

3/4 cup vegetable shortening, such as Crisco

4 teaspoons kosher salt

1/2 teaspoon freshly ground black pepper

1 cup sliced almonds

HEAT THE OVEN to 350°F. In the bowl of your stand mixer or in a large bowl, combine the yeast with 1 cup warm water. Add the flour, shortening, salt, black pepper, and almonds and stir to combine the ingredients. Using the dough hook of your mixer or your hands, knead the dough until it is smooth and elastic. Cover the bowl and let the dough rest for 15 minutes.

To shape the *taralle*: Grab about as much dough as will fit easily in the palm of your hand when closed. Roll the dough out into a rope 7 inches long. Twist the rope a few times and then join the two ends, pinching them, so that you have a circle. Put the circle on a baking sheet and continue shaping the remaining dough in the same manner.

Bake the *taralle* until golden and hard, 40 to 45 minutes. Remove them to a cooling rack. When completely cooled, store airtight.

VARIATION: For the more traditional fennel-flavored *taralle*, replace the black pepper and almonds with $1/4$ cup whole fennel seeds.

Chocolate Desserts

FOR MANY PEOPLE, DESSERT JUST ISN'T DESSERT UNLESS IT'S CHOCOLATE. So here you go. Recipes featuring chocolate in all kinds of ways: from the playful Chocolate Salami we serve as part of a plate of petits fours (which also includes the Gianduia Truffles on page 269) to a rich, dense, chocolate cake to—and the real chocoholics need to stand proud here—a Chocolate Soup. Those who like their chocolate fix served with a little restraint should try the Chocolate Chip–Pecan Biscotti.

Before you start melting your chocolate, consider a few things first. The best chocolate desserts, especially those that are primarily chocolate, begin with the best chocolate. So do taste the chocolate you're about to use in, say, the chocolate truffle cake; if it's not excellent, your cake won't be either. At the restaurant, we use the chocolate of the family-owned chocolatiers Michael Cluizel (shh . . . they're French). We also like our chocolate on the bitter side. Although you could probably substitute semisweet where I call for bittersweet, the results would be a little too cloying for me. In fact, we usually make the salami with unsweetened chocolate, but that's partly because we serve it with a few other very sweet treats, and its job in that case is to act as an almost savory break. To serve the Chocolate Salami on its own, it works better with bittersweet chocolate. We also almost always add coffee in some form to the chocolate to give it an ever deeper, toasty flavor.

BITTERSWEET CHOCOLATE
TRUFFLE CAKE

Serve this deliciously dense cake with the whiskied blackberries on page 287 for a truly dramatic dessert.

MAKES ONE **10**-INCH CAKE OR **6** TO **8** INDIVIDUAL CAKES

1/2 pound (**2** sticks) unsalted butter, plus more for preparing the pan

20 ounces bittersweet chocolate

7 large eggs, separated

1/4 cup dark rum

1/3 cup sugar

1/4 cup all-purpose flour, plus more for preparing the pan

Warm Blackberries with Whiskey (page 287)

PREHEAT THE OVEN to 325°F. Butter one 10-inch cake pan (at least 2¹/2 inches high) or six to eight individual rings, pans, or ramekins.

Using an actual double boiler or a bowl seated over—but not touching—simmering water in a saucepan, melt the chocolate and butter together, stirring often. Remove the bowl from the heat and let the chocolate cool a bit.

Meanwhile, in a large bowl, or in the bowl of a stand mixer, whisk the egg yolks and rum together until they reach ribbon stage—that is, a little of the egg drizzled from the whisk will hold its shape for a second or two before disappearing into the rest of the eggs. Add the cooled chocolate and butter mixture to the egg yolks; if it is still quite hot, begin by adding the chocolate in small amounts to temper the mixture and avoid cooking the eggs.

In a clean bowl using a clean whisk, whisk the egg whites until foamy. Add the sugar and continue to whisk until soft peaks hold their shape when you lift the stopped whisk out of the egg white mixture. Using a large flexible spatula, gently fold the egg white mixture into the chocolate mixture. Then, using the

same gentle action, fold the flour into the mixture as well. Fill the prepared pan or pans with the batter, leaving at least $1/2$ inch of room at the top. Bake until an inserted toothpick shows moist crumbs attached when removed from the cake, 45 minutes for a 10-inch cake, less time for smaller cakes.

NOTE At the restaurant we make individual cakes using PVC pipe to make the molds, cutting a 3-inch pipe into rings about 2 inches tall. The rings are buttered and floured and put on a baking sheet. The batter is poured into the rings, and once baked, the cakes are removed by cutting right through the rings. Individual metal rings would work, but you will have to run a knife inside the ring to remove the cakes. You could also try mini-springform pans, which run a bit larger in diameter and would yield fewer cakes, or even small ramekins.

CHOCOLATE SOUP

MAKES 1^1/2 CUPS

7 ounces bittersweet chocolate, chopped

1 cup half-and-half

3/4 teaspoon crushed black peppercorns

1^1/2 teaspoons crème de cassis

1^1/2 teaspoons espresso extract or coffee liqueur

PUT THE CHOCOLATE IN A LARGE BOWL. Combine the half-and-half and peppercorns in a saucepan and bring to a boil. Pour the hot half-and-half over the chocolate and whisk together thoroughly. Add the cassis and espresso extract. Pass the mixture through a fine strainer and serve warm. If serving as a "soup," pour about a half cup in a shallow bowl.

The soup will last for a few days in the refrigerator; simply reheat over low heat before serving.

This has become one of our signature desserts at L'Impero. A waiter comes to the table and places a shallow bowl in which a tiny panna cotta (page 274) and a tiny round of walnut cake (page 279) sit. He then pours this flavorful, molten chocolate into the dish so those tiny desserts become like islands in a sea of chocolate. You can do something similar either using those exact recipes or substituting a piece of your favorite nut or pound cake in place of the walnut cake, and adding some currants soaked in Italian brandy to the soup as we have done on occasion. You can also use the soup as an amazing chocolate sauce served over ice cream. The hint of black pepper and the cassis make this a sundae topping for grown-ups.

OLIVE OIL CHOCOLATE MOUSSE

Here olive oil takes the place of butter, adding a fruity undertone to the chocolate. My friend and former pastry chef, Heather Carlucci, based her recipe on an old Basque one. Hers does not include the whipped cream that's in this recipe because the mousse as she serves it would be layered with some vanilla bavarese (Italian for Bavarian cream) to lighten it. Adding whipped cream is a quicker and easier way to get a similar effect.

MAKES **8** SERVINGS

6 ounces bittersweet chocolate, chopped

3 tablespoons extra virgin olive oil

3 eggs, separated (see Note)

2 tablespoons confectioners' sugar, sifted

1/2 teaspoon vanilla extract, coffee extract, or coffee liqueur

1/2 cup heavy or whipping cream, plus additional whipped cream as a garnish, if you like

MELT THE CHOCOLATE using a double boiler or a bowl seated over some simmering water in a saucepan. (Or melt it in the microwave, if you like.) Let cool slightly. Whisk in the olive oil, a little at a time, until completely incorporated.

In a large bowl whisk together the egg yolks and confectioners' sugar until smooth and lighter in color. Add the extract. Add a little bit of the chocolate mixture to the egg yolks to temper them. Slowly whisk in the remaining chocolate.

Whisk the egg whites until soft peaks form. Gently fold the whites into the chocolate mixture. Whip the cream until soft peaks form, and gently fold it into the mixture. Divide the mousse among eight cups and refrigerate for at least 4 hours and up to 24 hours.

NOTE While salmonella risk from raw or undercooked eggs is extremely small, you may want to look for eggs pasteurized in the shell, a new consumer product becoming available nationally at supermarkets (see Sources).

CHOCOLATE SALAMI

> These slices of nut-studded chocolate really do look like salami. At the restaurant we make this with unsweetened chocolate in part because we use our sweet biscotti to make the crumbs that go into the salami and because we serve these slices along with other tiny sweet bites, making their bitterness a welcome respite. Bittersweet chocolate definitely makes these more appealing when served alone; a few pieces with an espresso make a wonderful ending to a large meal. For added drama, plate a few rounds, drizzle them with a little honey, and grind a bit of black pepper over them. These yield a lot, but you can freeze unsliced portions.

MAKES **100** PIECES

12 ounces bittersweet chocolate

1/2 pound unsalted butter

1 tablespoon honey (I especially like chestnut honey)

$1^1/_2$ tablespoons coffee extract or coffee liqueur, such as Kahlúa

2 egg yolks, beaten

1/2 cup almonds, chopped fine

1/2 cup pistachios, chopped fine

1 cup dried figs, chopped very fine

1 cup biscotti crumbs (such as the ones on page 268) or graham cracker crumbs

USING AN ACTUAL DOUBLE BOILER or a bowl seated over but not touching simmering water in a saucepan, melt the chocolate and butter together, stirring often. Remove the bowl from the heat and stir in the honey and coffee extract. Slowly add the egg yolks and stir well. Add the almonds, pistachios, and figs and stir to combine. Finally, add the biscotti or graham cracker crumbs and mix them in well.

Divide the mixture into four equal portions and, using plastic wrap as a guide, roll the portions into logs with a circumference the size of a quarter. Wrap the logs in plastic wrap and freeze them for 10 minutes before slicing the logs into pieces between $^1/_4$ and $^1/_2$ inch thick. Serve the pieces while still cool (or refrigerate them until serving) to ensure that they will be easy to pick up. You can keep the logs in the refrigerator for a few days before slicing and can freeze the logs, well wrapped, for a couple of months. Defrost deeply frozen logs in the refrigerator for a few hours before slicing.

Scott Conant's New Italian Cooking

CHOCOLATE CHIP–PECAN

BISCOTTI

There are a lot of good biscotti recipes out there; this one is kind of like a chocolate chip cookie for grown-ups—sweet but not too sweet with an excellently crisp texture. Biscotti will keep airtight for at least a week; you can also freeze them.

MAKES **20** BISCOTTI

4 ounces (**1** stick) unsalted butter, softened

1$\frac{1}{4}$ cups sugar, more for sprinkling

2 eggs, plus an additional egg for brushing

1 tablespoon vanilla extract

2$\frac{1}{2}$ cups (12$\frac{1}{4}$ ounces) all-purpose flour, more for flouring

1$\frac{1}{2}$ teaspoons baking powder

1/2 teaspoon salt

1/2 teaspoon ground cinnamon

1/2 cup old-fashioned rolled oats (not instant)

1/4 cup whole pecans

1/2 cup chocolate chips

HEAT THE OVEN to 325°F and line a baking sheet with parchment paper. In a large bowl, cream together the butter and sugar by hand or using the paddle attachment on a stand mixer. Add the eggs and vanilla and beat until fluffy. In a separate bowl, combine the flour, baking powder, salt, cinnamon, and oats. Add this to the butter-sugar mixture in a few additions. Finally, mix in the nuts and chocolate chips.

Dump the dough out onto a floured surface and roll into a log 12 inches long and 3 inches wide. Move the log to the baking sheet and flatten it slightly with your hands. Brush the top of the roll with a little beaten egg and sprinkle with sugar. Bake the log until firm and lightly browned. Remove it from the oven and allow it to cool. Reduce the oven temperature to 225°F. Slice the log crosswise into pieces between $\frac{1}{2}$ and $\frac{3}{4}$ inch thick. Return the pieces to the baking sheet and bake until the edges of the biscotti become dry and crispy, another 30 minutes.

GIANDUIA TRUFFLES

Though it seems as if the Swiss always get credit for it, we actually have Italy to thank for the creation of gianduia, the beguiling combination of toasted hazelnuts and chocolate. In the nineteenth century, a cocoa blockade prompted by the Napoleonic wars forced chocolatiers to find ways to stretch their scant inventory. In Piedmont, they turned to the hazelnuts that grow so well there. By blending a refined hazelnut paste into their chocolate they not only stretched their chocolate supplies but also created silky smooth bars of hazelnut-flavored chocolate. You can find gianduia, pronounced zhahan-DOO-yah and often spelled "gianduja," at some specialty stores and also through mail order (see Sources). An optional bit of hazelnut liqueur, such as Frangelico, will underscore the gianduia's flavor; dark rum also works well, giving the sweets a toasty, slightly boozy boost. Since these truffles are not dipped in a protective chocolate shell, they should be kept cool until ready to serve.

MAKES **36** TRUFFLES

1 cup heavy cream

9 ounces gianduia, chopped

3 ounces bittersweet chocolate, chopped

1$\frac{1}{2}$ teaspoons Frangelico or dark rum (optional)

1/2 cup unsweetened cocoa powder or finely ground toasted hazelnuts to roll the truffles in (optional)

HEAT THE HEAVY CREAM in a saucepan over medium heat. Add the gianduia and the bittersweet chocolate and melt, stirring constantly. Pour the mixture into a medium bowl and add the Frangelico or rum, if you're using it. Cover and chill until firm, 3 hours.

Line a baking sheet with wax paper or parchment paper. Using a teaspoon or melon baller, scoop some chocolate and shape it into a little ball. Roll the ball in the cocoa powder or the nuts, if you like, and then place it on the baking sheet. Continue making the truffles, leaving room between them on the baking sheet so they don't stick together. Chill the truffles until just before serving. *(continued)*

These can be made up to a week before serving and kept, covered in plastic, in the refrigerator. You can also freeze them well wrapped. Let them thaw for a few hours in the refrigerator before serving.

Fruits, Nuts, and Cream

OBVIOUSLY, LIFE WOULD BE A LITTLE BORING IF EVERY DESSERT WERE CHOCOLATE. And, though I haven't met one myself, I know there are actually people out there who don't even like chocolate. The desserts that follow feature such wonderful things as ripe seasonal fruits, toasted nuts, mascarpone cheese, citrus, cream. Although they may in fact contain the same amount of calories as the chocolate desserts, these desserts tend to feel a little lighter, and maybe a little more sophisticated. The Sesame Cannoli with Orange Mascarpone Mousse (page 285) has become a signature dessert of mine and is one of those dishes that looks really impressive but is not hard to make.

EXTRA VIRGIN OLIVE OIL CAKE

A mild, fruity olive oil is a good choice for this moist, fragrant cake. At the restaurant we bake small individual cakes. I'm a sucker for how sweet that looks on the plate. If you have small molds, you can divide the batter among them and begin checking on them for doneness after 15 minutes. The cake is delicious on its own, but it's even better with a dollop of lemon cream (recipe follows) and some macerated fruit (page 286).

SERVES **10**

2 cups all-purpose flour

1 tablespoon baking powder

Pinch of salt

1^1/2 cups sugar

4 large eggs

1/2 cup orange juice

3/4 cup extra virgin olive oil

3/4 teaspoon vanilla extract

HEAT THE OVEN to 350°F. Spray a 9- or 10-inch cake pan with vegetable oil spray or lightly oil it. Cut a piece of parchment to fit the bottom of the pan and lightly spray or oil it.

In a small bowl, whisk together the flour, baking powder, and salt. In a large bowl, whisk the sugar and eggs until the color lightens somewhat. Add the orange juice and whisk to combine. Add the olive oil and vanilla and whisk again to combine. Add the flour mixture in three additions, mixing well between each one. Pour the batter into the prepared pan and bake until a toothpick inserted toward the middle of the cake comes out clean, 45 to 50 minutes. Let cool on a rack for 10 minutes and then invert the cake onto a cooling rack. Wrap in plastic wrap when completely cool. The cake will keep for about two days. It also freezes really well wrapped in plastic wrap.

WHIPPED LEMON CREAM

This delicious dessert topping is essentially a classic lemon curd mixed with whipped cream. Since it's tough to divide a single egg, the recipe yields about twice as much lemon curd as you need for the cream. The lemon curd itself can be made days ahead and refrigerated or even frozen, and it goes with all kinds of desserts aside from the olive oil cake on page 272; you can even enjoy it spread on toast. After whipping the curd with the whipped cream, use it within a few hours.

MAKES **1** CUP OF CURD AND **2** CUPS OF WHIPPED LEMON CREAM

For the lemon curd

1 large egg

1 large egg yolk

1/2 cup sugar

Pinch of salt

Zest from 1 lemon

3 tablespoons unsalted butter, cut into pieces

1/2 cup fresh lemon juice, strained

For the whipped lemon cream

1/2 cup heavy or whipping cream

TO MAKE THE LEMON CURD: In a medium saucepan, whisk together the egg, egg yolk, sugar, salt, and zest until lightened in color. Put the pan over medium heat. Add the butter and lemon juice. Cook, whisking constantly, until the mixture is smooth and has thickened considerably. Test by dipping a spoon into it; the curd should coat the back of a spoon and stay put. This will take 5 to 10 minutes, depending on your heat, but don't let the curd boil. Strain the curd into a small bowl and put plastic wrap on its surface to prevent a skin from forming. Chill until very cold, at least an hour and up to a week if well wrapped.

To make the whipped lemon cream: With a whisk or stand mixer, whisk the cream until quite thick. Add 1/2 cup of the lemon curd and continue to whisk until soft peaks form. Serve immediately or chill and serve within a few hours.

CRÈME FRAÎCHE PANNA COTTA
WITH CARAMEL SAUCE

Panna cotta is a cooked cream dessert that tastes simultaneously luscious and light. We make tiny panna cottas to go in our chocolate soup, but made larger and topped with a caramel sauce, they taste wonderful on their own. Don't skimp on the gelatin. I'm sorry that you will have to open another envelope for just $^1/4$ teaspoon, but the panna cotta sets up beautifully with this extra bit and less well with the $2^1/2$ teaspoons that come in just one envelope.

MAKES 8 SERVINGS

For the caramel

3/4 cup sugar

1/4 cup heavy cream

Pinch of salt

For the panna cotta

$2^3/4$ teaspoons powdered gelatin

2/3 cup sweetened condensed milk

$1^1/2$ cups heavy cream

1/2 cup milk

1/2 cup crème fraîche

2 teaspoons vanilla extract

FOR THE CARAMEL: Have ready eight 4- to 6-ounce ramekins or other similar size molds. Heat the sugar and $^1/4$ cup water in a small saucepan and cook, swirling the pan by the handle, until a clear syrup forms. (Because you want the syrup to clarify before it boils, slide the pan off the burner as needed.) Increase the heat to high and cook the sugar until it turns a deep amber. (You can check the color by dripping a little onto a white plate.) As soon as the sugar has caramelized to the color you want, add the heavy cream. Be careful as the hot mixture will sputter. Stir in the salt and divide the caramel sauce among the ramekins. Allow the caramel to cool to room temperature.

For the panna cotta: Sprinkle the gelatin over the condensed milk and let stand to soften. Meanwhile, bring the cream and milk to a boil in a medium saucepan. Reduce the heat to medium and add the crème fraîche. Add the vanilla and condensed milk with the gelatin and stir until all of the

ingredients are well incorporated. Strain the mixture into a clean bowl, or even better, a liquid measuring cup with a spout. Divide the panna cotta mixture among the ramekins and refrigerate for at least 2 hours (and up to 24 hours) for the panna cotta to set up.

To serve, carefully turn the ramekin cup over and release the panna cotta onto a plate, letting the caramel sauce drip down over the panna cotta. (If it doesn't unmold easily, dip the ramekin in hot water, wipe it dry, and try again.)

NOTE To make 16 to 20 smaller panna cottas, use 2-ounce foil cups and place 1 teaspoon of caramel in the bottom of each cup.

CREAMY LEMON CHEESECAKE

When you cook cheesecake in a water bath, the results are different from cooking it in the traditional method. Instead of that dense, dry texture (which, admittedly, some people love), you get an extremely creamy cake that's pretty much the same texture in the middle as it is on the edges. A water bath is also very forgiving; you won't wreck the cake if it bakes an extra 5 or even 10 minutes. A water bath doesn't crisp a cheesecake crust as well as a dry, low oven would, but there's no crust on this cheesecake, so that's not a problem. If you want a little contrasting crunch, you can add a crust of sorts after the cake is baked by pressing your favorite cookie crumbs or biscotti crumbs into the sides of an unmolded, chilled cake before serving; you'll need 3/4 to 1 cup of crumbs to cover the sides completely. Serve the cake with some fresh raspberries.

MAKES **12** SERVINGS

1 tablespoon butter, at room temperature, for preparing the pan

16 ounces cream cheese, softened to room temperature

1 cup sugar

2 large eggs

4 large egg yolks

8 ounces sour cream

1/2 cup heavy cream

1/2 cup fresh lemon juice

HEAT THE OVEN to 250°F. Butter the sides of a 9-inch springform pan, going all the way to the top. (This helps prevent cracking.) Cut a round of parchment paper to fit the bottom of the pan and line the bottom of the pan with it. Wrap the outside of the pan with a double layer of heavy-duty aluminum foil to prevent leaking.

Using a stand or other electric mixer, beat together the cream cheese and sugar until very smooth. Beat in the eggs and egg yolks until the batter is smooth once again. (Scrape the sides of the bowl and then whisk occasionally.) Add the sour cream and heavy cream and whisk just until incorporated. (Too much whisking will make the cake puff up.) Add the lemon juice last and give the mixture a final whisk.

(continued)

Pour the batter into the springform pan. Set the pan in a larger roasting pan and surround it with 1 inch of very hot water. Bake the cheesecake until the center of the cake is dry to the touch but still jiggles a bit when the pan is shaken (the sides will puff up a tiny bit), 70 to 80 minutes. Remove the cake from the water bath and allow it to cool at room temperature; then refrigerate the cake for at least 6 hours.

To unmold the cheesecake, wet a towel with hot water and squeeze out the excess. Wipe the outside of the ring with the hot, moist towel. Run a paring knife or a thin metal spatula around the inside of the ring. Release the clasps and gently loosen the ring. If you want to put the cake on a serving plate, line a different plate with plastic wrap. Invert the cake onto the plastic-lined plate. Warm the bottom of the pan with the hot towel and then lift off the pan bottom. Invert the cake again onto its serving plate. You may need to smooth the edges of the cake with a metal spatula.

WALNUT AND BROWN
BUTTER CAKE

My friend and former pastry chef, Heather Carlucci, introduced us to this cake, which she would bake in a huge batch in a rectangular sheet pan. She would then cut out tiny circles of the cake to act as islands in our famous Chocolate Soup. The edges of the cake she left in the kitchen for the staff to snack on. Well, I had to tell the staff to please keep the cake scraps out of my sight. This cake, with its subtle toasted walnut flavor and moist buttery texture, is one of the few things I can't resist, especially when it's still warm from the oven. If you want to use just some of this in the Chocolate Soup on page 264, the rest freezes beautifully. A slice is excellent not only for dessert—try it with a glass of sweet Recioto della Valpolicella—but also as an afternoon treat with a cup of tea.

MAKES ONE **10**-INCH CAKE
TO SERVE **12**

1/2 pound (**2** sticks) unsalted butter, plus more for buttering the pan

4 ounces walnuts (or substitute hazelnuts or almonds)

3/4 cup (**3.75** ounces) all-purpose flour

3 cups (**12** ounces) confectioners' sugar, plus more for dusting

Pinch of salt

1 cup egg whites (from **8** large eggs)

Confectioners' sugar

IN A SAUCEPAN, melt the butter over medium heat and continue to cook it until it turns brown and smells quite nutty, being careful not to let it burn, 10 to 15 minutes. Remove it from the heat and let it cool to almost room temperature.

Meanwhile, heat the oven to 350°F. Butter the bottom of a 10-inch-round cake pan and line the bottom of the pan with parchment paper. Spread the walnuts out on a baking sheet and toast them in the oven until lightly browned and fragrant, 10 to 15 minutes. Let the walnuts cool, but leave the oven on.

Reserve 1/4 cup of the nuts and chop them finely by hand. Grind the rest of the toasted nuts in a food processor until finely ground.

(continued)

Sift the flour, confectioners' sugar, and salt together in a large bowl. Add the ground nuts and whisk to combine. Add the egg whites and whisk them together well with the dry ingredients. Slowly add the melted butter, whisking constantly until it is completely incorporated and no butter is floating on top of the mixture.

Pour the batter into the prepared pan and sprinkle the top with the reserved chopped nuts. Bake until the cake feels solid but still gives slightly when touched, 40 to 45 minutes. Let the cake cool in the pan for 10 minutes before inverting it onto a serving plate. Just before serving, dust the top with some sifted confectioners' sugar.

ORANGE COOKIES

These cookies are kind of homely, but I really like their pleasant light orange flavor and their crumbly, yet moist texture. They make a nice bright bite at the end of a meal and would go well with a glass of Vin Santo.

MAKES **50** COOKIES

3 cups all-purpose flour

1 tablespoon baking powder

1/2 teaspoon baking soda

Pinch of salt

1 teaspoon finely grated orange zest

1/2 cup orange juice, preferably fresh

1/2 cup vegetable oil, such as canola, corn, or grapeseed oil

1/2 cup sugar

1 large or extra-large egg

1/2 cup confectioners' sugar for icing

HEAT THE OVEN to 425°F. Lightly grease a couple of baking sheets.

In a bowl, whisk together the flour, baking powder, baking soda, and salt. In the bowl of a stand mixer using the paddle attachment or in a large bowl, mix together well the orange zest, orange juice, vegetable oil, sugar, and egg. Add the dry ingredients to the wet in a few additions, occasionally scraping the bowl. Continue to mix for a couple of minutes after all of the ingredients have been combined.

Roll the dough into balls 1 inch across and place on the baking sheets with some room between each ball. (They won't expand too much.) Bake until the bottoms of the cookies are lightly browned, 6 to 8 minutes. Cool the cookies on a wire rack.

In a small bowl, use a fork to combine the confectioners' sugar with just enough water to make a thick, opaque icing, 2 to 3 tablespoons. Dip the tops of the cooled cookies into the icing and let the icing harden for a minute or two. The cookies are best the day they're made but will last for a few days airtight. If you want to freeze some, freeze them before they are iced and ice them once they have thawed and come to room temperature.

INDIVIDUAL APPLE CROSTATAS

A crostata is a rustic Italian tart. As its name implies, it's all about the crust, which in this case is the perfect cross between a flaky piecrust and a tender cookie with an added kick of Marsala wine. We like to add a little Pecorino Romano to both the crust and to the topping. I think its sharpness adds an intriguing note. But it's not for everyone. For a straight-ahead sweet apple flavor, leave out the cheese.

MAKES **4** SERVINGS

For the pastry

1$\frac{1}{2}$ cups (**7.5** ounces) all-purpose flour

1 tablespoon cornmeal

1/4 cup sugar

1 teaspoon kosher salt

1/4 teaspoon baking soda

1/2 teaspoon baking powder

Zest of **1** lemon

4 ounces (**1** stick) unsalted butter, cut into small pieces and chilled

6 tablespoons heavy cream

1 tablespoon Marsala

2 tablespoons grated pecorino Romano (optional)

FOR THE PASTRY: In a large bowl or in the bowl of a food processor, combine the flour, cornmeal, sugar, salt, baking soda, baking powder, and lemon zest. Cut the butter into the dry ingredients until the mixture is crumbly by either pulsing it in the processor or using a pastry blender, a couple of knives, or your fingertips. If using a food processor, be sure not to overmix, which will cause the butter to soften too much. Add the heavy cream, Marsala, and the cheese, if you're using it. Pulse briefly just until moist clumps form or stir with a fork until just combined. Shape the dough into a ball or disk, wrap it well in plastic wrap, and refrigerate it for at least 1 hour and up to a day.

For the filling: Melt the 3 tablespoons of butter in a very large sauté pan over medium heat. Add the apples, increase the heat to medium-high, and cook, stirring occasionally, until the apples are lightly browned, 10 minutes. Add the sugar and cook, stirring, until thick and syrupy, 5 minutes. Transfer the apples to a bowl and let them cool to room temperature.

(continued)

For the filling

3 tablespoons unsalted butter

6 medium apples (**7** ounces each; Galas are nice), peeled and cut into **12** wedges each

1/2 cup sugar

2 tablespoons grated pecorino Romano (optional)

To bake the crostata: Heat the oven to 375°F. Line two baking sheets with parchment paper and flour a work surface well. Shape the tarts either by rolling each one individually or rolling out all of the dough and cutting out the circles. To roll each one out, divide the dough into four equal pieces and roll the dough into circles 7 inches across and between $1/8$ and $1/4$ inch thick (they don't have to be perfectly round). To cut out circles, use a sharp knife to make circles 7 inches across.

Top the dough rounds with the cooled apples, leaving a 1-inch border of dough empty. If using the pecorino, sprinkle about $1/2$ tablespoon over each crostata. Fold the edges of the rounds up and over the apples, pleating loosely. Carefully transfer the tart to the parchment-lined baking pan. Bake the crostata until the dough turns a deep golden brown, 22 to 27 minutes. Cool slightly and serve with additional grated pecorino, if you like.

SESAME CANNOLI WITH

ORANGE MASCARPONE MOUSSE

These are not your traditional fried cannoli stuffed with ricotta cheese. The baked shells have more in common with French tuilles, but the finished product—the crunch from the sesame and the creaminess of the filling—makes me think of Italy. Delicious on their own, they're even better served with some Balsamic Macerated Berries (recipe follows). You might want to buy your sesame seeds in bulk from a health food store, as you'll need a lot of them.

MAKES 6 SERVINGS

For the cannolis

8 ounces (1 stick) unsalted butter, melted

1^1/2 cups sugar

3/4 cup orange juice

7 ounces (1^2/3 cups) sesame seeds

8 ounces (1^3/4 cups) all-purpose flour

TO MAKE THE CANNOLIS: Combine the melted butter with the sugar, orange juice, and sesame seeds. Add the flour and mix with a wooden spoon until no lumps remain. Cover and chill in the refrigerator for at least 1 hour and up to three days.

Heat the oven to 375°F. Prepare a baking sheet: For the best results, use a nonstick mat, such as a Silpat. Parchment paper sprayed with nonstick spray is another option, but the parchment can wrinkle as you spread the batter. Using the back of an oiled spoon, spread about 1 tablespoon of dough into a thin round, 4 inches across. Bake until golden brown, 10 minutes. Bake only six or so rounds at a time because you need to shape them while hot. While the rounds are still hot and malleable, roll them around the handle of a wooden spoon into a cylinder, sliding them off when firm. (If the cookie becomes too crisp to shape, put it back in the oven for a few minutes. The batter will make about thirty cannolis, so don't worry if a few get sacrificed as you get the hang of making

For the filling

1/2 pound mascarpone cheese

1/2 cup sugar

1/2 cup orange juice

1/4 cup triple sec

2 cups heavy cream

Confectioners' sugar for dusting

Balsamic Macerated Berries (optional, recipe follows)

them.) Let the cannolis cool completely at room temperature and store in an airtight container until ready to fill; they're the most crisp on the day they're made, but they will last a couple of days in an airtight container.

To make the filling: In a stand mixer, whisk together the mascarpone, sugar, orange juice, and triple sec until creamy. Add the cream and whisk to stiff peaks. (You can make this earlier in the day and keep it refrigerated.) Using a pastry bag, fill the cannoli shells with the orange mousse filling. (You can fill these a few hours before serving them, but the closer you can fill them to actual serving the better, as the shells have the potential to soften.) Arrange the cannolis, four per plate, and dust them with some powdered sugar. Serve with some Balsamic Marinated Berries on the side, if you like.

BALSAMIC MARINATED BERRIES

MAKES **2** CUPS

1/2 pint raspberries

1/2 pint strawberries, hulled and left whole, halved, or quartered, depending on size

1/4 cup high-quality balsamic vinegar

1/4 cup orange juice, preferably fresh

Sugar to taste

AN HOUR BEFORE SERVING, combine the raspberries, strawberries, vinegar, and orange juice. Taste after 15 minutes and add a couple of teaspoons of sugar, if needed. Serve with the Extra Virgin Olive Oil Cake on page 272, Sesame Cannoli on page 285, or your own favorite ice cream or custard.

WARM BLACKBERRIES

WITH WHISKEY

These blackberries, flavored with a hit of alcohol, make a quick, sophisticated accompaniment for the Bittersweet Chocolate Truffle Cake on page 261. I reach for grappa when I make these, but I realize that most people are more likely to have a bottle of whiskey in the liquor cabinet than grappa, a fiery drink (some would argue it's barely drinkable) distilled from the solids left in the wine press. Serve the berries warm or at room temperature on the side, directly on the plate with the cake or—even more elegantly—in their own little dish. These are also delicious over vanilla ice cream.

1/4 cup whiskey (bourbon, Irish whiskey, Scotch) or grappa

1^1/2 teaspoons sugar

1/2 pint fresh blackberries, halved

IN A SMALL SKILLET, combine the whiskey or grappa with the sugar and cook over medium heat until the sugar has melted. Add the blackberries, gently tossing them with the melted sugar until warmed through but still in whole pieces, 5 minutes.

SOURCES

HERE ARE SOURCES for some of the specialty ingredients called for in this book. All of these pur-veyors offer many more products than those highlighted here, so you may want to spend a few minutes perusing their Web site or talking to them by phone after you have procured the item you're seeking. Don't be afraid of mail-ordering food; we chefs do it all the time (nowadays mostly online). The goods are packed superbly, and even perishables arrive in great shape. As for shipping, which can be pricy, especially for foods that must be sent overnight, you will generally get more bang for the buck by placing a larger order; a good idea is to go in on an order with a friend and split the cost. Finally, inventory changes: At press time these companies all carried these items; that they still do is a good bet, but not a guarantee.

ANCHOVIES: A great online site for many different Italian ingredients, including salt-packed and oil-cured anchovies, is www.ingredientsgourmet.com (646–250–8394). This site also offers re-gional specialties, including high-quality Italian cheeses.

BOTTARGA: Gustiamo imports all kinds of wonderful Italian products, including *bottarga* (grated and whole, tuna and mullet), plus risotto, pasta, and all kinds of salumi. Find them on the Web at www.gustiamo.com or call 877–907–2525.

CHESTNUT FLOUR: Formaggio Kitchen, which has retail stores in Boston and Cambridge, Massachusetts, sells chestnut flour as well as artisan Italian cheeses, high-quality anchovies, ca-pers, polenta, pasta, fregola, and preserves. Visit them at www.formaggiokitchen.com or call 888–212–3224.

COFFEE EXTRACT: You can find this flavoring at www.spicebarn.com (866–670–9040).

EGGS (PASTEURIZED IN THE SHELL): Look for Davidson's brand eggs, which are pasteurized in the shell and available at a growing number of supermarkets. For information, including where to purchase them near you, visit www.safeeggs.com or call 800–410–7619.

FOIE GRAS: Hudson Valley Foie Gras carries, as the name implies, foie gras as well as other duck products (www.hudsonvalleyfoiegras; 845–292–2500).

FREGOLA: Look for fregola (also called Sardinian couscous) at gourmet groceries. You can also mail order it from www.ingredientsgourmet.com (646–250–8394), www.gustiamo.com (877–907–2525), or www.buonitalia.com (212–633–9090).

GIANDUIA: You can find gianduia (hazelnut chocolate bars) for baking at some gourmet markets and at New York Baking Supplies (www.nycake.com; 800–942–2539). Or try www.chocosphere.com.

GLACE DE POULET GOLD: This is the commercially made chicken base that comes closest to my own chicken reduction. It's made by More Than Gourmet and is available at some gourmet groceries and through the company's Web site at www.morethangourmet.com.

GUANCIALE: I get my *guanciale* from Salumeria Biellese (212–736–7376) right here in New York City. Niman Ranch, based in California, also makes and sells it (www.nimanranch.com; 510–808–0340).

OLIVE OIL: Academia Barilla has started to carry a new line of artisan products that bear the Academia Barilla name, including olive oils from such regions as Tuscany, Puglia, and Liguria. All high in quality, they nonetheless offer very different flavors; for more information on these oils, check out Academia Barilla's Web site at www.academiabarilla.com. You can find the olive oil in specialty gourmet shops and online at www.agferrari.com (877–878–2783).

PANKO: These bread crumbs are popping up at more and more supermarkets and can be easily found at Asian groceries. You can also mail-order boxes from www.ethnicgrocer.com and www.cooking.com.

POLENTA BRAMATA: California-based A. G. Ferrari (www.agferrari.com; 877–878–2783) carries it as do many of the other Italian import sites already listed here.

PORK BELLY: Niman Ranch will ship a whole pork belly to you (www.nimanranch.com; 510–808–0340) if you can't find a local pig farmer.

RABBIT LEGS: Van Rex Gourmet Foods (www.vanrex.com), which recently opened in New York City, sells rabbit legs as well as all kinds of gourmet products. Call them at 718–784–4122 for a full list of products.

SAFFRON: You can buy saffron and all kinds of other spices from www.thespicehouse.com, which currently has three store locations: two in Illinois, Chicago (312–274–0378) and Evanston (847–328–3711), and one in Milwaukee (414–272–0977).

SEA SALT: From Sicilian sea salt to Australian River sea salt, Aspen-based Salt Traders (www.salttraders.com; 800–641–7258) offers all kinds of natural, hand-harvested salts as well as suggestions for how best to use and appreciate the salt's varied textures and flavors.

SPECK: Buon Italia, which has a retail outlet in Chelsea Market in New York City, is a great source for such products as speck, *guanciale*, and other cured meats and many other fine Italian products. Visit them at www.buonitalia.com or call 212–633–9090. Salumeria Biellese (212–736–7376) also carries delicious speck.

TRUFFLES, TRUFFLE OIL, AND OTHER TRUFFLE PRODUCTS: Urbani Truffles is a great source for truffles and truffle products as well as high-quality wild mushrooms (www.urbanitruffles.com; 215–699–8780).

VIALONE NANO: You can find my favorite rice for risotto at good gourmet shops and Italian markets, and through mail order, including A. G. Ferrari (www.agferrari.com; 877–878–2783) among the other Italian food sources listed here.

VINEGAR: Buon Italia (see Speck) also carries Trucioleto vinegar, a vinegar I use all of the time for cooking. Although inexpensive, this vinegar has a characteristically round flavor.

WINE (ITALIAN): Located in Union Square in the heart of New York City, Italian Wine Merchants, owned by my friend Sergio Esposito, is much more than simply a wine shop in that it represents to me the foremost expertise in Italian wines in this country. Certain states will allow you to mail order from Italian Wine Merchants, but even if you can't, do check out their Web site (www.italianwinemerchant.com) for more insight and information on Italian wines than you can imagine. For more information, call 212–473–2323.

Acknowledgments

My father always tells me that you are only as good as the people you surround yourself with. So here I give thanks to all the people who have made me "good" over the years. There were times in my career that I thought it would never work out. I thank God daily for his blessings. Again, to my mother and father, who struggled to make a better life for their children. Dr. and Mrs. Dattero got me through many rainy days; I love you both and cannot thank you enough. Howard Rourke, for his vision, integrity, and determination. Thank you to my business partners: Chris Cannon, thanks for your generosity, your loyalty, your friendship, and for believing in me and making me your business partner; Jane Epstein, I am blessed to have you in my life; Vicente Wolf, you are a genius—thanks for making me look good. My publicists: Philip Baltz (!), Becca Parrish, Tammy Walker, and Alison Good. Thanks to Joanne Smart for helping me express my thoughts on cooking, on food, and, occasionally, on life. Meg Suzuki for her excellent recipe testing and her fine wit. My publisher, Steve Rubin: I never want to let you down. My editor, Jennifer Josephy, for expertly navigating the waters. My agent—and friend—Patricia van der Leun. My manager, Scott Feldman at Two 12 Management. Maile Holck: I don't have the words to describe your importance in my life; if you didn't organize me, I would never have completed this book. Photographers Shimon and Tammar: Your work is amazing. I love working with you and benefiting from your combined vision. The Cannon Family for their generosity in letting a crew of people invade their home for a few days. I am fortunate for many, many things, and the staff at my restaurants is a big one. Many of these people have stuck around, trusting me, for a long time. Thank you all for your patience, hard work, and initiative, especially Tom Budny, John Paulus, Atelio Ramos, Chepi and Edwin, Jerry, and Orlando. My longtime friend and former pastry chef, Heather Carlucci. Chefs de cuisine Kevin Sipple, Paul Bently, and Craig Wallen. Also Jorge Espinosa, Junior, Abraham, Juan-Carlos, John, Poppy-chulo, and Domingo—the whole support system. Thanks to my good friend Sergio Esposito and his family for everything that they have done for me. John Nagler and Jay Veduccio for being there as sounding boards and advisors. My brother, Paul, and my sister, Rebecca, for all the encouragement and motivation they have given me over our lifetime. Also the DeAngelis family. Tom Black for letting me experience wines that I wouldn't otherwise have the chance to. Valentino, for getting me out of my whites.

Index

Index